MW00412182

you,
Improved

A DAILY DOSE
of INSPIRATION

by MARTHA KARELIUS

For my family

INTRODUCTION

"When we strive to become better than we are, everything around us becomes better, too." – Paul Coelho

It is possible to create your perfect life by consistently implementing small, positive steps to move you in the right direction. I hope this daily dose of thought provoking inspiration will motivate you to grow in every area of your life. Improvement comes when action is taken, and change occurs. Lasting change happens when small incremental changes are practiced daily.

This book will guide you to slowly, but surely, instill attainable and sustainable habits that can easily be assimilated into your current life. Just flip to today's date and enjoy your daily dose or binge read several pages at a time. Keep it by your bedside or somewhere close at hand and make good use of the opportunity every day for thoughtful reflection on concepts and actions that will make you better. Nothing would make me happier than to see old, well-worn copies of this book with dog-eared corners marking selected pages and numerous calls-to-action scribbled in the margins. Enjoy!

FRESH STARTS

"What the new year brings to you will depend a great deal on what you bring to the new year." – Vern McLellen

Happy New Year! The first day of the year is a clean slate and the perfect opportunity for fresh starts and new beginnings. It's time to shake off the 'what could have been' blues and intentionally close the door on the missteps and disappointments of yesterday. Today is the day to view the world through a new lens; one filled with hope, not regret.

There's always room for improvement. What would your life look like if you tried something new? It doesn't have to be life-changing like a new career or relationship. Even small changes make a big difference over time. Consider taking on a new hobby, health regime, or adventure. Stake your claim by crafting a clear and simple plan to live this day and each of the next 364 days with a vision of the new, improved you in the forefront of your mind.

It's the first page of your new book so be honest with yourself and crystal clear about what makes you happy. Thoughtfully design a life that will fulfill you and improve your outlook. Be brave, push your boundaries and never, ever let the fear of change or the fear of failure derail you. Avoid the temptation to dwell on the past or project too far into the future. Give it your best one day at a time and give up the idea of perfection. Not only is perfection unrealistic, it's quite unnecessary. Good is good enough, most days.

When you wake up every morning, make the decision to begin anew, adjust as needed, and create a joy filled life. Herein lies the difference between sleepwalking through life and truly living. Cheers to inspiration and implementation…one day at a time!

LET'S GO (GET ORGANIZED)

"Have nothing in your house that you do not know to be useful, or believe to be beautiful" – William Morris

January is National Get Organized (GO) Month, the perfect time to get your life and possessions in order. It's easy to accumulate 'stuff' over the holidays and tempting to store it all until next year. Out of sight, out of mind. The problem with that philosophy is the boxes stay in storage and multiply every year. Those cartons you assume contain items of values might be filled with outdated, unwanted 'treasures'. It's time to purge what you don't need and put systems in place to maintain what you do need.

Take time now to set up a file for all year-end statements, annual interest reports, and anything else that will be needed to prepare your personal income taxes. Papers are easily misplaced and wasting time looking for receipts you know are there, somewhere, can be very frustrating. When tax time approaches you will be in position to efficiently get the job done in a relatively painless and drama free manner.

Look at your belongings with new eyes. We become so accustomed to our possessions that we don't notice when they become worn or past their useful life. If necessary, call for a lifeline to help make hard decisions. Ask a friend to be candid about what you should eliminate and return the favor by helping them purge.

Organization does wonders to improve time management and productivity. Once you know what you own and why you own it, create storage solutions to make it easy to access items as needed. There should be a place for everything, and everything should be in its place. Empower yourself now by starting the year with manageable systems to maintain control and increase efficiency in your environment.

ONE WORD

"Your words have power. Speak words that are kind, loving, positive, uplifting, encouraging, and life-giving." – Unknown

Choose a word today that you will dedicate yourself to for the entire year. Clarify what you want most out of life and distill it into a single word representing your vision for the next twelve months. Carefully select the best word to express your personal intention. A word so powerful just seeing or hearing it will encourage you to pursue your goals with laser focus. Words inspire with amazing power, so choose wisely. A single word can evoke feelings that represent all you want to be, do, fulfill, or achieve.

What changes do you want to manifest this year? What kind of person will you need to be to influence those changes? What characteristics do people like that share? Make a list of words that clearly describe your intention. Carefully consider each word and through the process of elimination continue to refine the list until you find the perfect word.

Consider committing to a year of pure joy. Look for joy daily and purposely surround yourself with uplifting people and activities. Or dedicate this year to growth. Pledge to read more and learn more. Stretch yourself outside of your comfort zone at every opportunity. A year of pushing your limits would be very challenging, but ultimately very rewarding.

Once you have thoughtfully chosen one perfect word or phrase, share it with people you trust. Make a note of it and post it on your bathroom mirror, your desk, and the sun visor of your car. Set it as your computer and smartphone password. Keeping it at the forefront of your mind will prevent straying from or forgetting your one main purpose. One word can change your life.

TAKE THE LONG VIEW

"Think of the long view of life, not just what's going to happen today or tomorrow. Don't give up what you want in life for something you think you want now." – Richard G. Scott

Set your sights on your ultimate life goal and you won't be as affected by daily peaks and valleys and every small bump in the road. Long view thinking keeps you focused on the future. As an example of what life looks like in the long view look at a line graph that illustrates the value of stocks over time. On the short term the graph may show fluctuations in value, but over several years the results track steady and consistent growth. Life has similar ups and downs and it also improves incrementally over time. Every misstep, perceived slight, or missed opportunity isn't a setback. Learn the lesson and move forward focused on what's ahead. Attain future long-term success by continuing to grow and adjust along the way.

Slow down and look where you're going. Don't jump on a short-term fix if it won't benefit your end game. You find yourself in a career that is not fulfilling and have decided it is time to make a change. You're about to resign when your current employer offers you a better position. Short term thinking calls for accepting the new position which will trap you in the wrong profession. If you have your eye on the long game, it's easier to graciously turn it down and stay on track with your plan.

It is challenging, yet possible, to live in the moment while pursuing your vision for the future. Don't let life slip through your fingers while you're stuck in neutral. Look beyond today's difficulties with confidence and make decisions that lead to a brighter future.

AVOID COMPLACENCY

"Don't let your special character and values, the secret that you know and no one else does, the truth – don't let that get swallowed up by the great chewing complacency." – Aesop

In the beginning you struggled for success. At some point you reached a level of contentment, and once there, slid into complacency. Being comfortable with where you are in life is a good thing. Letting that comfortable feeling lull you into a false sense of security is not. Major corporations make this mistake all the time. They outpace their competitors in market share and profitability and, reveling in the lead, relax, lose their edge, and allow the competition to pass them by.

Picture your life in forward motion, driving you to be a better, happier, more successful version of you. Now picture yourself taking a break to enjoy the fruits of your labor. You lose momentum and begin to decline. If you're not rising, you're falling.

When you become satisfied with your achievements, it's easy to rest on your laurels and stop growing. The status quo refers to your existing state and it is not static. You must continually attempt to be the best you can be, in all areas of your life. Getting by is not good enough in today's competitive environment. Look for opportunities to improve, grow and make yourself more valuable. Interact with others in your field of interest and share ideas and opinions. Stay on top of technological advances that will add credibility and value. Be honest in your assessment. If you are where you are because you're comfortable, it's time to make a move and get uncomfortable to continue to thrive. Commit to one thing today that will get you out of your comfort zone and back on the road to success.

LESS IS MORE

"Often people attempt to live their lives backward, they try to have more things or more money in order to do more of what they want so they will be happier. The way it actually works is the reverse. You must first be who you really are then do what you need to do in order to have what you want." – Margaret Young

Think succinct, simple, and concise. Life doesn't have to be so complicated. People speak before they clarify their thoughts and feel the need to state their case several different ways to make their point. "In other words," "To make a long story short..."

Wouldn't it be refreshing to have a conversation with someone who expressed themselves one well thought out, articulate sentence at a time? The same goes for email and text exchanges. Brief and to the point gets the job done.

Daily life would be so much easier if there was a place for everything and everything was in its proper place. You could eliminate wasted time searching for the hammer you know is there and eventually buying another which will also get lost in the shuffle. Every space in your home does not need to be decorated. Closets and drawers do not have to be full. There is tremendous value in breathing space. Restaurants that offer a book instead of a page of menu selections or stores with displays jam-packed with merchandise can be overwhelming. We feel stressed and 'poisoned by possibilities' when faced with too many choices.

Focus on doing fewer things and doing them well. Live life purposely and use your time and energy to connect with people who are important to you. Quality over quantity in all things. Enrich your life by simplifying just one thing today and one more tomorrow, until you build the comfortable life of your dreams.

JUST DO IT

"When all is said and done, more is said than done." – Aesop

Do you have a life list tucked away somewhere that identifies places to visit, adventures to seek, or appealing opportunities calling your name? Today is the day to dig it out, choose one thing, and put the wheels in motion to make it happen. If it's a cost prohibitive, time consuming adventure you may need to modify your vision so that it's in line with who you are today and the resources available. Either dial back the elegant Mediterranean cruise dream and plan a more realistic vacation involving a backpack, air miles, and a Eurail pass, or up the ante, lose the backpack and set sail.

What you wanted then may look different now. Perhaps you've reached the stage in life where just the thought of extensive travel overwhelms you. A relaxing, reasonably priced Amtrak excursion or a road trip to a National Park might be exactly what you need. Start investigating ways to make it happen and adjust as necessary to fit your current lifestyle, energy level, and budget.

If your goal is to try something new every day, learn to play the piano, or speak fluent Spanish there are apps for that. Do your homework, research what it takes, and put a plan in place to make it happen. Watch YouTube instructional videos or use Google to locate helpful resources like webinars, live classes, or the perfect local tutor. Your prospects are endless.

Push yourself a little to live a richer, more interesting, and therefore, more rewarding life. If you continue to put off your dreams life will quickly pass you by. Commit to a project or adventure today and take the first step. Don't just talk about it, do it.

BE TRUE TO YOURSELF

*"To thine own self be true
And it must follow, as the night the day
Thou canst not then be false to any man."*
– William Shakespeare, *Hamlet*

Growing up we did our best to fit into the mold created for us by the authority figures in our lives, namely our parents and teachers. It was our only option, and by doing as we were told we fit in with our family and peers. We were blank slates waiting for our path to be made clear. That was then, and this is now. We know who we are and what makes us uniquely us and it is time to express and celebrate our individuality.

The time has never been better to dabble in areas that make your heart sing, even if circumstances require you to keep your day job. If you're crafty and feeling entrepreneurial check out the opportunities that Etsy offers. Work or volunteer part time in an area that interests you. Dust off your guitar and gather a few friends to make some music.

Years ago, you developed a reputation as the life of the party, but today pajamas and a good book beckon to you at the end of the day. There's no need to pretend you are looking forward to the next big event. Bow out and take the opportunity to feed your soul. Spend some time today reflecting on your happiest times, doing the things you enjoyed so much you lost track of time. Being true to yourself and honoring your needs will lead to a full and balanced life and allow you to enjoy honest relationships with the people who matter.

LOL

"I laughed so hard the tears ran down my legs." – Unknown

When was the last time you let go and dissolved in a fit of giggles or surrendered to a completely out of control, laugh out loud moment? It's probably been too long. Think back to your childhood when life was carefree, and laughter was contagious. Watch kids at play. They are happy for no reason at all and laugh just for the pure joy of it.

At some point our sense of duty and real-life responsibilities overcome our free spirit. Life is a serious matter, but laughter is still the best medicine. It benefits our body by helping us relax and enjoy a positive mood. It benefits our mind by expanding it to produce fresh ideas and a rosy outlook. And finally, the optimism generated by a hearty laugh nourishes our spirit and cleanses our soul.

We embrace this as fact and still manage to put a lid on our silliness. Stop and chuckle when you are tempted to indulge in unnecessary or petty drama. Be the first to poke fun at yourself when you suffer a gaffe. People will laugh along with you, which feels entirely different than being laughed at. Once you've cleared the air, step back, smile, and enjoy a fresh perspective.

Starting today, lighten up a little and LOL. This will open a world of joy and spark your creative side. Creativity ignites innovation which fuels even more joy and completes the happiness circle. Put a smile on your face and your personal relationships will improve and people will be drawn to you. Let's face it, fun is inspiring, and laughter is a powerful magnet. Go forward intentionally pursuing happiness. Begin the process right now and completely surrender to a good laugh.

HAPPY ACCIDENTS

"What people call serendipity sometimes is just having your eyes open."
– Jose Manuel Barroso

Serendipity is a wonderfully serendipitous word. The dictionary defines it as "the occurrence and development of events by chance in a happy or beneficial way". The word was coined in 1754 by Horace Walpole, an English writer. Walpole wrote a Persian fairy tale called The Three Princes of Serendip. Apparently, the princes were "always making discoveries, by accidents and sagacity, of things which they were not in quest of".

Life can be just like that - filled with surprises. You start out in the morning with a plan in place. Some days your expectations are met and some days they fall short. Many times, what we least expect happens instead, with much better results. Remember the meeting you were dreading? Yes, the one you were so grateful you attended where they announced an opportunity on the horizon that was a perfect fit for you.

Consider the scientist at 3M who failed in his attempt to formulate the super adhesive glue he was attempting to create. Instead he accidentally created a tacky reusable glue that he referred to as a "solution without a problem". He kept his eyes open for possibilities and the low tack version eventually became the indispensable post-it note. It took a little time to recognize the value of his discovery, but the result was indeed a very happy accident.

Be open to opportunities wherever and however they show up. Maybe it's just a coincidence when all the pieces suddenly fit together. Or perhaps serendipity showed up and aligned the stars to provide a happy ending. It doesn't matter how or why. Continue doing the right things and trust what you are looking for, or better, will show up in the right place at the right time. Let serendipity surprise and delight you today.

GRACIAS AND MERCI

"God gave you a gift of 86,400 seconds today. Have you used one to say, 'thank you'?" –William Arthur Ward

We teach our children to be polite and say 'please' and 'thank you' from a very young age. We understand the importance of good manners, but sometimes overlook opportunities to show our appreciation for others. Yes, it's in your admins job description to send an email to summarize the results of team meetings, but a little positive acknowledgment in front of the rest of the team is motivating and sets a good example. Everyone, including you, will benefit. People want to feel appreciated and those two small words expressed on a regular basis mean more than any others. Make it a habit to offer a sincere thank you to recognize a job well done every chance you get.

Don't underestimate the power of those two simple words. Some people go through life busy, important, and self-absorbed. They feel entitled, rather than grateful, when served by others. No one wins friends with that attitude, so help them out. If you feel unappreciated it's safe to say others do, too. Bring it to their attention by letting them know they hurt feelings by allowing kind acts to go unnoticed. Once you've opened their eyes you might be the first to hear the hoped-for words, 'thank you'.

When you show gratitude, you strengthen relationships and gain respect. People who feel appreciated will go the extra mile for you every time you need them because they know they're not being taken for granted. Inspire others by speaking from a grateful heart and expressing your own gratitude often. Just two little words. Be generous with anyone and everyone deserving a heartfelt thanks today.

USE YOUR WORDS

"The difference between the right word and the almost right word is the difference between lightening and the lightening bug."
– Mark Twain

There's nothing more satisfying than having the right word on the tip of your tongue when you want to express a thought. As you hem and haw looking for the perfect word your audience will either lose interest or try to finish your sentence for you. A larger vocabulary will give you a better understanding of what others are saying, and you will speak more confidently when you are able to convey your thoughts and ideas succinctly and effectively.

Words are fascinating. Your client suggested you were obfuscating. You're unfamiliar with the word and curious about what it means. You interrupt her rant to ask for the definition. She's caught by surprise but takes a breath and explains she thought you were being unclear and purposely trying to confuse the issue. She wants you to make yourself crystal clear, no obfuscation. Problem solved with a bonus - you added one new word to your vocabulary.

We know thousands of words and come across new ones every day. When you read a new word or hear a phrase you're unsure of it's tempting to skip past them, but you're missing a perfect opportunity to increase your vocabulary. Simply type the word into your smart phone, read the definition, and then try to use it in a sentence at your first opportunity. You can grow your word base in this way but consider increasing the pace of learning with a consistent, intentional plan. By committing to learn just one new word per day you will become a confident conversationalist and foster a lifetime habit of learning at the same time.

NO JUDGEMENT

"Love is the absence of judgment." – Dalai Lama

When a person labels actions as good/bad or right/wrong, they are judging others. The same applies when they can't see beyond the color of skin, body type, or sexual orientation. Many forms of self-expression leave individuals open to judgement. For example, what conclusion do you draw when you first meet someone with an excessive number of tattoos or piercings? How do you react to those with opposing political views or opinions? The rush to judgement is an inherent human characteristic and we are all guilty to some degree.

Some things may be viewed as clearly black or white. However, more often than not, there are extenuating circumstances that, if taken into consideration, will completely change your view and reveal many shades of gray.

Make an effort to lighten up on yourself, as well. Most of us hold the bar unrealistically high when measuring our own performance. We are critical of our size, accomplishments (or what we perceive as a lack thereof), and where we are or feel we should be on the corporate ladder. We compare our lives to the highlight reel of the lives of others and it's impossible to measure up. Give yourself credit for what you have accomplished/created/raised and show yourself a little self-love.

When you are tempted to judge, stop and consider other perspectives and see if your attitude softens. If you can see beyond your initial reaction and give others the benefit of the doubt you will begin to live a non-judgmental and more peaceful life. Acknowledge that your first impression is just that and not the entire story. Stand in their shoes and your mood might shift from negative to positive and open your mind and heart to acceptance and, yes, love.

TAKE THE HIGH ROAD

"Nothing gives one person so much advantage over another as to remain always cool and unruffled under all circumstances."
– Thomas Jefferson

Pick your battles. Do you want to be right or do you want to be happy? That's the question to ask yourself the next time someone hurts your feelings or treats you unfairly. You can make a point of being right and engage in an argument or let it go and take the 'high road'. The high road decision shows strength and maturity on your part. Approaching situations from a logical standpoint gives you the edge. Becoming a person who doesn't always take the bait will earn you great respect. The choice is yours.

When a situation escalates from a constructive exchange of opinions to an out and out confrontation, it's time to take a step back and resist the impulse to immediately lash out. This gives you time to get your thoughts together and gather a few more details. There's always more to the story, right? Try to view the situation from their perspective. Give yourself twenty-four hours and see if you still feel compelled to respond. A cooling off period will either allow you to let it go or give you the opportunity to express yourself in a calmer and more rational manner.

Many fires will put themselves out if left alone. Maybe they didn't mean what they said or perhaps it just came out wrong. If it's not a matter of high importance don't stoke the fire. There is no good reason to waste time and energy fighting a fight that isn't worth winning.

When you give up the need to be right you give yourself the right to be happy. And when you do dig your heels in, in a thoughtful, composed way, people will listen.

BELIEVE IN MIRACLES

"We live on a blue planet that circles around a ball of fire next to a moon that moves the sea, and you don't believe in miracles?"
– Unknown

Life is full of medical miracles and unexplained mysteries. Awe-inspiring events happen daily that defy logic or scientific explanation. I was enjoying a seemingly healthy existence in 2011 when I was diagnosed with leiomyosarcoma, a rare and aggressive form of cancer. The next two years were consumed by chemotherapy, radiation, and multiple surgeries. In 2013 I was preparing to start further rounds of chemotherapy when a PET scan came in clean, "no evidence of disease, resolved of cancer". Medically speaking it made no sense and in the big, cosmic picture it didn't need to. I accept it as a miracle.

A modern-day wonder has become known as 'the miracle on the Hudson'. US Airways Flight 1549 struck a flock of Canadian geese and lost power in both engines. Captain Chesley Sullenberger knew his only option was to land the plane on the Hudson River. All 155 souls on board were rescued by nearby boats. This might not be a phenomenon of biblical proportions, such as when Moses parted the Red Sea, but it makes one wonder how so many variables aligned so perfectly, with so little time. Certainly, credit is due to the quick-thinking crew for exemplary skill under pressure, and the passengers for remaining calm in a frightening situation but luck was also involved. Possibly in the form of a miracle.

It's not necessary to fully understand everything that happens in your lifetime. There are countless stories about inexplicable outcomes and impossible cures that serve as powerful reminders God is at work. Celebrate the mystery, believe, and ask for your miracle today.

CREATE YOUR LIFE LIST

"...sit down and take some time to discover yourself, to define what is really important to you, what your priorities are, what arouses your deepest passions. You should ask certain questions: What is the purpose of my life? What do I want from life? What are the things that I truly value, that are not done just to please or impress the people around me?"
– David Brooks, The Road to Character

There's no better time than now to determine your reason for living by creating a detailed life, or 'bucket', list. Don't lose another day waiting for the perfect moment. If you postpone truly living until X happens you will miss out on many wonderful opportunities along life's journey.

Invest a little time in self-discovery. Start by listing your interests and talents. Push yourself outside your comfort zone and give some serious consideration to these thought-provoking questions. What would you do if you won the lottery? What would come under the heading of "woulda, coulda, shoulda"? How do you want to be remembered?

Your bucket list is a work in progress. If you stay in curious mode, you will continually be adding new adventures and opportunities to your life list. When it grows longer by the day there's always something to look forward and aspire to. There are so many dreams worth chasing and the list of possibilities is endless. If you need more inspiration google 'bucket list'. The wealth of imaginative ideas will astound you. If you see anything that resonates with you add it to your own list.

Don't count on the universe to shape your life. Make your own luck by establishing goals, creating strategies to achieve them, and committing to whatever it takes to accomplish them. Do this and you will always have more dreams than memories.

THE POWER OF VISION BOARDS

"If you can imagine it, you can achieve it. If you can dream it, you can become it." – William Arthur Ward

Vision boards work. It's possible to manifest life events, relationships, personal growth, health and wellness, and much more using this simple visualization tool. Yesterday you made a list of things you want, places to visit, and success you want to achieve in every area of your life. Grab a stack of magazines and cut and paste to your heart's content and breathe life into it. Add mementos, quotes and any visual reminder that will keep your dreams in front of you while your subconscious works its magic.

There are no rules or restrictions in the creation of your vision. Just let your imagination soar. If you want to spend more time with family include happy photos of the clan. Yearning for an exotic vacation? Paste up travel brochures and maps to destinations on your bucket list and add clippings of the cruise ship or vehicle that will get you there. There's no shortage of images for the perfect room renovation or ideal body makeover. Sprinkle inspirational quotes and images throughout to keep your spirits high. Include pictures and descriptions of fitness, business, educational, recreational, and savings goals. You will be subconsciously reminded daily of everything conceivable that motivates and fulfills you.

Vision boards are beautiful reminders of all you hold dear and all that you want to manifest into your life. Keep yours close and it will send subliminal reminders to your brain day in and day out. Snap a photo and use it as a powerful screensaver for even deeper awareness. Think big, expect success, and trust in the universe. Thoughts are things and keeping those 'things' in view creates an easy, but powerful, way to bring your dreams to life.

FINISH WHAT YOU START

"It's not so important who starts the game but who finishes it."
– John Wooden

Are you easily inspired, but just as easily distracted? It's easy to start strong, but difficult to stay focused and cross the finish line. We all get weighed down by UFO's, unfinished opportunities. When UFO's pile up we feel overwhelmed and discouraged. It's difficult to abandon projects we have invested time and possibly money into, but sometimes it frees you up for something better. If you're stalled and getting nowhere, it might be time to cut your losses and scrap the project. If you decide to see it through, here are a few steps that will help you focus on the finish line:

- Ask yourself two very important questions before you enthusiastically embark on something new: "Do I really want/need to do this?" and "Is it aligned with my long-term goals?" If it's not going to impact your life or make a positive difference, press the pause button and look for a project or adventure that better serves your needs.
- Have a clear understanding of the resources, both time and money, that will be invested in the activity. This project may still have your name on it, but at a future date.
- Research the results of others who have gone down this road. Were they satisfied, and did they enjoy the outcome you are expecting?
- Create a timeline for the completion of the projects you take on. Break your plan down into manageable segments and set benchmarks to celebrate small successes along the way. The schedule may be adjusted as needed.
- Push through after the honeymoon period ends and find joy in finishing things that are important to you and will enhance your life.

Start now so you can finish.

WALK YOUR TALK

"The world is changed by your example, not your opinion."
– Paulo Coelho

Actions speak louder than words. Cliché, yes, but truer words were never spoken. When you say one thing and do another you lose credibility, trust, and followers. We earn (or lose) respect for the way we conduct our everyday lives. Your daily actions should reflect your values and beliefs. Don't just talk about how important your family is to you. Show it by investing time and paying attention to them or to whatever subject or project you profess to support. Inspire others by being human, not perfect. If you hit a wall, admit it and look for a solution instead of someone to blame.

There's no good substitute for stepping up, paying your dues, and applying the energy necessary to generate results that speak for themselves. Some individuals get through life by working every angle. Setbacks and failures are always someone else's fault. They indulge in little white lies to make their life sound more glamorous and interesting. They're too blinded by their own visions of grandeur to have an interest in small, steady growth. Big talkers don't motivate or inspire anyone of substance. You can see right through them. They are not admired as respected leaders or mentors. At the end of their career, or life, they will still be boasting about themselves without backing it up with any meaningful action.

Take time for thoughtful self-examination. If you consider yourself a caring parent/son/daughter/friend review recent interaction with important people in your life and see if that belief is based on reality. Review the causes you support. A little introspection will flush out areas that need realignment. It's time to commit to a life of action that's in sync with your words.

LIVE DELIBERATELY

"I went to the woods because I wanted to live deliberately, to front only the essential facts of life, and see if I could not learn what it had to teach, and not, when I came to die, discover that I had not lived."
— Henry David Thoreau

Life doesn't need to be so hectic or complicated. Take charge and design your best life by eliminating the non-essentials that sap your time and energy. Focus on important relationships and activities and let go of the ones that drain you. Commit to spending time with people and things that lift you up. Create breathing room by distancing yourself from clutter that serves no real purpose. It's not easy to do in today's 'more is better' climate, but it is possible if you resist the need to fill every moment in your calendar and every nook and cranny of your home.

Focus on the necessities by deliberately identifying your true values. Now embrace those values by making a list of the changes you can make to design the life you really want to live. To purposely manifest a fulfilling life, it helps to break it down into smaller increments. What does a perfect day look like to you? Intentionally fill your schedule with activities that reflect that vision. Start with one day and then string a few more together into meaningful weeks, months, and years.

If your career/acquaintances/hobbies are not satisfying, make some changes. Not just any changes...deliberate ones. Try something new, cultivate fresh relationships with like-minded people and thoughtfully plan projects or events to give you something to look forward to that will enrich your life. Once accomplished you will be able to look back and know you have not just passed the time but have truly and deliberately lived your best life.

LEAVE A LEGACY

"The purpose of life is not to be happy, but to matter– to be productive, to be useful, to have it make some difference that you have lived at all."
– Leo Rosten

How do you want to be remembered by those whose lives you touch during your lifetime? I'm not talking about bequeathing an inheritance or materials things to your heirs. I'm referring to your contribution to the world and the reasons why your life matters.

Most of us won't change the world, but in our own way we will change lives. You may have earned a reputation as someone who encourages others to be the best they can be or who influences people to find and follow their chosen path. Maybe you are admired as an individual with wonderful joie d 'vive and a kind spirit. We are many things and we can make a difference just by being ourselves.

Live an inspired life and you will be remembered for it. Pouring your energy into whatever you are passionate about will be enough to motivate others. Consider the critical role your Grandmother's recipes play in bringing the family together. The party wouldn't be the same without her baking legacy. Or the joy of planting and harvesting a 'victory' garden, a tradition Grandpa passed down to the grandkids. Memories of a life well lived are guaranteed to bring a smile to someone's face. Long after you are gone you will be quoted, stories will be shared, and those who knew you will want to follow in your footsteps.

Be mindful of the blessings in your life. Express gratitude for them and share the wealth with a smile, a compliment, or an offer of support. It doesn't matter if you are remembered for supporting people or your favorite causes. What's important is you will be remembered.

HEART VS. HEAD

"A good head and a good heart are always a formidable combination." – Nelson Mandela

We are faced with hundreds of decisions every day. If the decision is clear, or not very important, there's no need to overthink it. But what happens when we're faced with a real dilemma? Bigger, more difficult decisions require us to step back, weigh the facts, and honor the combined power of our heart and our head.

Decisions of the heart are inspired by emotion. A 'gut feeling' or your inner voice, intuition, speaks loud and clear and you should listen carefully to what it tells you. Your heart tempts you to throw caution to the wind and make frivolous, spur of the moment decisions that sound good at the time, but bad once your mind weighs in. Decisions of the head are based on logic and what you've learned through experience. Unknowns cause worry and the thought of change makes you fearful. Think things through, consider the pros and cons, and once you have examined the choices from every angle, cautiously move forward.

One sounds a little unsafe, and the other sounds a little too safe. Sometimes it seems there is no right answer. Your head feels it's a sound, rational decision and your heart is just not in it. Before committing, ask yourself if the decision you are about to make is aligned with and supports your true values.

Weigh your options, choose a path and move forward with no regrets. There will be time to adjust as you continue life's journey. Enjoy the process and recognize that when you honor your highest values your heart and mind work together, and the best option becomes clear. Go for it, you can't go wrong.

WRITE YOUR PERSONAL MISSION STATEMENT

"Without a mission statement, you may get to the top of the ladder and then realize it was leaning against the wrong building!"
– Dave Ramsey

You may prefer to call it your personal vision or personal belief system, but regardless of the title, a few thoughtful sentences become a powerful tool that will start and keep you on the road to success. A good mission statement concisely identifies your character and purpose in life and keeps you focused on the right things. It's important to identify what you represent and what you contribute to the world.

The Constitution doesn't require major re-writing or updating as the country grows and changes, because the American values described within it remain constant. Your personal mission statement will weather the years in the same way by defining not only who you are today, but who you will continue to be through all of life's changes.

You may feel purposeful and confident on your current path, but do you know where the path will take you or what you will do when you get there? You will if you follow your belief system and allow it to direct you through life passages. Consider it your personal North Star and let it guide you through all life decisions, big and small.

Begin the process by identifying your values and prioritizing your long-term goals. Consider what your contribution looks like. How will you make a difference? Will you leave your family/career/community in a better place when you're gone? Begin writing, revising, editing, and re-writing until your mission statement describes your essence and can be declared in a few well thought out sentences. Once you have a clear vision, live and breathe it every day and cherish the life you have created.

FIND THE GOLD

"Sincere compliments cost nothing and can accomplish so much. In ANY relationship, they are the applause that refreshes."
— Steve Goodier, Prescription for Peace

"Anyone can find the dirt in someone. Be the one that finds the gold" is a loosely translated version of Proverbs 11:27. Spreading joy costs nothing and comes back to you in spades. Start today and commit to giving a sincere compliment to at least one person every day. It will not only make their day, but it carries the added benefit of making your day, too. So be generous.

Don't overthink it. If you notice something praise-worthy, it deserves to be mentioned. You have no idea what the recipient is going through, but chances are your kind words will be a highlight of their day. You have the power to turn their day around and positively impact your outlook in the same breath.

Once you get used to freely complimenting you will find more and more opportunities to do so. If you walk away from a conversation thinking about how good someone looked, you loved their haircut, or they are looking fit and trim, go back and tell them. It's never too late to make someone's day. When you miss the chance to say it in person, write a quick note. "I want you to know that I couldn't help noticing (fill in the blank) when I saw you yesterday. I just thought I should let you know you look great." That's really all it takes to make a difference and change the world for the better, one compliment at a time.

Make compliments a part of your daily routine. Look for the best in people, mine for the gold and share your thoughts with them. You will create a positive mindset and generate happiness every single time.

DO YOUR PART

"Try to leave the Earth a better place than when you arrived."
– Sidney Sheldon

We hear a lot of talk about leaving a smaller 'carbon footprint' by using less energy and natural resources. It's easy to say, but in a world where cars and electric appliances are quite valuable, how and where do you begin to protect the earth's limited resources? The answer is start small and start at home.

If everyone commits to small changes, we can make a big difference. Californians recently lived through the longest drought on record and were subject to state-wide, mandatory cut-backs in water consumption. The results were dramatic. Some cities cut their water use by 30%, well over the reduction mandated. It was eye-opening to discover how much water was wasted in so many small ways. Simple painless adjustments like shorter showers and turning off the water while brushing teeth made a huge difference. Change came with awareness.

Turn off the lights when you leave a room. Your Dad drilled that into you when you were a kid. His motive was to save money by keeping the utility bills low, but it also conserves valuable resources. There are many easy adjustments that make a big difference. Set your heater a few degrees lower and your AC a few higher. Run the appliances only when you have full loads. Create less trash by eating fresh food that requires little or no packaging. Drink coffee from a reusable cup instead of a disposable one. Re-cycle, re-gift or donate what you don't need, and use your imagination to re-purpose items to give them a second life.

Simplify your life and save money while conserving vital assets. Begin today by committing to one small change. Stick with it until it becomes the new norm and in this small way change the world.

BUILD YOUR BRAND

"A brand is the set of expectations, memories, stories, and relationships that, taken together, account for a consumer's decision to choose one product or service over another." – Seth Godin

A personal brand is what comes to mind when your name comes up in conversation. Your reputation precedes you, now more than ever. We live in a world where every movement or misstep can, and will, be documented and shared without reservation. Rest assured that every prospective employer or date can, and most probably will, Google your name and within moments unearth the good, bad, and ugly following you. Don't underestimate the importance of managing your brand in today's culture, where oversharing seems to be the accepted norm.

You are blessed with unique strengths and challenges. It is important to present your honest self to the world but be aware of what you share. Stop and think before you post that hilarious photo or video of the girl's trip/guys getaway/office party. Will that story enhance your brand? If not, refrain from sharing it with the world. If you decide it's acceptable to post, stop and think before tagging others. It's their story to tell if they choose to tell it, not yours. They may have different boundaries or privacy needs and you don't want to be the one to compromise them. It will hurt your brand.

What comes to mind when people think of you? Authenticity and a little vulnerability never hurt anyone. You may not appeal to everyone, but people trust what is real. People are drawn to do business and develop relationships with people they trust. It might be time to refine and update the way the world sees you. Start a new story by replacing old memories with fresh, positive ones. Put your best self forward and the world will take notice.

BLANK CANVAS

"Life is a blank canvas, and you need to throw all the paint on it you can."
– Danny Kaye

Most days you get caught up in the tasks and commitments of everyday life and lose sight of creating the work of art that is your life. Every move you make contributes to the whole. Do you find yourself driving from point A to point B on automatic instead of soaking in the sights? Does each new day look just like the last? If you are stuck in the rut of a relationship that is going nowhere or a job that is neither challenging nor rewarding change it up. It's time to start living out loud and in color. Big, splashy, broad brush color! Fill every inch of your canvas with rich experiences and stimulating adventures.

Indulge in some 'free association' thinking. Find a word that best describes how things are now, then write the first word you think of that would enrich or improve your current world. Let your mind wander and compile a list of fun, innovative ways to brighten daily life. It is possible to re-invent yourself and design the life you want but didn't know you could have.

Imagine a new you, upbeat and optimistic, ready to sleep out under the stars or unplugged and curled up with a good book. Update your look, bring in fresh flowers, pump up the volume and fill your home and life with music. Re-think your relationships and the people you spend the most time with. Are they right for your life? Do they encourage growth and change? If not, paint them out of the picture.

Get started today. Take a blank canvas and create your own masterpiece. Brush on some paint and don't worry about making a mess, making mistakes, or what anyone else thinks. It's your canvas and your life.

ASK FOR DIRECTION(S)

"On the journey of life, it's okay to stop and ask for directions."
– Unknown

Think about how flattered you feel when someone asks your opinion or for assistance in an area where you have talent or expertise. You're more than happy to do what you can to help. It feels good to be offered an opportunity to contribute to your 'community'. You don't feel put-upon or think less of them because they need help. Most people simply want to extend a hand when given the chance.

Now consider what it feels like to be the one needing a little direction. You revert to that childish independent stage where you want to do it yourself. Maybe we can, but sometimes it would be so much easier, with such better results, if it was a collaborative effort. It can't hurt to ask others for their opinion and insight if you feel it would make a difference. If you're in need of advice, chances are good someone you know has already traveled that road and learned a lot from the bumps along the way. Wouldn't it be helpful to benefit from their knowledge and experience?

Is it pride, false pride, or just plain fear that's holding you back? It's normal to fear looking weak or unprepared but seeking help doesn't make you inadequate. Just the opposite is true. It shores you up and gives you confidence to move forward strengthened by the skills, connections, and resources of people you trust. Don't be afraid to expose your imperfections. No one is perfect.

Life's too short to know it all. Ask for assistance and know that we're stronger together. Decide today to push through the fear and reach out to someone who can and, most likely, would love to help.

IT'S TIME TO EXECUTE

"To me, ideas are worth nothing unless executed. They are just a multiplier. Execution is worth millions." – Steve Jobs

It's one thing to make a plan and quite another to make it happen. You have a great idea and build a complicated, more likely, overcomplicated plan of action around it, and are suddenly overwhelmed. This is where dreams die. You will never accomplish your goal and bring the idea to life without taking the first step.

The key to getting started is to keep it simple. Start with one clear idea. Break it down into an action plan with step by step line items that will take the project from start to finish. Set benchmarks to measure your success by creating a time frame for each phase.

If you have a goal to pay off your mortgage before retirement, the time to start is now. How many years will you work? If the magic number is fifteen years, you might amortize the balance of the mortgage over fifteen years and make larger monthly payments. Set up automatic withdrawals in an amount that fits your budget. Out of sight, out of mind. Start with the next payment due. If you don't, you risk others weighing in with their mortgage burning plan and the moment will pass without execution. Pull the trigger.

There are usually several ways to approach a project so pick one plan and commit to it without overthinking or second guessing your strategy. There's a Chinese proverb that says, "The best time to plant a tree was twenty years ago. The second-best time is now." There is something you have always wanted to do/ learn/create, some place to see, or something to accomplish. You could have started sooner, but there's still time. Make today the day you plant a tree.

WORRY IS A WASTE OF TIME

"If a problem is fixable, if a situation is such that you can do something about it, then there is no need to worry. If it's not fixable, then there is no help in worrying. There is no benefit in worrying whatsoever."
– His Holiness The Dalai Lama XIV

Are you a natural worrier? Do you waste time and many a good night's sleep fretting about things that never happen, are unimportant in the big picture, or are out of your control? The energy that goes into worrying is exhausting mentally and, when it interrupts sleep, it's exhausting physically.

Life comes with challenges, some real, some imagined. Make a 'worry list' of problems that are real, important, and within your control. Committing problems to paper releases anxiety and brings peace of mind. Anything imagined, trivial, or beyond your control does not meet the criteria and therefore, doesn't make the list. Past regrets or issues that may pose a problem in the future don't count. Focus on the present.

Identify and list your problems followed by a list of potential solutions. If, for example, you're buried in debt, create a strategy to dig out. Worry is not a plan. It's stressful and unproductive. Think of ways that would help shrink the debt. Make a list of unnecessary expenses by making simple changes, like dining in instead of out. Simplify and sell what you no longer need or use and contribute that cash to the cause. Find temporary part time work to add another stream of income and dedicate every dollar earned to dig out of debt, build a nest egg, and eliminate future financial worries.

Success breeds success. Proactively approaching problems will energize you. Embrace difficulties that provide opportunities for growth. Get started now. Toss out those worry beads and enjoy a good night's sleep.

NIMBY

"We live in a world in which we need to share responsibility. It's easy to say, "It's not my child, not my community, not my world, not my problem." Then there are those who see the need and respond. I consider those people my heroes." – Fred Rogers

NIMBY is an acronym for Not In My Backyard. A NIMBY refers to someone who is quick to champion change and development, as long as the change doesn't affect them personally. Wind turbines are one of the most cost-effective energy sources in use today and everyone seems to be in favor of them until a proposal is introduced to build in the sightline of a NIMBY. And then, suddenly, the neighbors join forces to prevent the unsightly wind farms from infringing on their currently attractive ecosystem.

Good neighbors maintain their landscape, keep an eye on each other's home when they're away, and promote Neighborhood Watch Programs to discourage crime. If we are to continue to be good neighbors we must do our part to make the world a better place for everyone, even if it means stepping back and letting progress intrude on our little corner of the earth.

Fred Rogers, of Mr. Rogers Neighborhood fame, was once introduced as "the best neighbor any of us has ever had". He was an advocate of the concept 'we're all in this together', which is the antithesis of the 'not in my backyard' culture. It was always a beautiful day in his neighborhood and he was always open to positive change. The world would be a better place if everyone followed his lead, took responsibility, and campaigned for the good of the whole, the greater good.

USE THE RIGHT TOOL

"I could make just such ones if I had tools, and I could make tools if I had tools to make them with." – Eli Whitney

How many fingernails will you break before you learn to start with the right tool instead of resorting to it after all else failed and you're beyond frustrated? When a package arrives at your door it is typically secured with industrial packing tape reinforced with fiberglass filament. That's the secret weapon many vendors use to ensure their products arrive in one well wrapped piece. Experience, if not old-fashioned common sense, should have you reaching for an actual cutting device to remove the tape. Should you use scissors, a knife, or the tool designed specifically for the job, a box cutter?

Start by considering your resources and then decide what is best for you. If you own a box cutter, look no further. If you don't, make the best choice from the assortment of possibilities available. Every day requires the use of an assortment of different tools. There are usually many options and you can always find something new and improved to do the job.

You tried to embrace technology by using electronic tools to manage your schedule and to-do's, but found tablets lack the satisfaction of crossings items off one by one. You have settled on a combination of traditional and cloud-based systems, preferring to write lists and chart your daily plan on paper and track progress and development on the web. There is no one right way to do most things. Consider your needs first and then choose the best option. Think in terms of effectiveness and efficiency. Use the right tool to get the job done in the best way, with the least stress, in the shortest amount of time.

BE AN IDEA MACHINE

"To get a great idea, come up with lots of them." – Thomas Edison

If you want to enjoy personal growth and an exciting future create the habit of generating new ideas. Flex your idea muscle first thing every morning and at any other time, day or night, when inspiration strikes. Maintain a journal to record random ideas that might have an impact on your relationships, inspire current or new business ventures, or trouble shoot a problem you are facing. Write down the good with the bad. It's an exercise in brainstorming, therefore, every idea counts. A lukewarm idea might be the steppingstone to an amazing one.

The more you do it, the easier it gets. Start with one concept, open your mind, and free-associate ideas around the issue. Be creative and let energy and ideas flow. If you're not feeling creative, try surfing the web or reading a chapter of a business or motivational book. Once you create the habit of generating ideas it will be easier to jump start any sector of life where you might be feeling stuck. Simply reviewing your list of fresh, stimulating opportunities may be all the inspiration you need to spark the next lightbulb moment.

Not all ideas will serve a purpose in your own life, but they may serve the needs of an associate, family member, or friend. Think of it as today's version of clipping items from the newspaper and sending it to someone who might find it interesting. Making room in your life for people with different passions and interests will expose your world to a fresh perspective, offering even more and varied food for thought. Begin with the phrase, "Here is my new idea for today..." Start now and repeat daily.

READY, AIM, FIRE

"To me, ideas are worth nothing unless executed. They are just a multiplier. Execution is worth millions." – Steve Jobs

Ready.

Now that you have exercised and toned your idea muscle it's time to make some decisions about which ideas are launch worthy. Determine where you will invest time, energy and monetary resources to bring ideas to life and which ones will remain dreams. Be very clear about the outcome you expect. If you go to the effort of developing and nurturing it to reality what purpose will it serve? Will it simplify your life? Enhance your relationships? Elevate your business to the next level? The more clarity you have around the expected results the easier it will be to see the project through to completion.

Aim.

It's important to spend some time vetting the idea before you take a leap of faith. Ask people you trust if it really holds water. Sometimes we are blinded by our passion and overlook or ignore holes in our plans. Maybe there's already a product or service available to serve the purpose if you tweak it a little. Don't overthink it or try to perfect it at this point. Once you have launched your idea you can regularly measure, review, and make corrections and adjustments as needed. If you have studied and scrutinized the idea from all angles and it still appears to be viable it's time to execute.

Fire.

Now is the time to stop being a dreamer and start being a doer. Doers have concrete plans with a time frame attached. How much and by when? Set benchmarks along the way to measure progress. Your original idea may morph into something even bigger and better than you originally imagined. You will never know if you don't pull the trigger.

STOP TRYING

"There's a difference between interest and commitment. When you're interested in doing something, you do it only when it's convenient. When you're committed to something, you accept no excuses - only results."
– Ken Blanchard

Think about the hesitation you feel when someone says they will try to do something, such as, "try to come to your party". Take that as a 'no'. If they can't commit, the courteous thing to do is to extend their regrets, allowing you to update the guest list with definite attendees.

Trying should not be confused with doing. Trying is not action. It lacks commitment and it doesn't get the job done. Doing is the only thing that will advance you toward the goal. Approach every obligation or objective with confidence it will be successful completed. If you aren't sure, ask for help or look for other solutions.

Three little letters can make all the difference between success and failure. Listen to the difference between "I am going to lose weight" vs. "I am going to try to lose weight." Now fill in the blanks with whatever has been holding you back: I'm going to _____ vs. I'm going to try to _____. Total commitment will put your mind in action mode with success in clear sight. Your subconscious is a powerful thing. Once you're fully committed to success it will get to work on your goal.

Trying is a default excuse that sets the stage for failure. The wise Jedi Master, Yoda, expressed this best in The Empire Strikes Back when he said, "Do or do not. There is no try". This doesn't mean you will succeed every time, but you will enjoy a much healthier success rate if you state your intention as a non-negotiable. Don't just try it. Dig your heels in with resolute determination and do it.

LET IT GO

"Some people believe holding on and hanging in there are signs of great strength. However, there are times when it takes much more strength to know when to let go and then do it." – Ann Landers

Are you weighed down by heartache or anger following a failed relationship? Are you nursing wounds inflicted by unkind or thoughtless words? Life doesn't always go as planned and when that happens we risk injury and collateral damage. It's important to let go of past feelings and resentment or you run the risk of letting them consume you. Your former partner is probably not spending much time pining for you and the person who hurt your feelings may not even realize they did. If the only one suffering is you, it's time to let it go.

We grow and evolve, and sometimes relationships, careers, or interests should change because they no longer fit our needs. Take a step back and consider what you want out of life. Now look at the people you spend time with and what you spend time doing. Focus on what you can do to improve the situation instead of maintaining status quo, making excuses, or suffering in silence. If you're not truly happy right where you are, consider what you can do to shake things up and get moving in the right direction.

Not every relationship is meant to last forever. Build some memories, acknowledge the good that came from it, gather your strength, and move on. When you let go of people and things no longer aligned with your values you are energized and able to attract relationships and choices that are a better fit. It's time to let go of whatever is keeping you up at night and make room for the life you deserve.

LEARN TO SAY NO

"The difference between successful people and really successful people is that really successful people say no to almost everything."
– Warren Buffett

Simplify your life and ease stress by learning to say 'no'. It feels so good to be needed that 'yes' rolls off your tongue each time you are asked to chair a committee, check someone's work, or spearhead a new project. You want to be included but spreading yourself too thin causes you to feel overwhelmed and resentful. These feelings can be avoided with a series of gracious, but firm 'no's'.

It sounds easy enough to donate a little time and talent, but once committed the pressure is on. Be clear about your availability and interest. Adding one more 'must do' to your 'to-do' list automatically demotes the things you really want or need to do to the bottom of the list.

Time is your most precious commodity. There's a finite amount available so choose to use it doing what is important to you. Evaluate every opportunity that comes your way by asking if it will add value to or impact your life, in a positive way. If it won't, a polite, but confident 'no' is the best answer. If that's too hard offer an alternative solution. When people understand your house-of-cards life risks collapse if you try to squeeze in one more thing they will respect your decision. No further excuses or apologies will be necessary.

It's up to you to decide how to allocate limited time and energy. When you commit to activities that don't benefit your life it takes the focus and productivity away from things that do. The next time someone asks for your commitment to their cause, take a breath, think about your personal limitations, and consider responding with a polite, positive negative.

SAY YES TO LIFE

"Just say yes and you'll figure it out afterward," – Tina Fey

Yesterday you learned to say 'no' to things that hold you back and today is about saying 'yes' to life. Opportunity knocks at the most inconvenient times. It shows up when you're too busy, not feeling adventurous, stretched too thin, or simply afraid you will get in over your head. But what if opportunity appeared at just the right time? Would you recognize it and opt in or play it safe and wait for the next big break?

What's the worst that can happen? Failure is a possibility when we try something new, but the risk of failure lurks even in the safety zone. Corporations re-size and lay off long-term employees just before retirement, long after entrepreneurial prospects have passed them by. If you don't try you risk being overlooked in the next round. Missed opportunities don't encourage or increase more prospects. Once you close the door, complacency and 'what if' blues settle in. Good is good enough. No need to expect more, but, what if? What might your life look like now if you had answered the knock?

What's the best that can happen? When you are a 'yes' to life you attract positive, exciting choices. No more sitting on the sidelines of life. A 'yes' will spark your creativity and inspire you to do more, be more, and live a rich, robust life. If an opportunity really interests you, step out of your comfort zone and commit with absolute confidence that you are up to the challenge.

How will you ever know your true limits if you don't stretch yourself and welcome every possibility with open arms? Living your best version of life requires a little blind faith, crossed fingers, and following your intuition. Say yes! You have everything to gain.

FORGIVE

"Let us forgive each other. Only then will we live in peace."
– Leo Tolstoy

When someone disappoints or treats you badly you feel hurt and angry. That's normal. If you hold on to negative feelings they begin to wear on you, poison your attitude, and the bad guys win. Let go of the bitterness and resentment caused by others and you win. It is therapeutic to forgive, move on, and allow the healing to begin. Here are a few thoughts on forgiveness:

- It's not necessary to let the offenders know you forgive them. Some people and things can be left in the past. Going back may risk opening old wounds.
- Whether you let them know personally or simply set yourself free, you are not giving them an out. What they did was wrong and forgiving them does not change that.
- Forgive does not mean forget. As you move through life and experience different relationships, careers, and personal growth, you recognize behavior and situations that are acceptable and others you won't tolerate. Live and learn. With each bruise you establish healthier boundaries for personal self-preservation.
- Forgiveness is not important for the sake of the offender. Forgiveness is important for your own peace of mind, happiness, and well-being.

The next time you bristle when something triggers a past hurt, be the bigger person and offer up forgiveness. And while you're in compassionate mode, spread the love and accept a little self-forgiveness for any part you may have played. We all make mistakes. Acknowledge

them and move on to more positive and uplifting relationships.

BUSY VS PRODUCTIVE

"It's not enough to be busy. So are the ants. The question is, what are we busy about?" – Henry David Thoreau

Ask almost anyone to describe their life today and you are likely to hear one of two current default complaints: "I'm too busy!" or "There's not enough time to get it all done!" Busyness is a smoke-screen that keeps us safely in our comfort zone, and not having enough time is a popular, but not valid excuse. There is enough time. We just don't use it wisely or on the right things. Staying busy is easy. Focusing your energy on priorities and tirelessly working toward your goals is more difficult and doing it will protect you from distractions and procrastination.

We have become a nation of multi-tasking, unfocused individuals flaunting over-scheduled lives like they are a badge of honor. Busy people feel the need to tell you just how overbooked they are. Productive people don't talk about it, they let the results speak for themselves. Talking to someone who claims to be so busy they can't come up for air can be intimidating. They must be very popular, successful, or interesting. But when you take a step back and look at what you accomplish on any given day without unnecessary drama, you realize you are doing okay.

Regularly review your to-do list, identify your number one priority, and tackle it first. When that task is completed, repeat the process. Every time you add something to your schedule ask yourself if it will be the most productive use of your time or will move you closer to your goals. At the end of the day you will enjoy a gratifying sense of accomplishment knowing you completed exactly what needed to be done. Be honest with yourself, stay on track, and you will soon be enjoying stress-free, rewarding results.

STOP COMPLAINING

"Complaining about a problem without a solution is called whining."
– Teddy Roosevelt

It's easy to get into the habit of complaining about life's problems, big and small. "My wife doesn't understand me". "My husband cares more about his his work than me". "The copier is jammed again". It's an endless litany of complaints from people who really have a pretty great life if they would just take a step back and view it through a new lens.

Chronic complaining is a bad habit, but one that can easily be reversed. Instead of complaining about the tedium of your day, recognize daily routines as peaceful rituals. When you find yourself in whining and complaining mode take a little time for introspection and investigate what is really bothering you. Don't focus on irritants and disappointments. Once you identify the root of the problem, work on a solution.

You might be tempted to push back in a negative manner when you're afraid. Face your fear and fix it. Perhaps you are simply overtired or overwhelmed with life. Let go of extracurricular activities and focus on just what needs to be done to get through the day. If you find yourself in the presence of an energy vampire, someone in negative mode who is draining your energy, try to find out what they are going through. Reach out to them with an offer of support. It might be all they need to turn themselves around. A good friend will return the favor when you feel the need to vent or could use a helping hand.

There is joy in daily living if you look for it. Ask yourself: Do I want to continue living with a negative attitude or do I want to be happy? Choose happy and find joy.

FIND YOUR TRIBE

"Be careful who you call your friends. I'd rather have four quarters than one hundred pennies." – Al Capone

Thank your lucky stars for the friends who come to the rescue, no questions asked, regardless of the time they get the call. Consider yourself blessed to have a handful of friends like that during your lifetime. They are the same people who accept you at face value and never expect you to change to fit their mold. They are your tribe.

You may refer to them as your circle, network, or family. When you are with people who share the same values it's possible to let down your guard and relax. There's a level of safety and comfort sharing ideas with trusted individuals.

Be aware of the vibes you put out to attract the right community. Spending time complaining that life's not fair will attract like-minded people who support the belief and you will find yourself stuck with a tribe of whiners. Look for people who are similar or who possess attributes you admire. Identify commonalities in outlook and interests, both professionally and personally. Be optimistic, hopeful and mindful of what it is you really want. Put it out there and attract people who will build you up and encourage the best possible you. It's reciprocal, do the same for them.

Building a tribe is an on-going, lifelong process. Through growth and change you might decide to open the circle to a broader, more diverse group or become more focused and pickier about who you let in. It's okay to recognize and acknowledge you have outgrown your childhood BFF if you no longer share the same standards and beliefs. If you are authentic, confident and continue looking, you will find the perfect tribe.

SLAY YOUR DRAGONS

"Slay that dragon once, and he will never have power over you again."
– Steven Pressfield

Life is fraught with issues capable of shaking your self-confidence and taking the wind right out of your sails. Sometimes it feels as if you're fighting dragons on all fronts. The longer you live the more realistic you are about the ebb and flow of life. When faced with scary things your critical inner voice will sometimes fuel the fear rather than alleviate it. When you can stare down those fears, you have slayed your dragons and earn the right to be the knight in shining armor in your own personal fairy tale. But how do you do it?

First, honestly assess your challenges. Once you identify what you fear or what's holding you back it's all about mindset, attitude, and mental strength. A positive outlook and a little self-love can overcome almost anything. Start your day with a comfortable and comforting ritual that centers you and affirms your strength and capability. Read a few pages of an excellent book that speaks to your soul. Meditate, or check in with an accountability partner who has your best interest at heart. Exercise will get your endorphins singing your praises and quiet that annoying inner voice that warns you of potential failure and imminent danger lurking around the next corner.

Be gentle and understand that life comes jammed packed with the good, the bad, and the downright ugly. Take it one day at a time and when you get off course, recognize it, and re-align yourself with what is really important. Stand up to what haunts you, the familiar fears, as well as the yet unidentified. Don't worry about what you can't control as you move forward with confidence to claim your destiny.

SLOW DOWN

"There is more to life than simply increasing its speed."
– Mahatma Gandhi

Slow down...you're moving too fast. It's a fact: If you drive ten miles at 65 miles per hour instead of the posted speed limit of 55 miles per hour you will save one minute and fourteen seconds. Not enough time to risk a speeding ticket or the stress generated when racing to get someplace on time. And speaking of driving, it's not necessary, or beneficial, to cut in front of one car after another to position yourself a few car lengths closer to the destination. The effort will frequently find those same pushy drivers sitting next to you at the red light.

Instead of rushing through life take a little time to look around and appreciate the beauty of your surroundings. Eat a little slower. Chew your food and savor the experience. This will add a few relaxing minutes to your mealtime and when you're not wolfing your food it might be easier to connect with whoever is sitting across the table. Focus on the person or people you are with and enjoy the opportunity to share time with them.

Give yourself a much-deserved break. Schedule uncommitted white space into your daily schedule to simply breathe to allow your brain and body a chance to restore and refresh. Simplify and do less. You can't slow down when there are more items on your to-do list than there are hours in the day. Stop trying to multitask. You're much more efficient when mindful and focused on one task at a time. Learn to linger in the moment. There's no need to rush through life in the pursuit of happiness. Find happiness along the way and relish every unhurried minute of it.

THE POWER OF LOVE

"Love is a canvas furnished by nature and embroidered by imagination."
– Voltaire

Valentine's Day is primarily associated with romantic love involving hearts-and-flowers, chocolates, and candlelight dinners. You look forward to celebrating the love of your life in special ways. But don't overlook the many other ways to love and make the day mean so much more to so many more.

Valentine's Day hype is focused on the love-struck romantic kind of love, but it's a perfect time to honor the bonds created by the companionship of friends. You love the people you can relax with and share comfortable downtime. These are unique and special relationships. No pressure, no competition, just friends being friends or much-loved siblings who are always there for you. Family and best friends are forever and should be cherished on this day. It's a time for friends to rededicate themselves to friendships and families to share their love over favorite meals and traditions as a way of marking the occasion.

Acknowledge the people you enjoy, look up to, or trust. Act like the school kids and exchange cartoon pop-outs, handmade Valentine cards, or heart shaped candy and sugary pink treats.

Thank your mentors and cheerleaders with sappy cards letting them know how important they are to you.

This may be a day designed to highlight romantic relationships, but it's so much more. It is a red-letter day because it's the one that reminds you to be grateful for the love you have in all of its many forms and to reach out and celebrate those relationships. Make this day count by reminding the people you hold dear how important they are. Start today, but don't be afraid to tell them how much you appreciate and love them every day. Love is all you need.

SELF-COMPASSION

"If your compassion does not include yourself it is incomplete."
– Jack Kornfield, Author Buddha's Little Instruction Book

You're quick to excuse the shortfalls and folly of others but expect and accept nothing less than perfection on the home front. The incessant chatter in your head can be mean spirited and discouraging. It's time to give yourself a break by reframing and redirecting self-talk into positive reinforcement and admit that you are, after all, only human.

There are two inner voices for every story. One points out you dropped the ball and the other recognizes you did some things right and learned from the process. You show up for a job interview noticeably unprepared. You can beat yourself up or admit the mistake, consider it a practice run, and vow to never let it happen again. Before the next opportunity appears invest some time and energy into script practice and become familiar with the prospective company's mission statement, values, and goals. Anticipate questions the interviewer might ask and be prepared to respond with confidence. Treat yourself like you would a friend and offer encouragement about what you did right and reassurance you will never 'wing it' again.

Self-compassion should not be confused with self-pity. It doesn't involve wallowing or feeling sorry for yourself. It's the same empathy you extend towards others when things go wrong, turned inward. It's a kinder, gentler way to live than constantly judging and falling short. Indulge in a little hopeful optimism things will improve.

Find one small success and grow from there. Build self-esteem by becoming your own best advocate. Pat yourself on the back with pride, become a personal cheerleader, and celebrate all that is positive. Learn from mistakes, out shout that inner critic, and try, try again. No one likes a bully.

PRIORITIES TAKE PRECEDENCE

"The key is not to prioritize what's on your schedule, but to schedule your priorities." – Stephen Covey

The most important use of time is spent doing things that reflect personal values and move you closer to your goals. The only way to be sure the important things are done is to prioritize the time spent on each task. Re-visit your goals and concentrate on doing the things that will make a difference. Avoid distractions and stick to your priorities to maximize available time, energy, and effort.

You're pulled in too many directions with too much to do and not enough time to do it. Lists become the critical first step to prioritizing. Make a list of action items related to advancing your career and to maintaining life balance by finding ways to schedule family and relationship building time. It's very important to include all-important personal time to avoid the feeling of resentment that creeps in when you do too much giving and too little replenishing of your own body, mind, and spirit.

Throughout the day ask yourself the question: "Is what I am doing right now moving me closer to or farther from my goals?" The answer will help you devote time to the things that really matter. It's not about being busier or working faster. It's about focusing on the right things. It's very easy to get distracted and off course. By working on the most important activities you will achieve more of what you want which will energize you to pursue even more interests.

At the end of the day you will feel tired but accomplished. There won't be any stress or anxiety about what didn't get done because you concentrated on what was needed to create the life you want to live.

BE THE CHANGE

"Carry out a random act of kindness, with no expectation of reward, safe in the knowledge that one day someone might do the same for you."
– Princess Diana

National Random Acts of Kindness Day garners more attention and spreads more joy every year. It is celebrated by individuals, families and groups across the nation to encourage selfless, unexpected acts of kindness.

Just one small gesture can change your world and the world around you in an instant. If you're having a bad day quickly turn it around by doing something nice for someone else for no reason other than to put a smile on their face, and your own. Whenever we make an effort to positively impact those around us, even in a very small way, everyone involved benefits. There is definitely a strong connection between being kind to others and being healthy, confident, and well-balanced.

Spread cheer today with unexpected acts of kindness. You might start by tucking a love note in your children's or spouse's lunch box. Make a donation to a favorite cause, write a note of encouragement to someone who's going through a tough time. Pick up the tab for coffee or lunch or leave a generous tip at dinner and jot 'thanks for the great service' on the receipt. If in fact, you didn't experience five-star service, the lucky patrons at the next seating will benefit.

It's easy to get caught up in making it through the day and overlook the remarkable benefit of the even tiniest act of kindness. A smile or a sincere compliment is simple and easy to give and can produce a sunnier outlook in an instant. Start now and change your day, and the world, for the better.

YOUR NON-NEGOTIABLES

"It has been said that success only shows up when determination does…but it must be powered by a non-negotiable decision."
— Doug Firebaugh

Make a list of your non-negotiables. These are the beliefs that are ingrained deep inside, make you who you are, and never change no matter what happens. Base them on your values and personal line in the sand. Here are a few possibilities for your 'always' list to get you started:

Always tell the truth. This is not about harmless little white lies or lies of omission about things that are better left unsaid. It's about truth and honesty. The truth not only sets you free, it builds trust and respect with others. *Always look on the bright side.* Not every relationship, plan, or day, goes as desired. Life is a balancing act and you have choices. Find the silver lining and make the best of it. *Always be learning.* Stay relevant, feed your passion, stimulate your brain, and generally make life more interesting for yourself and others by committing to learn something new every day. *Always try your best.* Set and keep your standards high. You will inspire others, become a great role-model, and live up to your full potential. *Always have goals.* Goals breathe life into dreams. They give direction and instill focus, accountability, and motivation. If you don't know where you're going you will never know when you arrive. *Always believe in yourself.* Approach life with a can-do attitude. Self-esteem soars, others look up to you, and success follows. *Always be kind.* Kindness is contagious. When you extend a hand or show compassion it builds self-confidence in the recipient and in you.

Look around and see the endless opportunities to reach out in kindness and help someone. What's on your 'always' list?

THE OTHER SIDE OF NON-NEGOTIABLES

"I am not a product of my circumstances. I am a product of my decisions." –Stephen Covey

Yesterday was about things to commit to doing at all times. Today let's explore the opposite side of your 'always' non-negotiables and build a personal 'never' list. This is a list of things you will never do, at any time, under any circumstances.

Never ignore your moral compass. It's located deep in the soul, guarding the vault of principles you hold dear. It guides you to exhibit upright ethical behavior and to make good decisions reflecting those values and should be held in the highest regard. *Never spend more than you have.* Out-spending your income leads to a debt-ridden, stressful financial life with no safety net when things go wrong. Create new habits like paying yourself first and get a taste of how satisfying saving feels. *Never take your health for granted.* Health is wealth and a precious gift indeed. Do what it takes to maintain a healthy body and mind. Eat right, exercise, and get enough sleep. Give thanks every day for good health. *Never forget your manners.* Good manners are an indication of good character. Make the effort to be courteous and respectful and let people know you value them. *Never give up without trying.* Don't cave in and say 'I can't' before trying. Success comes in 'cans', not 'can't'. *Never litter.* It's easy to avoid creating litter but take it one step further. If you see litter pick it up and dispose of it properly. This a beautiful planet deserving of respect. *Never cheat.* Not on your diet, taxes, or anything else. Shortcuts and sidesteps have a way of catching up to you eventually and cheaters never prosper.

Create a personal list of non-negotiables and start living them today.

LOVE THE ONES YOU'RE WITH

"Do your little bit of good where you are; it's those little bits of good put together that overwhelm the world." – Desmond Tutu

You can choose your friends, but family represents the luck of the draw. Your relatives represent a cast of characters with individual beliefs, passions, and goals…or the lack thereof. Outside relationships, on the other hand, are based on mutual interests. So, it's a fact - devoting more time to family than friends might mean more time with people you have little in common with, even though you are connected by all important blood lines and family ties.

Outside the home you are kind, patient and generally try to present yourself in the best light. It's all about making a good first and lasting impression. But at home the unfortunate truth is your family might not always get the best you have to offer. It's easy to become impatient with the people most important to you, while kind and understanding to total strangers. You might find yourselves taking each other for granted or arguing over every little thing. You know the storm will blow over this time like it always has in the past. The truth is the family bond is strong enough to keep the clan together, history will repeat itself, and family will forgive family.

Familiarity can breed contempt particularly when you don't share similar views, but try to look past the quirks and shortcomings and take a look in your own backyard through a new lens. See your family from a fresh, new perspective. Make an effort to really listen to what they have to say, try to understand the world the way they view it, and "do your little bit of good" for the ones you're with.

FORWARD IS FORWARD

"It does not matter how slowly you go as long as you do not stop."
– Confucius

Life is not about speed. It is about consistent, steady forward progress. Remember Aesop's Fable, The Tortoise and The Hare? The Hare was clearly the favorite to win, but he squandered his talent and napped while the Tortoise plugged away and crossed the finish line. Confidence is good, but over-confidence lulls you into thinking you don't need to prepare, strategize, or in this case, even show up. You're tempted to relax knowing 'you've got this', and along comes a younger, hungrier contender who wins the race, the business, or whatever you stand to lose.

It was the Hare's race to lose. You might be armed with everything necessary to succeed, but if you fail to execute or stop short of completing the job, you lose. The Hare started strong but didn't finish. Sound familiar? You also get excited, pull the trigger, and then become sidetracked. Sometimes you almost reach the summit, take a breath, and stop trying. Resting on laurels gets you nowhere, fast.

It was the Tortoise's race to win. Slow and steady really does win the race. Slow progress is better than no progress. The Tortoise faced certain defeat based on talent and capabilities, but he believed in himself, did the best he could do, and his persistence paid off. He didn't worry about his competitor or wonder how he was doing. He cared only about what he needed to do to get the job done.

Life is a competition with yourself more than anyone else. Set a goal, prepare to win, visualize the result, and then start the journey. Run your own race. Give it everything you've got and don't stop until you reach the goal. Get ready. Get set. Go.

IF WE HAD MORE TIME

"One day you will wake up and there won't be any more time to do the things you've always wanted. Do it now." – Paulo Coelho

What would you do with an extra three hours per week? That might be just enough time to rekindle a friendship or schedule regular visits with a loved one you've been missing. It might free up time to sign up and take a class or join a group of like-minded individuals to share ideas and expertise. Catch up on your reading, meditate, volunteer, workout, breathe. It's remarkable what can be accomplished in just a few hours. If only there was a little more time in the day.

So, make the time. Carve out a little here and a little there and commit your 'found' time to the things you've always wanted to do, if only…

One small way to find time is to get up a little earlier in the morning. You may feel like you're stretched to the limit, but you won't miss a few lost minutes of sleep. Consider limiting television viewing time, curtailing a social media habit, or eating lunch in so you can leave work a little early. Assess your workload and delegate wherever possible, both at home and the office. An extra few minutes here and there will add up to blocks of time that can be spent on more important things.

Start today to do less of what doesn't matter and more of what does. Time is a nonrenewable resource. Use it or lose it. Stop doing things that aren't necessary or no longer bring you joy. Give up commitments that have run their course and/or do nothing to enrich your life. Spend more time doing the things you love, with the people you love to be with.

DO THE WRITE THING

"Writing in a journal each day, with a structured, strategic process allows you to direct your focus to what you did accomplish, what you're grateful for, and what you're committed to doing better tomorrow. Thus, you more deeply enjoy your journey each day, feel good about any forward progress you made, and use a heightened level of clarity to accelerate your results."
– Hal Elrod, Author, The Miracle Morning

When you were a pre-teen did you record all of life's happenings (real or imagined) in a personal diary complete with lock and tiny key? If so, you guarded that diary with your life, convinced everyone was trying to pick the lock and discover those all-important secrets. It's a safe bet the individuals you were afraid would snoop were being completely honest when they assured you they had no interest in it. If you weren't a risk taker or very adventurous no one other than you would find any interest in it, although it served a good purpose.

Writing then and now sheds light on your hopes and dreams, eventually identifying the path you will take to realize them. By expressing thoughts and feelings in written words you mindfully acknowledge what is important, what is stressful, and what brings happiness. It's an outlet to vent, identify emotions and clarity life goals. The results are for your eyes only so what do you have to lose?

A very effective journaling system is 'stream of consciousness' writing. Sit down with paper and pen and let your mind wander. Jot down whatever comes to mind, as quickly as you can, without over-thinking it or searching for just the right word. You will improve over time and release and strengthen the creative powers within you. Journaling at the end of each day will clear your mind and make way for a peaceful night's sleep.

NEVER SAY NEVER

"Never say never, because limits, like fears, are often just an illusion."
– Michael Jordon

As a teenager you probably thought your parents were uncool and outdated. You were determined never to act like them until, inevitably, you reached a certain age and became them. How many times have you sworn you would never fill-in-the-blank and found yourself having to eat those very words? Through growth comes change, and what looked like an impossibility one day becomes reality the next.

You dig in your heels and take a firm stance based on knowledge and past experience. As a newlywed you may have proclaimed, "No child of mine will ever play with toy guns", oblivious to a future darling little guy who innocently delights in noisy shoot outs with friends. That was all in fun as a kid, but as he grows into an adult his perspective changes and by the time he has his own children he might sound just like you. Something he was sure he would never do.

You entertained big ideas about a successful career and vowed to settle for nothing less than your very high goals. Then you achieved the dream and realized it wasn't for you. Or it's still your passion, but jobs are scarce, and you settle for work that was never in the grand plan.

So much of life is out of your control and decisions can be complicated. When given a choice look at the situation through more experienced eyes and realize that what was previously unacceptable, turns out to be the best solution in light of current circumstances. It's okay to change partners, parties, religions, and your mind if it's the best choice. No one knows what the future will bring so soften up those cast in stone beliefs and keep an open mind.

TRUST YOUR INSTINCTS

"Follow your instincts. That's where true wisdom manifests itself."
– Oprah Winfrey

Think of all the things you would miss out on in life if you were afraid to trust a hunch or acknowledge a gut feeling. Your mind is like antennas, constantly on the alert for signs that may be unseen and unspoken but are very real. They come through as 'feelings' or that insistent little voice in your head that is definitely worth listening to.

What if you swear never to fall in love again after someone you thought was 'the one' broke off the relationship? All of a sudden there's a new set of rules, you've sworn off the dating scene, willing to risk missing out on an even greater relationship a little farther down the road of life. Good friends will understand and support the decision, until that day when a trusted acquaintance encourages you to take a chance and it suddenly just feels right. By following your instinct you're open to the opportunity to meet the real 'one' or the best one for now. It could happen, but only by having faith in that elusive sixth sense.

Combine what your instinct says with what you have learned through experience and general knowledge and decisions become clear and easy. If you're weighing your options and alarm bells are going off in your head or the hair on the back of your neck is tingling the answer is a swift and definitive 'NO'. If everything resonates, there's no resistance, and it just feels right it's an easy 'YES' with no hesitation or misgivings and no need to seek advice or opinions from your support group. When it's right, it's right and every fiber in your body will confirm it. Don't be afraid to trust your gut.

RESPECT STARTS WITH YOU

If you want to be respected by others, the great thing is to respect yourself.
Only by that, only by self-respect will you compel others to respect you."
– Fyodor Dostoyevsky

We teach our children to respect their elders which includes nearly every person who touches their life. They are asked to respect parents, teachers, playground monitors, coaches, and so on, without question. That's not a bad thing but teaching self-respect at the same time would be a very good thing. Would the bullies in the schoolyard need a target if they felt better about themselves?

Self-respect is a critical factor that prepares you to face the world head on. If it wasn't fostered during formative years, now is the perfect time to address it. The first step toward nurturing self-respect is defining your personal values. Be careful not to let the opinions of others weigh in during this process. These are your values and should be the basis for every decision made or action taken. When you have a clear understanding of what you stand for, face the world with pride and confidence. You're living with integrity – presenting the world the authentic you.

Self-respect provides the self-confidence necessary to make good choices and the strength to stand by those choices, if challenged. Base your actions on sound personal values, not on the fear that you won't be accepted. When you demonstrate self-respect, you are positioned to respect others, or to keep a respectful distance from them, depending on the choices they make for themselves. There's no need to find fault, place blame, or indulge in gossip to make yourself look or feel better.

Take some time today to count your blessings. Be the head cheerleader, first in line every morning to hold yourself in the highest regard, confidently worthy of respect.

You've earned it and deserve it.

THE BUTTERFLY EFFECT

"That small difference made all the difference." – Johnny Rich, Author of The Human Script

One small cause can have an enormous effect. The butterfly effect theory explains how a minor change in one system can influence major changes in that same system as it further develops. The classic example of the theory describes a butterfly flapping its wings in one part of the world which eventually triggers severe weather conditions in another part of the world. An almost imperceptible action can affect very noticeable results given time.

Tired of being a couch potato, but can't seem to get off the sofa? Maybe this will motivate you. Studies have shown that marching in place during television's commercial breaks will burn calories and begin the process that will soon become a habit if practiced on a regular basis. That very simple 'flapping of wings' could soon lead to an evening stroll, short walks around the neighborhood, participation in a 5K event, and perhaps even a marathon. It could happen. As strength and stamina builds you will feel better about yourself, have more energy, and improve your self-confidence which could lead to growth in all areas of life.

Most great things start small. A slight move in the right direction could lead to significant life changes. In the example above you are more likely to succeed by walking in place in front of the flat screen than by hiring a trainer, hitting the track, and burning yourself out. Pick the pace that will allow you to maintain your enthusiasm for years to come. Planning and executing at an entry level causes gradual growth which will lead to lasting change.

Be the butterfly. Flap your wings and make your own weather. It might take a little time, but it will happen.

MIND OVER MATTER

"Be who you are and say what you feel, because those who mind don't matter and those who matter don't mind." – Dr. Seuss

Your mind is a very powerful thing. An optimistic attitude can aid healing, reduce or eliminate even the most serious symptoms, strengthen your immune system, and generally make the world a better place. In other words, positive thinking is crucial to your overall wellbeing. A negative attitude is just as powerful and can be counted on to exacerbate what ails you in every area of life. The evidence is overwhelming that minds can influence physiological and psychological life change and it's up to you to cause them to change for the better.

There are endless studies verifying the mind/body connection. It's a known fact that placebos often bring the same results as miracle drugs based on nothing other than the patient's expectation. Belief in the power of the pill, regardless of the ingredients, causes the body's chemistry to produce the desired medical result. The magic of mind over matter.

Watch an Olympic skier psyching up for an epic downhill journey. They close their eyes, get inside their head, and virtually experience the run from start to finish. Watch their head bob as they move and sway, nailing every bump and turn on the simulated track. They are ready to race it when it's their turn based on the thrill of victory they already experienced in their mind.

There's no need to wait until you're facing a life-threatening illness or life changing circumstance. Start with a committed decision, form a strategy around it, and believe it will happen. Put your powerful, creative mind to work today to positively create a life that matters. Expect and accept nothing less than success.

TAKE A LEAP

"Happy Leap Day. A day where 'this time last year' and 'this time next year' does not apply" – Anonymous

Every four years you are gifted with an extra day. It seems 24 hours times 365 doesn't quite add up to a full year. That adds up to six extra hours at the end of each year that are bundled together every four years to provide one more day. If today is that day you have some decisions to make. You don't want to squander your bonus day so how can you make the absolute best use of your time?

This might be a perfect day to catch up. You could use the extra day to check off those pesky to-do's that keep moving down the list or take on something as mundane as cleaning your closet and organizing the house. Those aren't exciting choices but sometimes getting your house in order, literally or figuratively, will fulfill and refresh you more than anything else.

On a more fun note consider indulging in a favorite creative outlet, like painting, music, or writing. Possibly some well-deserved pampering at the local spa is in your future. Look over your bucket list and see if this is the day to experience a once in a lifetime event. The sky's the limit on this rare day.

February 29th is an auspicious date to celebrate a birth. Leap Year babies get to celebrate on the day before or after on non-leap years, and then party four times as hard on actual Leap Days. That's pretty special, but there's one more advantage for the ladies. If you've been waiting patiently for a marriage proposal that hasn't come, take advantage of an old Celtic tradition that allows you to propose to the man of your dreams on this day. Take a leap of faith and make the most of this Leap Year.

EVERY DAY STARTS AT ZERO

"With the new day comes new strength and new thoughts."
– Eleanor Roosevelt

Yesterday may have been something less than a stellar day, definitely not one for the record books. It happens. But yesterday is gone and today is a new day, a new beginning, one that's brimming with endless possibilities. It's up to you to decide how this day will be different, more positive, or more productive. Embrace the opportunity to learn something new, meet someone new, or explore uncharted territory.

Each morning your day re-sets to zero and with planning and a little focused discipline it can quickly rate a ten. What changes will you make to enrich your life today? Commit right now to start living this and every day as if it were your last. Let the people you love know it. Reach out to someone you've lost touch with and reconnect. Be the bigger person, mend fences, and extend an olive branch where, and if, needed. You don't always have to be right. Sometimes it's enough just to be happy. When you learn to let things go you experience serenity and peace of mind. This allows you to make and savor wonderful memories, to be fully present in every moment, and appreciate the 'now' along the way.

You are the only one in control of your life and the way you choose to spend each day dictates how exciting, challenging, and interesting your life will be. Set your intentions to turn this page in your book of life into something promising and adventurous. Make a list of your expectations and begin with a mindset of success and positivity. When you do this your day will reflect that mindset making it possible to manifest a positive outcome.

THE POWER OF THE WRITTEN WORD

"The more that you read, the more things you will know, the more that you learn, the more places you'll go." – Dr. Seuss

Reading is a tremendous source of growth, inspiration, and creativity and can be one of the great joys of life. Not everyone enjoys reading and many who do simply cannot find the time. There are alternate ways to enjoy the written word, such as listening to books while driving or working out. If you like to read, but don't have the luxury of time, there are apps that provide 'compressed knowledge' by distilling books to short summaries.

Reading is a daily habit shared by leaders and other successful people worldwide. You are a leader in some capacity and, as such, should make an effort to read. If you are a parent, you have committed to the most important and daunting leadership role of your life. There are hundreds of excellent books to help you in that role. Read business books and increase your value to the organization. People are thirsting for leadership and reading will prepare you to step up. Educational books, how-to's, and self-improvement publications change lives and a good novel will transport you to another time and place.

If reading is not currently part of your daily agenda commit to at least a few pages every day. Listening to books, speed reading, or taking advantage of the highlights of the abridged version are equally valuable ways to stimulate your brain. Books provide valuable information to tuck away and use later as an ice-breaker or conversation starter. Dust off your library card and borrow actual books or download an unlimited assortment of works the library offers on-line.

You read this page! Now keep going…happy reading!

WAKE-UP CALLS

"In the absence of wake-up calls, many of us never really confront the critical issues of life." – Stephen Covey, First Things First

Remember the glory days when you stayed fit and trim without lifting a finger? You took it for granted, became complacent, and over the years, added a few pounds in all the wrong places. The much-anticipated class reunion invitation has arrived and the walk you just took down memory lane left you winded. Unless you start today and make some drastic changes your classmates will reunite with a much less hale, somewhat hardier version of you. In that moment you realize it's time to renew your lapsed gym membership and stock up on crash diet staples. That is a wake-up call.

If you are living your life on auto pilot take a moment to consider what would wake you up. It usually takes a significant occurrence like a serious health issue or the loss of a job, relationship or close friend to snap us out of our comfort zone. Don't wait for a life-changing event to rise above merely existing and start truly living, to stop dreaming and start doing. The time will never be perfect and there will never be enough money. The litany of excuses is endless so eliminate them, face the fear, and start chasing your dreams now. Make a plan and begin to take the actions necessary to turn your visions into reality.

You only live once. Stop going through the motions of daily life and commit to spending your time on earth living life to the fullest. Continuing to delay happiness until some indefinite future date may have you looking back with misgivings and regret. Answer the call and start fully living today.

BE A GOOD STEWARD OF YOUR LIFE

"Be a good steward of your gifts. Protect your time. Feed your inner life. Avoid too much noise. Read good books, have good sentences in your ears. Be by yourself as often as you can. Walk. Take the phone off the hook. Work regular hours." – Jane Kenyon

A good steward responsibly manages and cares for the resources entrusted to them. When you take full responsibility for your life and make good choices you feel fulfilled and in control. Every choice made and every action taken makes a difference. Decide to be a productive contributor and commit to excellence in all areas of your life.

You are in charge of your body and should nourish it with healthy food and regular exercise to keep it strong and fit. Protect your mind with positive thoughts by reading excellent books and committing to constant learning.

God provides material things with the expectation you will accept full responsibility for them. Good stewardship requires maintaining your home and personal environment in the best possible condition. Keep your car clean and in top running condition. Likewise, all possessions should be treated with care and maintenance should be timely, not deferred. It's just the right thing to do.

He also blessed humans with various other gifts. Enhance and refine your special talents and abilities until they are the best they can be. If you're interested in the arts, sports, or hobbies commit to whatever must be done to perfect your part. Work on enriching and improving personal relationships. Be a good steward by deliberately allocating time to development and growth. Every action you take affects progress either positively or negatively so make good choices this day and every day.

STRENGTH THROUGH ADVERSITY

"Hang in there. Trust that those winds of adversity are blowing away what's not needed while making you stronger." – Anonymous

Biosphere 2 is a replication of earth, constructed under a huge glass dome. The interior is a closed ecological system with purified air and water and an artificially controlled agricultural system featuring perfect weather conditions. It was designed to allow the study of the planet's living systems to find out exactly how they work. After collecting data for several years scientists were amazed to discover the negative effect those 'perfect' growing conditions had on trees.

Saplings inside the biosphere grew very fast and then collapsed. They soon realized trees require the stress of wind for survival. In natural habitats, wind blows against them creating the need for deeper roots to withstand the pressure. A stronger root system supports the weight of the trunk as the tree grows taller. Trees in the biosphere did not thrive simply because they lacked adverse conditions.

Who hasn't, at one time or another, longed for a wind free, utopian existence? But that's not how real-life works, and everyone must run the gauntlet of tough times. Sometimes it seems as if the storms and stress will never subside. When life tests your spirit stand firm, make good decisions, and adapt as needed. Learn to be flexible when faced with circumstances that are unwelcome or out of your control.

If you spend your days sheltered from life, you will miss important lessons that can only be learned when faced with adversity. A wise man once said, "What doesn't kill you makes you stronger". It's true. Each lesson of life strengthens and prepares you for the next one. Welcome the challenges, face them head on, and stand tall and strong.

WELCOME WHIMSY

"Living a life fully engaged and full of whimsy and the kind of things that love does is something most people plan to do, but along the way they just kind of forget." – Bob Goff, Author of Love Does

When was the last time you did something purely 'on a whim? Maybe you jumped on a plane at the last minute to take advantage of a terrific travel opportunity or played hooky and headed to the beach when the sun finally broke through the gloom. It was exhilarating, but it probably doesn't happen often. At least, not often enough. Life gets busy and you are responsible, an admirable trait most of the time, but every now and then a little impulsive behavior is just what's needed to zest things up.

You experience down times that are lackluster or uninspired. You love to be organized and pride yourself on the ability to plan every detail of life. You are a steadfast and dependable rule follower, a solid citizen living an efficient, well-organized life. A pop of spontaneity now and then would certainly get those juices flowing. If you're bored it's the perfect time to get busy and to do something outside the normal routine. An outing or adventure purely whimsical in nature, even once, will renew your enthusiasm and reboot your mindset.

Change your morning routine and enjoy a cup of coffee in bed, leisurely. Schedule your workout at a different time or in a different place. A change of scenery might inspire fun. Indulge in some luxurious downtime. Sleep in, day dream, or sit down and write a letter. Make a list of things you have been meaning to do when there's time and schedule one right now. Intentionally do something today just for the sheer fun of it.

NO LIMITS

"There are no great limits to growth because there are no limits of human intelligence, imagination, and wonder." – Ronald Reagan

From day one your brother was the smart one and you were the pretty one. Or he was good at sports and you were the smart one. Now you're grown and still gorgeous, but beauty does not define you and you really want to take up tennis. In either case you internalized the beliefs from early childhood and they are still embedded in your psyche today. "I can't..." or "I'm not..." are natural responses that, left unchallenged, will limit success, joy, and potential.

It didn't just happen in childhood. You continued questioning your abilities and value throughout life, limiting options and restricting growth. You've tried to move up the corporate ladder on several occasions, but the promotion is always awarded to someone else. It's easy to convince yourself you're not good enough because that's what it feels like when you're passed over. But you are good enough. The right position might be just around the corner. Believe in yourself and choose to wait for the next opportunity where you are or look for a better one elsewhere. Apply the same option to relationships and other interests and the prospects are unlimited.

What's holding you back? It's time to re-wire your brain and take a chance. Identify the demons and face them head on. Is this a personal belief or did your parents or others convince you? Write down what you currently believe to be true. Now write down what you know or have learned about yourself and your abilities. You may find the opinions carried for so long are illusions, after all, and not the truth. Think about what life would be like if you implemented a new truth around those misbeliefs. Live the new truth and know for sure the sky's the limit.

GIRL POWER

"A woman is like a tea bag – you never know how strong she is until she gets in hot water." – Irish Proverb

International Women's Day celebrates women everywhere to positively bridge the gender gap and raise awareness of the ongoing disparity between the sexes. The holiday was founded in 1909 and celebrates noteworthy achievements by women politically, economically, and socially. It was established to inspire women's empowerment and individuality and to fast-track parity with men.

The gender pay gap is real. Women are no longer content just to stay home and cook up the bacon. They represent almost half the workforce, which means that about half the time they bring it home, too. A man employed in the same role as a woman, with the same title, and equivalent experience and education earns twenty-three percent more today than his female counterpart. You've come a long way, baby, but there's a lot more work to be done.

If protest marches aren't your thing, International Women's Day can be celebrated in a number of gracious ways. Women celebrate this day by coming together and networking with peers to share awareness, support, and empower one another. Attend and contribute to women's events and conferences. Reach out to the significant females in your life with a note of thanks or a small gift. Express gratitude for the self-confidence you enjoy because of their belief in you. Plan a 'girl's night out' and connect with your favorite ladies for some serious girl talk.

This is not us against them, male vs. female, he said/she said. Every individual deserves to be treated impartially and compensated based on merits, not gender. Combine forces, be inclusive and invite a few of your favorite guys to join the fun. Bridge the gap, and begin to change the world.

GET ON WITH LIFE

"Cry me a river, build a bridge, and get over it." – Justin Timberlake

Life is too short to be wasted worrying about something that has already happened. When you get stuck in that rut emotions take control and you're not open to what might be an even better situation. If you don't like the way your last relationship ended take what you learned from the experience and put your energy into establishing a healthier one. Still smarting from being passed over for a leadership position at work? Don't sit and stew about it. Take positive action. Share your goals with someone who can help you. Ask them to keep you in mind for the next opportunity or to groom you for advancement if you are lacking in skills or experience. Prepare yourself in advance to be the next best choice.

How you react to the hand your dealt is entirely up to you. Take charge of your life and make the decision to move forward. Stop complaining and blaming your circumstances on others. You alone are responsible for your life and through positive action can get out of neutral and into high gear. There's no time to worry or wallow when you're focused on productive behavior.

Well-intentioned family and friends freely give advice without really knowing the whole story. Listen to the voice of reason in your head and follow your heart. Be your own best advocate and make certain the outcome is different next time. Get up and get over it. Do it now because once you do you'll be too busy being happy to pay any attention to what hurt so much in the first place. Move past it or move through it, but whatever it takes, move on.

BE PRESENT

"If you want to be happy, do not dwell in the past, do not worry about the future, focus on living fully in the present." – Roy T. Bennett, The Light in the Heart

Life is made up of a series of moments and those moments are easily missed if you are constantly looking forward to what is just around the bend. Let your thoughts race ahead and you miss the turn or the important point in a conversation. When your attention is not future focused it gets stuck on rewind and trapped in the endless loop of your past. Everything is clear in hindsight, planning ahead is virtuous, but the present is where life happens, with or without you.

You're driving through town one lovely spring afternoon and your young daughter comments on the gorgeous flowers you just drove past. Sadly, you didn't even notice them. Driving along lost in thought, worrying about something that happened in the past or anticipating a future event you're rarely, if ever, fully present. It's a safe bet you're living life on autopilot.

Being present is not easy. Life is filled with distractions and countless minor details that constantly vie for attention. Start small. Practice mindfulness by consciously directing your attention to the here and now. If you find yourself finishing a meal without really tasting it or arriving at your destination with no recollection of how you got from point A to point B this is for you. Take time to enjoy mealtimes without phones or external distractions. Deliberately engage in every part of the day by pausing long enough to savor meals, pay attention, and appreciate your surroundings. Literally take time to stop and smell the roses. Be mindful and inspired, one moment at a time.

HOPE IS NOT A VERB

"Life's not about expecting, hoping and wishing, it's about doing, being and becoming."– Mike Dooley

Alexander Pope spoke for all with his words, "Hope springs eternal in the human breast..." Without hope you have nothing. However, hope, without action, won't get you anywhere. Combine the word with any verb and the process is started. A sound plan put into action will make it happen. Ah, but that's where things go sideways and become a wish and a prayer. Begin by asking yourself, "How will I get from where I am today to where I want to be?"

If this is the year you hope to pay off your credit cards, decisions must be made. How will you do it? What is your plan of action? One strategy might involve paying off the account with the highest fees first, then the next highest, and so on. Another possible approach would require opening a new account offering zero interest for a set period. By consolidating all your high interest cards onto the no interest one every dollar paid would reduce the debt. Consider all options and choose the one that will work best for you. Once that's done earmark how much you are willing and able to commit, and how often. Apply the same methodical formula to achieve your weight loss/workout regimen/retirement savings goals. There are usually several possible ways to transform hope into reality, but you won't get to square one if decisions aren't made and action isn't taken.

Don't ever give up hope. It's where growth, improvement and a better life take wing. Hope change will occur, hope things will improve and then do what it takes to manifest your dreams, one well planned action at a time.

PERFECTION IS OVERRATED

"Perfection is not attainable, but if we chase perfection we can catch excellence." – Vince Lombardi

Try as you might to reach it, perfection will always be just a little out of reach, thwarted by those annoying imperfections. And that's okay. You're convinced you would be truly happy if only you were thinner, smarter, richer, or better looking. In other words, perfect. The thinnest people in the world aren't the happiest. No one is happy when they're hungry. The smartest people aren't very relatable which can leave them pretty lonely. A quick check of the headlines confirms every day the rich/beautiful people live complicated lives fraught with problems on many levels.

Seeking perfection is stressful and the search becomes an endless cycle. You strive for perfection, fall short because you're human, try to live with disappointment, and then start again. You assure yourself this time you will achieve your unreachable goal. It may be time to admit you're not intended to be a perfect creature, just a little better today than yesterday.

It's not easy to change your mindset from nothing-less-than-flawless to perfectly imperfect, but give it a chance. Relax and embrace the real flawed and fabulous you. When your body is healthy and fit, it becomes the size it's intended to be. Likewise, it's not necessary to be the smartest, richest, or most beautiful. You can educate yourself and ask for help from others, as needed. You are rich in life experiences and enjoy the wealth of wonderful relationships. Recognize the real you is lovable and people who love you think you're beautiful. You accept all of the imperfect others in your life. It's time to give them a chance to get to know and love you just the way you are.

LOOK FOR CLUES

"Success leaves clues, and if you sow the same seeds, you'll reap the same rewards." – Brad Thor

Clues will smooth the road to success and can be found all around you. Avoid trial and error by simply following the clues left by innovators who paved the way for the rest. There's no need to completely reinvent the wheel when pursuing a new interest or career. Chances are good at least one person has already prevailed in that arena and dropped a few clues to guide you. Model your project on their plan and bypass the angst and frustration of the learning curve. Use established and perfected processes to guide you on the chosen path.

The first step is to define your dreams and goals. What exactly do you want to achieve? Once the objective is clear find someone who has attained success in that area. Select mentors who share your values, ethics, and passion. Gather all the information possible about them and the story of their success. Most confident, accomplished individuals will provide material and data to help and encourage others. They may direct your focus to the resources that matter (time, energy, action, and funding), and minimize the struggles that often block the road to success.

You can follow the clues through Internet searches, books, You-Tube videos, webinars, and personal interviews. It's possible to produce a perfect soufflé without suffering the disappointment of the deflated ones, or to dominate in the complex world of business without losing your shirt in the process. Follow the tried and true methods others have established, adopt strategies that work, and sidestep the pitfalls they encountered along the way. There will still be bumps, but with a previously tested roadmap it will be a smoother ride. Look for clues, they're everywhere.

BE COACHABLE

"My best skill was that I was coachable. I was a sponge and aggressive to learn." – Michael Jordon

There's no one right way to do most things. Sometimes you get stuck and won't consider needed changes because 'your way is the best way'. This might have more to do with avoiding change, or not wanting to appear vulnerable, than true belief. When you're too close to the problem your perspective is narrow, and you miss the big picture. It's easier to spot weakness and areas needing improvement from the outside looking in. Being coachable means you are receptive to the idea that a fresh approach and refined skills will make you better.

Coachable people have awareness, determination, and a positive attitude toward life. They are more likely to succeed because they respect the experience and skills of others. They are constantly striving to up their game by holding themselves accountable to meeting deadlines and getting things done. Athletes are the first coachable group of individuals who come to mind, but a good mentor can improve any area of life. Fitness instructors provide the consistent support necessary to help achieve and sustain health goals. Life coaches keep you centered and guide you through personal challenges. Business coaches clarify the vision needed to strategically build a profitable organization and provide the structure and incentive to maintain it.

Anyone who wants to succeed in business, health, relationships, or life in general should consider reaching out for the innovative concepts and inspiration coaching brings. Knowing someone is on your side, encouraging and cheering you on is empowering. Your coach might help you build a better mousetrap or open your eyes to new and easier paths to success. Be open to the possibilities. Be coachable.

LIFE IS MESSY

"Life itself is a haphazard, untidy, messy affair." – Dorothy Day

Every holiday event or party you plan looks great on paper. You spend time creating ambitious gift lists, making elaborate menus, and organizing activities, confidently incorporating many little details to guarantee a memorable event. And then the big day arrives, somehow sooner than expected, and the unfinished over-zealous lists are slashed, eliminating all but the absolute necessities. The menu is simplified and the table that should have been gloriously decorated in advance (according to the plan) has been relegated to a hastily set up do-it-yourself buffet. You justify the lack of planned activities by convincing yourself the guests would rather chat amongst themselves.

Messy can be spontaneous, unpredictable, and fun. You covered the messiness so well at the last event that you've been asked to help with a niece's birthday party. You arrive to find fifteen seven-year olds waiting for the party to begin. Your only option is to pump up the music, morph into DJ mode, and let the karaoke begin. It's still referred to as the 'best party ever'.

Relationships can become complicated and messy. We're all wired differently making it difficult to mesh completely with anyone else. There will be frayed edges, frayed nerves, and yes, a lot of messiness. Do the best you can and enjoy the journey. Happiness is the goal, not perfection.

Best laid plans will be derailed, and over complicated events are just that. Your house will never be completely clean, tax deadlines will be extended, and your garden will attract bugs. It happens. The next time you think everything should fit perfectly into its assigned place give yourself a break. Jump right in and embrace the messiness of it all. Sift through the piles and find your joy.

GET YOUR BEAUTY SLEEP

"Sleep is that golden chain that ties health and our bodies together."
– Thomas Dekker

Sleep deprivation is a chronic problem in this busy, over-complicated world. You learn to get by with fewer hours of sleep and convince yourself it won't hurt to burn the candle at both ends. But when you do so you risk your health and wellbeing. Your body enters repair and restore mode while you sleep. The memory and learning center of the brain is actively committing recent information to memory. A very successful study technique involves reading through test material just before bedtime. The brain sorts and stores what is needed overnight and the information is readily available for the upcoming test. It's a much gentler solution than pulling a sleep depriving all-night study session.

You make more errors when you're overtired and, admit it, you become short tempered and irritable. Who feels like going the extra mile when they don't even have enough energy to enjoy their morning mile? There's no get-up-and-go for the activities you usually look forward to with joyful anticipation. In slumber your blood pressure drops and brain waves, breathing, and heart rates slow. Blood is pumped to heal tissue and re-build muscle while organs and major systems get much-needed rest. When you run on empty sleep-wise your bodies' restorative processes are interrupted. Getting a good night's rest wards off illness because more virus and bacteria-fighting white cells are being made while you doze. And best of all, sleep helps keep the weight off. If you're not down for a long enough count you won't have time to process and store carbohydrates or regulate hormones to manage your appetite and metabolism. So, commit to seven+ hours of sleep and you will be smarter, thinner, and much more fun! Sweet dreams...

MAKE YOUR OWN LUCK

"I am a great believer in luck, and I find that the harder I work the more I have of it." – Thomas Jefferson

On St. Patrick's Day we roll out our brogue and talk about the 'luck of the Irish'. Until recent years the Irish seemed to lead a pretty hardscrabble existence. Year after year they toiled to coax potatoes out of the rocky landscape until the crops failed and The Great Potato Famine forced many to flee to America where they hoped for an easier life. The adventurous ones continued west to the gold rush eager to strike it rich. Many of the hardest working, and therefore, most successful miners were of Irish descent. Instead of giving them credit for their tenacity and determination they were dismissed as 'lucky'.

Chance sometimes works in your favor, but you can't rely on the outcome of unexpected or accidental events. The only way to ensure success is to take responsibility for your own actions. With a little foresight and carefully laid plans you can create more opportunities for things to go right and cause others to marvel at just how lucky you are. There are no short cuts. Being in the right place at the right time might be a stroke of luck or it could be the result of extensive research and planning. If you put in the time and effort you will increase the chance to be the 'right place/right time' individual.

Luck is an unpredictable occurrence, out of your control and it can go either way. It's the luck of the draw, bad or good. Take control of your life, set the stage for success by doing more than required and make your own luck. Good luck to you on this day, and keep in mind, "if you're lucky enough to be Irish, then you're lucky enough!"

AGE GRACEFULLY

"There is a fountain of youth: it is your mind, your talents, the creativity you bring to your life and the lives of people you love. When you learn to tap this source, you will truly have defeated age." – Sophia Loren

You would be extremely lucky and very happy to enjoy a long, healthy life without going through the actual aging process. Unfortunately, physiological changes are inevitable. Gravity takes its toll, waists thicken, thought processes slow, and strength and energy ebb. It's a predictable part of the lifecycle, but there are some steps you can take now to maintain quality of life through your golden years.

Implementing good nutrition is key to aging gracefully. A healthy diet offers many benefits resulting in less illness and more energy. You feel better when you enjoy a clean, simple diet. When you feel better, you look better.

Regular exercise is one of the most important things you can do to maintain a healthy body and mind at any age. It benefits how we feel physically, mentally, and emotionally. Your metabolism slows down after forty, causing weight gain making it even more important to get up and move around. When you look better, you feel better.

It's just as important to exercise your brain as it is your body. Some mental ups and downs are lifestyle related and preventable. Reading, writing, puzzles, and word games are activities that will keep your mind alert. Tune in, stay on top of current events, and remain relevant. It's never too late to learn something new to stay sharp and make you more interesting in the process. Let the days gracefully turn into years and enjoy every minute of the journey. Laugh a lot, give thanks, and keep your heart and spirit young.

FIND YOUR NORTH STAR

"It's about finding your values and committing to them. It's about finding your North Star. It's about making choices. Some are easy. Some are hard. And some will make you question everything."
– Tim Cook, CEO of Apple

The North Star is one of the first stars you learn to recognize as a child. It's the brightest star in the sky and takes center stage in the galaxy, remaining virtually stationary while the entire northern star system gravitates around it. Sailors have depended on it for centuries as a beacon for navigational guidance. The North Star is a pretty big deal.

What is your North Star? What one thing keeps you up at night, gets you up in the morning, and your whole world revolves around? Find it and you have identified your passion and your life's mission. Like the real North Star, it's a fixed purpose that may evolve as you change and grow but will remain essentially the same throughout your life. Follow it faithfully and stay on your own true course.

Real life contains roadblocks and detours which sometimes send you down a different path. You get caught up in the minutiae of day to day living and your goals have more to do with getting through life than conquering it. It's easy to get mired in a daily routine of career/kids/bills/errands which conflicts with or hinders your life's mission. When this happens recommit to your values and single-mindedly reconnect with your personal beliefs. Let the North Star aim you in the right direction and guide you toward your life path. Don't give up or give in. The storm will pass, the clouds will clear, and you will find your guiding light. Keep it in your sights every single day.

CELEBRATE HAPPINESS

"Happiness is not a goal...it's a by-product of a life well lived."
– Eleanor Roosevelt

In 2013 the UN General Assembly declared March 20 International Happiness Day. The happiness and well-being of humanity has now taken center stage and is celebrated around the globe on this day. The members of the Assembly recognize governance must involve more than upholding the law and maintaining the status quo. In conjunction with a day of happiness they launched 17 Sustainable Development Goals to "end poverty, reduce inequality, and protect our planet". This represents a cosmic shift that directs energy and focus to two separate fronts while working toward one common goal. Progress is not just about growing the economy. It's about growing the economy and increasing happiness as a basic human right. UN Secretary General Ban Ki Moon stated, "Social, economic, and environmental well-being are indivisible. Together they define gross global happiness."

The world is getting smaller. Humans are better together, and a day dedicated to happiness reminds us to reach out and connect with others in a positive way. Identify what makes you feel happy and content and share the feeling. It can be as simple as spending time with friends, enjoying a good laugh, or giving someone a big bear hug. It's about caring, support, and feeling like you're a part of something. People want and deserve to feel included. No one is happy when they're lonely. Starting today proactively find people to connect with, not in a social media kind of way, but in a warm human way.

If it's an important priority for the leaders of 160 countries, it should be at the top of your goal list as well. Together we can change the world in a very happy way.

SPRING BREAK

"Spring is nature's way of saying. 'Let's party!'" – Robin Williams

Goodbye winter, hello spring! The vernal, or spring, equinox is finally here bringing a balance of light and darkness. The days are warmer, and the sun moves higher in the sky providing extra hours to enjoy the outdoors. Your outlook is brighter as sunshine brings out the beauty of the season and chases away the winter blues.

Nature's miracles are happening all around, and you don't want to miss a minute. Find every excuse to go outside and revel in the fresh and new. Look up. Birds celebrate with song from dawn until dusk and butterflies shed their cocoons and take wing. Look around. Bulbs are springing up everywhere. Trees and perennials are leafing out and adding much needed color to the recently drab landscape.

Spring feels hopeful and hope, after all, springs eternal. It puts a bounce in your step and possibility in your heart as the world stirs and wakes up. Moods lift as bulky layers are replaced with the lighter, brighter clothing of spring. Smiles come more easily.

The return of spring should be celebrated on many levels. Treat all your senses to a little springtime today. Watch for the first glimpse of growth in the garden and puffy white clouds in a backlit blue sky. Listen for the happy sounds of the birds and the bees. Feel the sun on your skin. Open your windows and breathe in the fresh scented air. Bring a little more of the outdoors in and let a bouquet of fresh flowers erase the last remnants of winter. Taste the essence of spring by treating yourself to fresh berries for breakfast, over ice cream for dessert, or get the spring break party started with ice cream over berries for breakfast. Why not?

RETHINK SUCCESS

"Rethink success: Few people will ever discover that the most important business they will ever run...is their life!" – Tony Dovale, Author of SoulShift

Remember when you launched into adult life armed with ambitious hopes and dreams? You turned visions into goals and goals into action. One victory led to another until the bar was set pretty high. Your home and lifestyle improved with every step up the corporate ladder.

Or maybe, like so many, you aimed unrealistically high and fell flat. It happens. Either way it's time to take a fresh look at what success really looks like at this point in your life. If you are enjoying a big lifestyle, as well as the career that provides it, you may be exactly where you want to be, doing exactly what you want to do. But if the long hours and time away from family and fun cause resentment, look for solutions. When the car is almost paid for and you've been eyeing the latest model, weigh the options. A pink slip in hand might look better now than a new car and more responsibility. Just a thought.

Making enough money to support a comfortable lifestyle is admirable. But the next step up doesn't have to be bigger or more. Consider what life would look like if you maintained your current lifestyle and found a way to earn the same income working fewer hours. Live more/work less vs. work more/live less sounds a lot like success.

There are other ways to measure success besides money and possessions. Happiness, close family relationships, and personal well-being are significant benchmarks of success. Conspicuous consumption is so last year...and the Joneses you've been trying to keep up with might be deep in debt. It's your life, spend it wisely.

EXPECT THE BEST

"What day is it?"
It's today," squeaked Piglet.
My favorite day," said Pooh."
– A.A. Milne

Optimists are the glass half full people who go through life with the expectation things will turn out right. When they don't turn out as planned an optimist will somehow find the silver lining. They choose to either accept the disappointing result as a lesson learned or spin it until they find a win.

Optimism is a choice. Choose to look on the bright side of life. It's just as easy to find the negative or glass half empty in the situation, but optimists choose to acknowledge a positive outcome. They look for solutions instead of simply giving up when life gets difficult. A pessimist will throw in the towel and move on instead of trying a new technique or asking for help. Positive attitudes greatly improve coping ability and give you the strength necessary to face problems head on. And solve them.

Positivity is contagious. Hang around doom and gloom and it rubs off on you. Surround yourself with happy, upbeat people and you can't help but feel that way yourself. If you're struggling to find the sunny side, start with a smile. Paste one on even if you don't have anything to smile about. Once you look happy you'll start to feel happy. It's just that simple. Everyone who sees you will smile back and before you know it you'll be back on top with the attitude needed to win the day.

Look for the good in everything today. Rise above the fray and choose happiness. Resist the urge to criticize, judge, or find fault with others. You will experience less stress which leads to better health, confidence, and energy, simply by expecting the best.

LISTEN TO YOUR BODY

"The body never lies." – Martha Graham

Driver personalities are revered today. Go, go, go, and don't slow down or you'll be left behind. Your mind feels the pressure and sends a message to your body that a little stress eating would feel good right now. You don't indulge because of concern about your body image, which piles on additional stress. Your mind and body are in constant communication so pay attention to the signals.

It's okay to admit you're worn out and would love a nap, or hungry and snacking between meals. You're a unique individual with different restorative and fueling requirements. Some people thrive on less sleep or fewer calories, but most people pay dearly for discounting the importance of sufficient rest and nourishment. Replenish, as needed.

You know when you've pushed your body too far, but sometimes it feels good to test the limits and pay for it the next day. It's easy enough to figure out why your legs ache when you climb the stairs after a record number of squats, but random pains are rarely random. They mean something and it's important to discover the cause. Favor a sore foot long enough and it will trigger pain in your hips. That's understandable. The same pain with no clear explanation might indicate a larger problem and should not be ignored. Likewise, inexplicable weight loss might sound like an answer to prayers, but if you maintain consistent diet and exercise programs a noticeable change in weight, up or down, could indicate a problem, and should be brought to the attention of a doctor. Learn to recognize the signs and take precautions to resolve problems while they are manageable. Listen carefully. Your body is talking to you right now.

COLOR THERAPY

"Your attitude is like a box of crayons that color your world. Constantly color your picture gray, and your picture will always be bleak. Try adding some bright colors to the picture by including humor, and your picture begins to lighten up." – Allen Klein

Teachers of toddlers and young children know how important it is to wear bright, upbeat colors if they want a classroom or play yard filled with bright, upbeat youngsters. On days they select primarily dark outfits a little black cloud hovers overhead, and blah gray brings out the sulky or listless side unless offset with something more vibrant.

Take a lesson from the kids. Color is a big part of energy and mood. Pink is the preferred color for prison walls because of its soothing effect on the inmates, and it can do the same for you. A pop of yellow acts like a ray of sunshine and red will either excite or alarm you. Think fire trucks, flashing red lights, and red-light districts. Blue calms and speaks to honesty. If you are designing a new corporate logo, consider blue to display your trustworthiness. Also, a blue suit will give you a confidence boost when attending an important business meeting.

It's warming up outside. It's time to act like a caterpillar and shed your drab winter outerwear. Rearrange your closet and move the dark colors out and your brighter, lighter wardrobe in. Make a happy statement and celebrate spring by dressing in the colors you find outside in gardens, lush lawns, and the bright blue sky.

Color is subjective and the role it plays can change depending on personal preference, but experts agree it impacts emotions and influences mood. Look around and identify areas and items that could use a change of color to bring out the best in you.

THE JOY OF WAITING

"The idea of waiting for something makes it more exciting."
– Andy Warhol

Anticipation of a future event is an important part of life because it adds a little drama and excitement to what otherwise might be ordinary, everyday activities. Your life takes on a rhythm which could easily become a rut. You go to work, come home, run errands, visit friends, and so on. Humans are wired to anticipate positive events, so keep life interesting by scheduling fun at a later date to keep you on pins and needles in the meantime. A little forward planning will add a lot of pleasure to your life.

Spontaneity can provide unexpected fun and acting on impulse will surprise and delight, but having something to look forward to multiplies the pleasure by adding anticipation to the mix. Purchasing advance tickets for a popular concert or play makes waiting part of the total package. Working out the final details of your summer vacation in February gives you months to savor the joy you know the trip will bring.

It's sometimes better to tell the honoree a party is being planned for them than to wait nervously in the dark and shriek "SURPRISE" when they innocently open the door. What if they don't show up as planned or they arrive dressed inappropriately? Keeping the secret during the planning stages is nerve-wracking and can back-fire if they think no one remembered their big day or achievement. Chances are good they were on to you already and were dreading having to fake a shocked/surprised/grateful response. It seems so much kinder and gentler to allow them to look forward to the party, excited and looking their best.

Schedule at least one thing today that you will look forward to with barely contained excitement. Now sit back and enjoy the wait.

SELF WORTH

"The best investment you can make is in yourself." – Warren Buffett

Invest in yourself through education or personal development and raise the bar on your value as a human being. Enhancing your self-worth demonstrates self-love which is a critical component of happiness and guarantees a huge return on investment. Don't sell yourself short. There's nothing to give to others if you aren't fulfilled yourself.

Personal well-being in the form of physical and mental health should be at the top of your list, priority one. Pump up the bike tires or invest in a gym membership, personal trainer, or a new pair of hiking boots. Exercise is excellent for the body, as well as the mind. It energizes, de-stresses, and releases lovely endorphins that will enable you to embrace the day with confidence and peace of mind.

Evaluate your skills and talents and sign up for a class or seminar that will take you to the next level. Stay on the cutting edge of innovation in areas of interest and become the go-to expert in your field. It takes persistence and constant learning to remain relevant in today's fast paced world. The only way to stay ahead is to commit to consistent and on-going investment in continuing education.

Invest in a coach or find an accountability partner. Share your goals with them and strategically and intentionally create a plan for successful implementation. Invest in yourself business-wise and other-wise and become a better version each day of the person you were the day before. Your energy and confidence will attract like-minded people to you. Review your goals and get started. Go big and invest whatever it takes to improve in all areas of life. You're worth it and your value is increasing by the day.

BE AN ACTIVE LISTENER

"Since in order to speak, one must first listen, learn to speak by listening." – Rumi

High speed communication is available at your fingertips literally 24/7, but the high-tech options are no substitute for a two way, live and in color, conversation. You can effect positive change simply by becoming a good verbal communicator. The most effective way to have successful and effective conversations is to become an active listener. Active listening requires concentrating on the words being spoken, not the ones you expect to hear. It requires taking a break from the phone and computer, making eye contact with the speaker, and devoting your full attention to the conversation. If you need more information wait until they have stopped speaking to ask clarifying questions. It takes practice to fully connect, understand what was said, and form an appropriate response.

As you listen with your ears, watch with your eyes. What is the speaker's body language saying? Encourage them to continue by responding with a nod to indicate you are interested and give them permission to open up and communicate even more honestly. Imagine being able to express your thoughts to a loved one, spouse, or boss while being given their full attention. It would inspire trust, and by doing so, strengthen your relationship. Connecting in this way reduces the opportunity for misunderstandings and false assumptions. Try this technique when settling a conflict. A straightforward exchange of thoughts and feelings, asked/answered/problem solved. There are two sides to every story. Starting today, make the effort to hear what the other side is saying by tuning in and really hearing what is said.

EXIT STRATEGY

"It doesn't matter when we start, it doesn't matter where we start, all that matters is that we start." – Simon Sinek, Author

It's never too early or too late to start saving for retirement. Preparing financially for retirement might be more challenging today than it's ever been. People are living longer than ever and must support themselves for an increasing number of years. If your current plan is to work until the bitter end you might want to give that a little more thought. Working until your dying day would not be a bad thing, as long as you enjoy what you are doing, and remain healthy while doing it. However, given that health is an unknown, without the safety net of a retirement plan, you could find yourself in an untenable and unsustainable situation.

If you don't start planning for it today, when will you? Tomorrow might be your current plan, but what happens when life changes and tomorrow never comes? It's possible to start with a few dollars, and by funding your account consistently, set yourself up for the most important asset in your later years—peace of mind. Once you find the discipline needed to put money aside, and realize the effects of compounding interest, saving for the future becomes a gratifying game.

Do something today your future self will thank you for. Don't wait for the stars to align to design the life you want to live. Be disciplined, focused, and committed to financial planning for the future. Starting right now revisit your hopes-and-dreams list and allocate funds to those priorities. No matter how old you are, it's later than you think. Put some goals in place that will set you up for a life of contentment and serenity in your golden years.

ACCEPTANCE

"The greatest gift you can give to others is the gift of unconditional love and acceptance." – Brian Tracy

You look forward to having children to share your passion for football/golf/food/dance or whatever gives you greatest joy. It can be quite a disappointment to find those children have absolutely no interest or affinity for sports of any kind or they are picky eaters with two left feet. It's difficult to resist the urge to direct them to the pastimes and interests that make your heart sing but resist you must. If you continually try to clone them into mini versions of you, they will never blossom into the best version of themselves.

If they decide to take piano lessons, join a sports team, or follow their passion du jour, do whatever you can to make it happen. Practice acceptance by introducing a variety of subjects until you find activities that light them up. Think of it as 'falling forward'. If, and when, they lose interest, have them fulfill the commitment and fall forward to the next activity and give it the trial and error test.

Being curious and trying new things allows individuals to fine-tune talents and uncover hidden strengths and skills. Practice will allow pastimes to blossom into lifelong passions. It is amazing how often experimenting with something that doesn't resonate at the time will, at some future date, be put to good use. Even a minimal amount of knowledge, acquired while dabbling, offers an opportunity to become a big part of life at a later date.

Unconditional love means you accept others as they are and not as you want them to be. Everyone is unique in their own way and through acceptance you honor and encourage the quirks and idiosyncrasies that define them.

CHANGE YOUR CHI

"The best way to find out what we really need is to get rid of what we don't." – Marie Kondo, The Life-Changing Magic of Tidying Up: The Japanese Art of Decluttering and Organizing

Don't underestimate the energizing influence of Feng Shui and the positivity released through the 'power of placement'. Feng Shui is based on the premise that the arrangement of furniture and objects in your home or office affects the chi, or energy flow. It's possible to make simple changes in your personal environment to lift and enhance the chi. Energy, whether it's good or bad, will directly affect and impact your thoughts and actions. The more positive you feel, the more centered and content you will be throughout life.

Feng Shui is not a religion nor is it a passing fad. It is an art and a science that has been practiced in China for over 3,000 years. Instill balance and harmony in life by repositioning what you already own to allow the energy to flow. Begin the process by paring down excess possessions no longer needed or used. Look at everything as if you're seeing it for the first time. If an object is beautiful or means something special find a conspicuous place to display it. Every time you view it you will feel joy which in turn will brighten the whole room.

Lighten up. Raise the blinds and open the windows. Let in as much natural light and fresh air as possible. Pump it up by adding splashes of rich, invigorating color. Making a few simple changes will create a vibrant, airy atmosphere and improve the chi in your surroundings. The energy will lift and change with each adjustment. Create good chi and a balanced environment by inviting harmony and peace into your surroundings and life today.

MIND YOUR MANNERS

"Good manners will open doors that the best education cannot."
– Clarence Thomas

Good etiquette goes beyond a simple 'please' or 'thank you'. The basics are important, but courteous behavior goes much deeper. It comes down to respect for others, as well as, ourselves. It is simply treating people the way you would like them to treat you.

Demonstrate consideration for others by making eye contact, listening while they speak, and waiting until they finish before responding. Say 'excuse me' when walking in front of someone and 'I'm sorry' when you step on toes and an apology is necessary. Rise to the occasion by standing when you shake hands, greet someone, or bid them farewell and offer your seat to someone older who is standing. Understanding and practicing the art of sharing serves well throughout life. Make it a habit to graciously give credit where it's due, share knowledge, toys, recipes, tools, and above all, ideas.

Give your children a positive advantage by teaching them at a young age to be courteous and considerate. Well-mannered and respectful children make a better first impression, are more likeable, and are better equipped with basic life skills. Lead by example and your own polite behavior will set the standard for the household. Let the family know what you expect of them and offer positive reinforcement for good behavior.

Proper etiquette has relaxed considerably in recent years, but a little awareness of the needs of others will raise the bar once again. People who demonstrate sincere concern and consideration stand out. The use of good manners puts the needs of others before your own. Demonstrate authentic kindness and respect and make the people you interact with feel good while enjoying the added benefit of making yourself feel good, too.

LIVE OUT LOUD

"I don't want to get to the end of my life and find that I just lived the length of it. I want to have lived the width of it as well."
– Diane Ackerman, Author and Poet

Living out loud means pushing yourself every day to live life to the fullest with no regrets, reservations, or excuses. Some adventurous individuals pull up stakes, selling or bequeathing all of their worldly possessions with the exception of what will fit in a backpack. Off they go on an extended journey of adventure while you watch wistfully from the sidelines. What's preventing you from following their lead and living the life you want to live?

If there is something you have always wanted to do, put a plan in place now to make it happen. Backpacking might not appeal, but a rail, road, or mission trip might be calling your name. Champion a cause that is important to you. Put your whole self in and live on purpose, no apologies.

Set goals about the direction of the journey you will take rather than just the final destination. Make intentional and resolute choices on the road to your bliss. If you focus on the fun and the 'living' that will happen along the way, the pursuit will bring ample pleasure. Relish every step of the process and share your joy with others along the way.

Proactively design and manifest the life of your dreams. If you don't follow a plan you run the risk of going down the wrong road and ending at a default destination. It's your life so why not live it out loud and in color? Choose a path that delights, intrigues, and inspires growth. Engage and enjoy every step of the fascinating and meaningful journey.

GRACE NOTES

"You can't have peace if you don't understand grace." – Joyce Meyers, Charismatic Christian Author

In music, grace notes or 'ornaments' are added to embellish the melody and add interest and emotional expression to a musical arrangement. They are not essential to the score, however. Their purpose is simply to decorate or enhance it. What would happen if you applied that same term to everyday life and improved your environment with a few gracious touches?

Flowers are an easy way to instill an element of grace. Fresh flowers bring beauty to any living space. A showy, commercial arrangement is not required to make a difference. One simple bud is enough. Snip a single rose or sprig of lavender from your garden. It's so easy to add a little life, a pop of color, and a lovely scent to any room. A bowl of fresh fruit, especially bright yellow lemons, set out on a counter, will create the same effect.

Small, thoughtful gestures will add a note of grace to any day. Unexpected courtesies can instantly brighten someone's mood and positively adjust their attitude. Make someone's day by offering small, but mighty, daily acts of kindness. Tucking a note of encouragement in a child's pocket on oral report day will reassure, encourage, and ease their nerves. Turning down your partners' side of the bed or laying out a warm robe and slippers at the end of a particularly stressful day will ease anyone's pent up pressure and tension.

Turn on some tunes. Never underestimate the power of music to smooth life out, restore energy, and lift spirits. Listening to music while you go about your day is a definite mood enhancer. Brew a cup of tea or coffee, sit down with a favorite book, and allow peace to grace your day.

YOU, ONLY BETTER

"They always say that time changes things, but actually you have to change them yourself." – Andy Warhol

A makeover shouldn't change you into someone else – it should lead to a better you. Take inventory of all areas of your life that would benefit from a new look. A few changes will leave you feeling balanced, centered, and energized. Renewed confidence will empower you to think bigger and reach for higher goals.

How do you want to look and feel every day? The way you present yourself to the world speaks volumes about who you are. Re-think your wardrobe or hairstyle. If you have become too comfortable and casual you may want to step up your game. Today's relaxed atmosphere doesn't require power dressing, but it is important to dress suitably for your age, body type, and environment. Look at your current wardrobe objectively and upgrade or purge as needed.

If you have been trying to transform your body into something it isn't, set a more reasonable goal. Aim for fit and healthy. You will experience more success if you realistically honor your true body type. Increase daily exercise to bring peace of mind, reduce stress, and improve overall well-being.

Clean and reorganize your work area. Remove stacks of paper or books and mementos that distract you from important projects and goals. Make sure your desk is uncluttered and motivates rather than frustrates. Go through the same process throughout your home. If you're unsure where or how to begin, ask someone who has your best interest at heart for an honest evaluation. They have a fresh perspective and will gladly do their part to make you a better you.

CLOSE THE LOOP

"I think it's very important to have a feedback loop, where you're constantly thinking about what you've done and how you could be doing it better."
– Elon Musk

You do the tasks required of you and confidently pass the baton to the next member of the team to do their part. You expected a successful outcome but realize days later that no one 'closed the loop' or confirmed the results. One minute it's checked off your list as completed and the next you are worried it's stuck in limbo.

Communication is key to reducing misunderstandings, dropped balls, and loose ends. When you make a request or give instructions it's safe to assume the job will be done, but unless someone circles back to confirm execution there is no way to know. The concept is as simple as 'asked and answered', but very often no one answers. It's called a loop for a reason: Directive out, job completed, check, next.

One way to eliminate problems is to have the receiver of instructions repeat what they heard back to you. People often hear different words than were actually spoken. You learned this lesson as a child playing the game 'telephone'. Whisper a few words in one ear and pass it on until the message has completely changed. A quick reiteration of what was heard compared to what was said confirms everyone is in the loop from the start.

A 'feedback loop' refers to a technique used to regularly review what has been done and rates the results. Pay careful attention to feedback about recent activity and use those responses to improve the process and enjoy a better outcome. Is it possible to be more efficient or effective and, if so, what changes would bring better results? Maintain a positive feedback loop and, over time, success will feed success.

GROW SOMETHING EDIBLE

"Last night we had three small zucchinis for dinner that were grown within fifty feet of our back door. I estimate they cost somewhere in the neighborhood of $371.49 each." – Andy Rooney

There is nothing more rewarding than dining on fruits or vegetables fresh from your very own garden. There's also nothing quite as frustrating as nurturing them from seed to harvest. Doesn't your heart break for the farmers of the world when you walk outside after a windstorm to find every possibility for fruit has been blown from the trees and your next opportunity for success is another year away?

You feel the same way about the amazing heirloom tomato crop the squirrels decimated and the zucchini plants that produced an abundance of squash flowers, but not a single squash. It's possible to buy fresh vegetables for substantially less than the cost required to create beds, prepare the soil, buy the plants, and stay ahead of the aphids, caterpillars, and snails. But, hope springs eternal, and every year you optimistically plant your garden.

Every now and then, against all odds, you manage to grow something edible and the slightest success renews your spirit. One season might bring a bumper crop of cucumbers so robust you can almost hear them growing overnight. You feel like a very successful grower as you enjoy home grown cucumber salads and refrigerator pickles for months. The following spring you confidently plant little cucumber seedlings and harvested not one cuke all season.

Give farming another chance. It's like gambling...it hooks you. No matter how small your space it's possible to plant and grow a variety of edible greens. There's something so satisfying about snipping fresh herbs for your culinary creations. The secret is persistence. If at first you don't succeed, try, try again.

WHO CARES

"The greatest wealth is health." – Virgil

World Health Day is celebrated annually on this day to raise awareness to the significance of health and wellness on a global level. The day is sponsored by the World Health Organization (WHO) to strengthen health systems and reduce health risks worldwide. It's a day to recognize shared developments, breakthroughs, and strategies and improve the overall well-being of mankind.

That's the big picture. On an individual level it's the perfect time to schedule a check-up with your doctor to update tests or screenings that are age and stage appropriate. Early detection is key. No one wants to walk in healthy and walk out with a diagnosis, but if disease is caught in the early stages the treatment is generally easier and the prognosis much more promising.

Your body is your temple and it's on you to protect it to the best of your ability. Of course, it's not possible to guarantee a disease-free existence, but there are definitely ways to minimize the risks. If you smoke, stop. If you're sedentary, start moving. Eat your fruits and veggies. Prepare smaller portions and think twice before you have just one more drink. Mental health plays a critical part in your quality of life so do what you can to avoid anxiety and stress. Go out and play. Surround yourself with up-lifting, positive people. Smile even if you don't feel like it and laugh out loud every chance you get.

Adopt a health-giving lifestyle and you will increase your chances for a full active life, sufficiently energized to keep up with your kids, and their kids. Adlai Stevenson said it best, "It is not the years in your life but the life in your years that counts."

To your continued good health!

BODY LANGUAGE

"I speak two languages, Body and English." – Mae West

You say one thing with words, but the unspoken element of communication tells a completely different story. The way you hold your body, make eye contact (or don't), gestures, and facial expressions tell the true story. The body doesn't lie.

Pay attention to the nonverbal signals and learn to read between the verbal lines. If you are in a conversation with someone who is leaning back in their chair with arms crossed it's safe to say they feel resistance and words alone will not win them over. Do a quick check of the language your own body is speaking. Facial expressions set the tone before you speak. A confident smile creates immediate rapport and a creased brow speaks so loudly others may not hear what you have to say. Relax, lean in, and try to convey an approachable, positive visual message as you deliver your words.

In the past, speakers were able to rate their audience engagement based on the amount of notebook scribbling going on. People stayed tuned in by taking notes along with a bit of doodling in the margins. Today, it's very clear the speaker has lost the audience when everyone is peering into their lap, catching up on emails and social media. Attention spans are shorter than ever and it's difficult to hold people's interest. Nonverbal interaction with the listener through movement and gestures, as well as posing questions or asking for opinions helps maintain a connection.

If you're checking the time, sighing, or indulging in the ultimate nonverbal communication, eye-rolling, while reading this, you may be underestimating the importance of body language in today's world. Being approachable, moderating your tone and other nonverbal clues, along with the actual spoken word, will give you a practical advantage in your daily interactions with others.

THE CALM AND THE STORM

"Solitude matters, and for some people, it's the air they breathe."
– Susan Cain, Author Quiet: The Power of Introverts in a World
That Can't Stop Talking

Is the upcoming weekend calling you to party like a rock star and paint the town red or is it enticing you with comfy sweats, solitude, and a good book? Extremely outgoing individuals are at one end of the spectrum and quiet introverts the other. Everyone else falls somewhere in the middle, preferring to balance robust adventure with peace and solitude.

Introverts find the world a very noisy place. They do well in social situations, but at a cost. They favor one-on-one, in-depth discussions and avoid small talk and beauty parlor chitchat whenever possible. True introverts are book smart, reserved, and deliberate in pursuit of their goals. Introverts generate energy from the inside out. A day in the workplace glad-handing and networking drains their energy. Once the exhausting day is done, some reflective alone time is necessary to refuel and restore.

Extroverts rely on a large group of friends and acquaintances to energize them. They are assertive, optimistic, welcome high-stake ventures, and tempt fate. They are team players and thrive in leadership positions. Extraverts love the limelight, but once it fades they are easily bored and in hot pursuit of the next stimulating experience or shot of adrenaline.

No matter how you respond to the world around you, it's important to be mindful and attentive to your needs and those of others. If alone time fills you up, carve some out every day. If you need more interaction than your partner does, give them some space and join a club, gym, or sports team to blow off steam. Be respectful and understanding of the needs of people around you. A little empathy and thoughtfulness strengthens and celebrates the difference.

HARMONY AND RIVALRY

"You don't choose your family. They are God's gift to you, as you are to them." – Desmond Tutu

Siblings are sometimes considered best friends and other times they have so little in common they may as well be strangers. Either way, if you have siblings there's a good chance you were thick as thieves as you snooped through Mom's closet for a peek at Santa's gifts, so carefully hidden before Christmas. Or maybe you covered for one another when your parents were out of town and one, or all of you, took advantage of the opportunity to test established boundaries. If you are blessed with siblings, you understand some days you can't live with them and others you can't live without them.

Growing up it was impossible to bask in your parents undivided attention. They had to share their love even though you were sure you were the favorite. Competition for recognition often extends beyond Mom and Dad. You may have aced every spelling bee, but your brother's athleticism, encouraged by cheers from the sidelines, is so much more exciting. You're proud of him, but understandably a little jealous. It's tempting to criticize in an attempt to level the playing field, but the minute someone else finds fault you rush to his defense. That's the beauty of the love/hate sibling relationship.

If you are lucky enough to have a brother or sister, today is the day to bury hatchets, count your blessings, and extend a healing olive branch. You managed to survive the talent competition, it's no longer necessary to vie for parental attention, and all those mini-skirmishes were really pretty juvenile. Take time to honor your relationship. Give them a call, send a card, or spend time together reminiscing about the good, old days.

YOU BETTER BELIEVE IT

"The future belongs to those who believe in the beauty of their dreams."
– Eleanor Roosevelt

There's a lot of talk about hope, as in hoping something will work out or come together successfully, but commitment and belief don't come as easily or as often. Consider these two thoughts: "I hope I will be promoted to the new position at work" vs. "I believe I will be promoted to the new position at work". There is a definite difference. Hope expresses an element of uncertainty or doubt. Belief demonstrates determination. Don't stop believing.

Believers are not victims, they are doers. They don't look for easy outs or reasons why a situation won't work for them. As long as you trust your judgement and are willing to try new approaches until one works, you will succeed. Believe that you can reach your goals and you're halfway there.

Being hopeful is optimistic, upbeat, and positive, but it is an emotion and not something that proactively drives you toward your goals. You cross your fingers and hope for the best, even when you aren't in a position of strength or in control of the outcome. Only when you are 'all in' and 100% committed to making something happen will you be able to reach the desired outcome and manifest your dreams. By taking ownership, maintaining faith in the outcome, and striking out confidently in search of your dreams, you are controlling your destiny.

The major difference between successful people and unsuccessful people has little to do with opportunity, means, or intellect. It's directly related to their belief in themselves. They believe they alone are responsible for bringing their dreams to life. The combination of unwavering confidence and resolute belief will make all the difference in your life

RESIST RESISTANCE

"When you meet obstacles with gratitude, your perception starts to shift, resistance loses its power, and grace finds a home within you."
– Oprah Winfrey

Something must be done. You might even be looking forward to doing it and still struggle to start. Resistance pushes back all day. You sit down with good intentions to complete the task at hand and then allow life to get in the way. Emails to check, reminders pop up, phone calls to be returned, appointments to set. The distractions are endless. It's up to you to stay on track and resist the temptation to stall.

You resist change even when you know it is the necessary ingredient for growth. Fear of the unknown, a painful learning curve, and leaving your comfort zone, all contribute to the self-sabotage of resisting the inevitable. Why is it so difficult to 'just do it'?

Resistance manifests itself in countless ways. Some days are fraught with delays, procrastination, and feet dragging until you're completely under the gun to perform. You plod along making very little progress until finally the end is in view. Only then do you shake off inertia and pick up enough speed to complete the job. Or you simply ignore the task and hope it goes away.

Resistance is hard wired in humans. Identifying the source of resistance is the first step toward finding a viable solution. If you struggle through daily activities only to look back and realize they weren't so bad, it's time to analyze the reasons why. Possibly you really don't want what you're working toward or you're aiming for something to make you happier/stronger/more successful and you are afraid it might not be the answer. Resist resisting this message. Acknowledge what's holding you back, and why. Shake off the shackles and move forward with confidence.

FIND YOUR ALOHA SPIRIT

"In Hawaii, we greet friends, loved ones or strangers with Aloha, which means love. Aloha is the key word to the universal spirit of real hospitality, which makes Hawaii renowned as the world's center of understanding and fellowship. Try meeting or leaving people with Aloha. You'll be surprised by their reaction. I believe it and it is my creed. Aloha to you."
– Duke Kahanamoku

Hawaiians welcome friends and strangers with 'Aloha' when greeting them and again in farewell. It's a lovely and gracious salutation, but it's so much more than just a word. It's a way of life. The Way of Aloha expresses the spirit of the islands and permeates the daily work, play, relationships, and beliefs of the islanders. The dictionary assigns many loving, giving verbs to the definition of the spirit of Aloha, but it's difficult to define the essence of it in words. At its core it's about opening your heart with love, grace, and gratitude. It's about living a life of empathy and compassion for others and showing respect for all living things.

And there's more. Aloha is about ethics and guidelines for everyday life. It's about making decisions for the good of the whole; inclusive and unselfish, healing and strengthening. It lifts the spirit with love and forgiveness.

You don't have to be an Islander to foster the 'Aloha Spirit'. Slow down and think about what you can give from your heart today that will make a difference in the world, or in just one life. You reap what you sow. Give abundantly and you will be blessed abundantly. This peaceful state of mind relieves stress and opens the floodgates of happiness. If you want to live a happy, satisfied life start by spreading a little Aloha today and every day.

Mahalo.

THE GOLDEN RULE

"We have committed the golden rule to memory; let us now commit it to life." – Edwin Markham

"And as ye would that men should do to you, do ye also to them likewise" is a quote from the King James version of the Bible. It's paraphrased in the teachings of all major religions including Judaism, Islam, Buddhism, Sikhism, and Hinduism. Historically significant philosophers, like Confucius, Socrates, and Gandhi have also weighed in with similar words. It's safe to say that this principle is universally accepted as the number one rule that, if followed, would make the world a better place.

The message is straightforward. There's nothing ambivalent or confusing about it, and yet, treating others as you would like to be treated trips people up from time to time. When you do the right thing, you inspire others to pay the goodness forward. It starts with you. Speak respectfully, stay humble, and be a friend. People will be motivated to return the favor or to mirror your 'Golden Rule' conduct when the opportunity presents itself. You will become a living, breathing example of how to live an exemplary life.

Look for an opportunity today to do something kind or make someone happy. Stand in someone else's shoes to better understand what they might be going through. Think about how you would feel if you were them and act accordingly.

Commit today to living a life guided by the Golden Rule. The world needs more people to commit their lives to this simple belief. Don't over-think or over-complicate it. Here's one small way to make a difference today: If you don't have something nice to say, don't say anything at all. It's simple. Treat others as you want to be treated...excellent words for everyone to live by.

BEWARE THE IDES OF APRIL

"Taxes are the price we pay for a civilized society."
– Oliver Wendall Holmes, Jr.

Tax season is a painful time for many people. It's discouraging to see such a large percentage of hard-earned income earmarked to support the federal and state governments. As much as you dread the process, it's necessary, as a good citizen, to pay your fair share in support of the management system that shapes society. Your taxes contribute to government employee salaries, Social Security, Medicare, Medicaid, Defense, and various government agencies that serve to keep the administrative lights on. Someone must fund the running of the nation, and, in all fairness, it falls on "we, the people" to keep the home fires burning.

There is, however, always room for improvement. The government budget can be reined in much like you manage your personal budget. Trim the fat, cut costs wherever possible, and maybe even turn a few of those administrative lights out. If you have an idea or comment about fiscal responsibility or anything else government related use your vote and use your voice. Reach out to representatives at all levels and let them know what's on your mind. It may feel like one vote or one comment won't make a difference, but your opinion may just be the tipping point that causes change to happen. Policymakers listen to their constituents and hearing an opinion from a voice of reason would be welcome.

Tax Day is here, like it or not. Determine what you owe, write your check, and put a stop to the angst and anxiety the deadline creates. Like ripping off a Band-Aid, there will be pain, but it will be over quickly. Thank you for contributing your share and using your voice to improve and advance America's 'civilized society'.

SAVING GRACE

"Grace is not a short prayer you say before the dinner; it is a way to live." – Paulo Coelho

You experience grace when you can give yourself a break and admit you are human. Living in judgement guarantees you will always come up short. No one is, or ever will be, perfect. Relax, forgive, let a little grace into your life, and be your human best. Living in a state of grace gives you a better look at the 'long view' perspective of life. Life is perfectly imperfect, and it is unfolding as it should, when it should. Relax, let go, and enjoy the flow.

Something good comes from everything. Call it a silver lining, or better yet, your saving grace. There's at least one good quality, characteristic, or outcome in every situation. Like the unexpected rain that might have ruined the otherwise perfectly planned no-rain-contingency wedding. It didn't dampen anyone's spirits because, by the grace of God, it started to pour after the garden ceremony when the guests were safely inside the reception hall. That saving grace.

Grace conveys happiness and acknowledges life is good just as it is, but there might still be a little room for improvement. It offers serenity and expectation simultaneously and encourages you to remain patient even as you push forward. You don't always have to be right and it's not necessary to insist on the last word every time. Be open to new ideas and listen respectfully to the opinions of others. They may not change your mind, but you will be reminded that a grace filled life is open to options.

Graciously accept the life that is yours even as you strive to polish and refine it. Greet each day with optimism, understanding, and yes, grace.

HAPPY MAIL

"Making the extra effort to say thanks in a genuine, personal manner goes a long way. It is pleasurable to do, and it encourages more of the same good behavior." – Richard Branson

When was the last time you opened your mailbox and found a hand-written note among the bills and circulars? Most likely you pulled it out and opened it first. You smiled then and just thinking about it now makes you smile all over again. It's truly a gift from a friend. The only thing better than receiving this gift is giving it. Add joy to your life, as well as the lives of your friends, family, and colleagues, at every possible opportunity. The secret is to be prepared.

Make the process easy by stocking up on notecards to write a quick three line note whenever you think of it, without having to add 'buy cards' to your to-do list. Keep stamps and pens with the notes and have everything close at hand at all times. Being prepared overcomes the biggest hurdle. You can write a note or two when waiting for appointments, watching TV, over your morning coffee, or whenever you have a few free minutes.

Writing notes has become something of a lost art that absolutely should be revived and promoted. It's an excellent way to build relationships and keep in touch in a significant, personal way. You can easily send a quick text, email, or private message on social media, but it feels good to know the recipient has a completely different response when your message arrives in their mailbox. It's very likely the bright spot in their day.

Send someone an unexpected gift today, but instead of picking up your phone or powering up your computer, put pen to paper, write a few sincere, meaningful lines, and make their day.

JUST IMAGINE

"The world is but a canvas to our imagination."
– Henry David Thoreau

Human beings have the unique ability to take a known concept and through thoughtful 'imaging' create something totally new and different. There's no limit to what you can conceive simply by using your imagination. It gets full credit as the creative force behind the invention of the wheel, sending a man to the moon, and every new idea, theory, or breakthrough in between. In the words of Walt Disney, the most famous Imagineer of all, "If you can dream it, you can do it."

It's fascinating to listen to the conversation of children at play. They love to make-believe and spin fanciful tales. Play sparks curiosity and wonder as their imaginations soar. Watch the magic happen as an empty box becomes a fort/playhouse/race car. Or how the young personalities transform when they 'become' one of the superheroes in the costume collection. Take a page from their pretend playbook and dream/visualize/imagine reinventing reality.

Tap into your imagination and dream. Solve a problem, simplify a process, or build a better mousetrap. Thoughts are things, so think big. Innovation happens when you noodle ideas around and test the boundaries of the known by pushing through to the unknown. Ask "what if?", and let your mind find the answer.

Indulge in a little daydreaming and reimagine the world, not as you know it, but as you want it to be. Put your creative powers of imagination to work by visualizing opportunities for advancement or improvement. What can you do differently to realize a different outcome? Refine your mental picture to include as much detail as possible. Use this visionary gift to seek out possibilities in all areas and in this way manifest the life of your dreams.

I'M POSSIBLE

"Impossible is just a word thrown around by small men who find it easier to live in the world they've been given than to explore the power they have to change it. Impossible is not a fact. It's an opinion. Impossible is potential. Impossible is temporary. Impossible is nothing."
– Muhammad Ali

If you think something is impossible you give up without even trying. But look at the word through new eyes and see within it "I'm possible" and you are encouraged and empowered to go forward. Be a 'yes' to life. Anything is possible once you make the decision to accomplish it, no matter what mountains stand between you and the goal. Say 'I can' if it's something you really want to do. You are the final decision maker, no excuses.

When a challenge or problem seems insurmountable, break it down. By eliminating or overcoming small obstacles even the most overwhelming problems become manageable. Running a marathon might seem impossible, but with proper training and gradually building distance and endurance, some of the least likely runners have crossed the daunting finish line. Start with the first step, take a quick walk, and improve from there.

You love to say you will exercise, read, or hone your skills and talents, but there's never enough time. The truth is you have time and fail to make that pursuit or activity a priority. Overcoming the time obstacle requires the same approach as running a marathon. Start small and improve little by little. Take a walk first thing in the morning or exercise during television commercials. Read a few pages while you enjoy your coffee. Catch up on your hobby, brush up on your instrument and be The Little Engine That Could. "I think I can, I think I can, I think I can."

You're possible.

WORDS TO LIVE BY

"If you fail, never give up because F.A.I.L. means "First Attempt In Learning"; End is not the end, in fact E.N.D. means "Effort Never Dies"; If you get No as an answer, remember N.O. means "Next Opportunity". So let's be positive." – President of India, A P J Abdul Kalam

If at first you don't succeed, try, try again. Those who don't fail regularly, are not pushing hard enough to succeed. Unless you have incredible beginners' luck you will not hit the bull's eye with your first arrow. 'First Attempts In Learning' often end shy of the goal, but anything worth doing takes practice, practice, practice. Multiple attempts will get you to the goal so never give up, get out of your safe zone, and take that necessary leap of faith.

'Effort Never Dies'. Success comes to those who persevere. If you feel you have reached the end of the rope, go back and try a new strategy. It takes determination and tenacity to repeatedly push through challenges and setbacks. Do it as often as it takes to break through whatever is holding you back.

When one door closes the 'Next Opportunity" is behind another door. Keep knocking until you find it. If it's not the happy ending you imagined re-think the results. Many times, the successful ending we were looking for is concealed by another, possibly better, outcome. Recognize and welcome the wins however they present themselves.

Choose to be positive, expect success, effect success. Focus on the good and what is possible. Think yourself through first attempts, give never ending effort, and welcome the next opportunity. If the results look a little different than you imagined there's a good chance they are a better version of your initial goals. Give thanks and live by the words 'all things are possible' to those who have the courage to try.

THOUGHTS ON ETHICS

"Ethics is knowing the difference between what you have a right to do and what is right to do." – Potter Stewart

Ethical people rely on their moral compass to determine the difference when they are faced with a choice between what is right, and anything less. At its core, being ethical means obeying the laws, but beyond that it means avoiding gray areas and cutting corners to get things done. People who are always looking for short cuts and angles aren't necessarily unethical, but they wouldn't come to mind as examples of virtuous behavior.

Be the person at the top of the list by doing the right thing when no one is watching. Making good choices without fanfare or accolades demonstrates utmost integrity and personal ethics. You're living up to your own high standards, not to impress others, but to live your best life. You find a twenty dollars bill in the aisle of the grocery store. You subscribe to the, 'finders' keepers, losers weepers' philosophy for a moment before you realize you may have the right, but that doesn't make it right. You give the money to the manager who puts it in his pocket. Both sides of the ethics question were demonstrated in this scenario, but you feel good knowing you did the right thing.

Being ethical requires honesty and fair play at all times. It means taking responsibility for your actions and decisions, and the results of those actions and decisions. Everyone makes mistakes and it takes character and strength to admit errors or bad judgment. Step up, own up, and accept the consequences. When you shield others from the blame, you earn respect and trust, and strengthen your reputation as someone who sets a high bar when it comes to personal integrity and ethics, qualities that are paramount ingredients for long term success.

SAVE THE PLANET

"When one tugs at a single thing in nature, he finds it attached to the rest of the world." – John Muir

There was a time, not all that long ago, when it was acceptable to throw cigarette butts and gum wrappers out the car window. It might sound like an innocuous bad habit, but it more likely indicated a larger, universal environmental problem. That same family car burned leaded gas, emitting smog producing exhaust that blanketed our cities preventing children from outdoor play on the worst days. Industries recklessly polluted the rivers, people blatantly wasted natural resources, and everyone seemed to take the earth for granted. Until one day folks woke up, assessed the damage, and put sweeping changes in place that began to turn the tide. Just in time.

This day was set aside to celebrate planet earth and to raise public awareness of the fine balance required to maintain a healthy, sustainable environment. Once the conversation was started, more voices were heard, more action was taken, with more significant results.

For almost five decades people have worked hard to reduce exhaust emission and successfully improved the quality of the air we breathe. Our water is no longer polluted, littering is not acceptable, and we diligently rethink, reuse, and recycle. But as successful as we have been to date we continue to face tremendous challenges like climate change and clean energy.

Join over one billion others worldwide to demonstrate your support for global environmental protection. It's not okay to wear out the planet we call home expecting future generations to fix it. You can make a difference by planting a tree, cleaning the beaches or making the commitment to effect 'green' changes in your own household today and every day.

LESSONS FROM OUR CHILDREN

"A child can teach an adult three things: to be happy for no reason, to always be busy with something, and to know how to demand with all his might that which he desires." – Paulo Coelho

There's so much to be learned from children. They wake up smiling and full of anticipation for what each wondrous day will bring. Yesterday is a memory to a child, and today is filled with promise. Most days you wake up overwhelmed, dreading what lies ahead. You might smile more if you could get past yesterday and enjoy today.

Kids giggle for no reason, finding joy in simple things. They love to run, climb, ride bikes, and get sweaty. You call it a workout, kids call it play. They are open to new adventure and inclusive of everyone. A straightforward question, "Hi. My name is Billy. Do you want to play with me?" is enough to start a friendship. It's just that easy. When and why did adults start taking themselves so seriously?

Kids are forthright and unselfconscious. They speak the truth with no hidden agenda. It's easier to be confident when you haven't faced failure or embarrassment, but maybe grownups could learn to let some things go. Forgive, forget, and start fresh.

Children question everything. 'Why' is followed by 'why not' and 'are we there yet?' They are persistent and tenacious, qualities that make them the world's best salespeople. Adults give up after the first no, when determination might be all that's needed to advance the ball.

Think back to your youth when every day brought new opportunities and summer vacation stretched an eternity. Resist the urge to schedule every minute only to wonder where the day/week/year went. Slow life down by savoring the moments, enjoying the beauty, and living in the here and now.

DISCIPLINE

"One of the most important keys to success is having the discipline to do what you know you should do, even when you don't feel like doing it."
– Unknown

Do you start your day feeling passionate and determined and end it surrounded by loose ends and unfinished projects? If so, you're not alone. Starting something is easy, seeing it to the finish line is a challenge. It's easy to become distracted by the many shiny objects you encounter during the day and difficult to know where to focus attention. When you do settle down to work you have a very short attention span and lose interest in anything that doesn't offer instant gratification. Discipline requires a daily plan that is followed persistently with patience.

Everyone struggles with focus from time to time so when you find yourself floundering try a new approach to pique interest and renew energy. If you have lost momentum strengthen your resolve through collaboration. Identify mentors in your sphere of influence who can re-direct your attention. Consider reaching out to an accountability partner or hiring a coach to professionally guide you. Set firm deadlines and stick to them by assigning a consequence when you don't do the job or a reward if you accomplish it in a timely manner.

Every day matters. Miss just one and passion, energy, and enthusiasm begin to ebb. Put a plan in place and track time spent and benchmarks met on the road to success. Progress is an excellent motivator. Once you have made headway, stop your work on a high note so you're excited to get back to it the next day. Resuming the process just before a breakthrough adds much needed incentive. Be disciplined and committed to what must be done every day, whether you feel like it or not.

WRITE A NEW STORY

"When we deny the story, it defines us. When we own the story, we can write a brave new ending." – Brene Brown, Author

You believe your day to day story mirrors reality, but maybe seeing life through your own lens distorts the truth a bit, as if you're viewing it through a funhouse mirror. Use caution when writing your tale, but don't be too hard on yourself. Self-talk sometimes isn't the most supportive. You are the author of your own life story so if things aren't going as well as expected, write a new one with a happier, more successful, ending.

You wake up one day and your spouse asks for a divorce. You overeat, drink yourself silly, drunk text the perpetrator, and cry on anyone and everyone's shoulder. At least for a while. Eventually it's time to admit it was inevitable, a fait accompli, and move on. Close the outdated book and consider writing the next chapter on a fresh subject, with new players. Don't let the tale end on a low note.

Let go of false hope and recognize reconciliation is not an option. Gather your self-respect and focus all your energy on a future where you are the central character, the victor, not the victim. Either foster a mutually respectful relationship or learn to be content on your own and build a full, satisfying life around the people and things that bring joy.

If you are ready to write a new story, make it a jumping off point to new ventures and amazing adventures. Spark up a new love interest or re-kindle one from the past. Introduce a plot twist, create a festive, interesting narrative, and by all means, feel free to embellish. It's your story. Write well and edit often.

CAUTION SPEEDBUMP AHEAD

"Speed bumps, I was thinking, you know, you're driving along, everything's OK, and then there's a speed bump to go, 'Slow down.' Go over it real slowly, and you hit the pedal, and you keep going, and I just thought it was kind of a nice metaphor for life." – Teri Garr

Life is not a bowl of cherries. Everyone faces their share of challenges, disappointments, and problems. There's nothing to be gained by wallowing in sorrow or lamenting the 'why'. It's not just you. No one gets out unscathed.

You prepare for the worst, steel yourself to face adversity, and are still blindsided from time to time. Think speedbump, not roadblock. There's either a solution, workaround, or a real life-changing, not life-threatening, lesson to be learned. You're not living if you don't encounter road hazards that look a lot like health issues, relationship problems, financial set-backs, or any number of other unexpected problems. It's up to you to choose how to handle them. Will you pull over to avoid them and do nothing? Or slow down, face the fear, find the best solution, and resume speed once you're past it?

Don't try to face difficulties alone if you can enlist the help of friends and family. They can be experts at damage control and looking at problems in a realistic light. You might feel like you're facing an overwhelming obstacle when it's really just a little bump in the road. Focus on the outcome, not the stumbling block.

Challenge builds character and fuels growth that wouldn't happen without the opportunity difficulties present. Problems force you to test your strength and discover the powerful person you are. Realize you can face anything life throws your way. Now all that's left to do is slow down and enjoy the ride.

DON'T CURB YOUR ENTHUSIASM

"Wherever you go, go with all your heart." – Confucius

The decision is yours. You can choose to be the fountain, or you can choose to be the drain. Fountains are upbeat and do what they can to encourage others to enjoy a happy, fulfilled life. Contagious enthusiasm elevates the mood of everyone it touches before it comes full circle back to you. It's impossible to be down in the presence of someone who is confident, cheerful, and excited to be alive.

Drains are negative and, well, draining. No matter how much upside you see they focus on the downside. Their lives are fraught with drama, on-again off-again relationships, and self-sabotage. They share their constant turmoil to gain attention and, in the process, manage to throw a wet blanket on any enthusiasm or positivity in their path. Not all days can be great, but some good can be found in every day if you look for it. Align yourself with optimists who choose the bright side, and steer clear of doom and gloom pessimists.

It's easy to be energized and enthusiastic when things are going right and a little more difficult when things are slipping sideways. Adjust your attitude by focusing on one action that will move you in the direction of your goals. Recommit to your purpose and take one deliberate step at a time. Positive achievement will energize and inspire you.

You chose to be the fountain so reach out and sprinkle some hope and optimism on others. Find someone who needs a helping hand, lift their spirits, and turn the day around. A positive outlook and a few encouraging words will empower and enthuse people you touch and replenish passion and excitement in the process. Enthusiasm is contagious. Catch some today.

THE RIPPLE EFFECT

"Remember there's no such thing as a small act of kindness. Every act creates a ripple with no logical end." – Scott Adams

One good deed certainly deserves another, but what if, instead of repaying the benefactor, you surprised someone completely unsuspecting with a gift of kindness? They would be pleased and would feel obliged to do something nice in return, preferably for somebody new. And so it goes rippling along, spreading wider and wider circles of happiness.

The wave of good deeds being paid forward has reached over eighty countries and, on this official Pay It Forward Day, is expected to become a tsunami inspiring over ten million acts of kindness. What a wonderful world it would be if each day from now on millions of people paid kindness forward and made the life of one person better. The good deeds would continue 'with no logical end' in sight. Lives, and the world, would definitely be changed for the better.

If you're not sure where to start you can give it some thought while you hold the door open a little longer than usual to help a young mother push a stroller through. Consider small, but effective, gestures like baking cookies and sharing them with your neighbors or coworkers, bringing soup to someone nursing a cold, or offering to help a co-worker who is struggling with a difficult project. When they offer to return the favor ask them to pay it forward and resolve one more need. One small act of kindness might be all it takes to lift another's spirit or brighten an otherwise gloomy day.

Join the millions today who are determined to change the world one good deed at a time. Spread the word, share the love, and make a difference.

LIFE HAPPENS

"Life is 10% what happens to you and 90% how you react to it."
– Charles R. Swindoll

On the way to your long-anticipated vacation you come down with the flu, which sadly scuttles those well laid plans. You return home to a flood in the laundry room and your vacation fund must be repurposed to repair the leak and remediate the water damage. Illness and cancelled plans sometimes turn out to be blessings in disguise. There are two ways to look at that scenario. You can fume, complain and claim nothing ever goes right or view the frustrations as life managing to work out exactly as needed.

Before you spend time moaning and lamenting, understand and acknowledge that life happens to everyone. Admittedly there are times when you could have planned ahead and avoided a situation, but other times you're simply in the wrong place at the wrong time. Instead of becoming bitter over unanticipated events prepare for the inevitable pitfalls and misfortunes of life. Take responsibility by putting solid back up plans in place. Review your insurance policies to make sure they provide sufficient coverage where needed. Create a rainy-day fund to cover surprise expenditures. Big ticket items like cars need regular tune-ups and replacement tires, appliances wear out, and baby always needs a new pair of shoes. Planning for the worst, combined with a little forward thinking, will minimize risk, optimize opportunity, and allow you to genuinely hope for the best.

John Lennon said, "life is what happens while you are busy making other plans". Count on life to surprise, divert, and re-direct you...the long way around. That's life. Make the best of it. Stay ahead of it whenever possible, remain flexible, and don't become a victim of what comes your way.

MEASURE PROGRESS

Life is not about being perfect. It's about being the best you can be every day. You may have fallen a little short, shelved your New Year's Resolutions, and dialed back those slightly overzealous goals, but you still managed to make some progress. Bring your daily best and watch the growth and transformation evolve one day at a time.

You do what you measure. Once you've set goals, make a plan of action that will get you there. If your goal is to walk ten miles a week, use a pedometer to measure the best walking trails and neighborhood 'loops'. Identify one, two, and three-mile routes and start tallying the miles weekly. Numbers don't lie. If it turns out you're kidding yourself about the amount of ground covered, it might be necessary to schedule time on Saturday to take a 'make-up' walk to reach your goal.

Set benchmarks to track your success. It's important to analyze progress and evaluate systems to encourage improvement. Isolate the area of your life you wish to improve and create step-by-step procedures and timelines. Check you progress at each level and adjust as necessary. Once measured you can decide to continue at the same rate, step the pace up or down, or replace the process with something that might be a better fit for you.

If you can count it, you can do it. Create a master checklist of activities and stick to it through thick and thin. Track your daily habits and be laser focused on the commitments. Identify weekly, monthly, and quarterly targets to review and measure progress. When you reach a milestone, send up a flare, reward yourself, and celebrate progress, if not perfection.

CELEBRATE MAY

"As full of spirit as the month of May, and as gorgeous as the sun in Midsummer." – William Shakespeare

May Day is a festive spring holiday celebrating nature's awakening and fresh, new beginnings. When I was a child our May Day event involved colorful dresses, bright ribbons, and fresh flowers woven into our braided hair. We skipped around the maypole until our ribbons were hopelessly tangled. I don't think we fully understood the purpose, but as far as little girls are concerned floral crowns and dance routines spell p-a-r-t-y.

The name May is derived from Maia, the Roman goddess of fertility and growth. It's the perfect word to depict the season when birds hatch, flowers bloom, and the world is lush and full of hope. In what way will you celebrate this month of change and growth? What new challenge is calling your name?

Someone very wise once said "Find three hobbies you love: one to make money, one to keep you in shape, and one to be creative." Is your career a perfect fit or is it time for a change? Your job should be fulfilling and bring you joy. The same advice goes for exercising. There are many ways to keep physically fit. Do you prefer working out with friends or are you happiest exercising alone? Choose a team sport or join a class to interact with others or jog/hike/swim your way quietly to a personal best. Finally, flex your creative muscles in ways that make your heart sing. Make the time and put in the effort to pursue and express your own individual passions.

Commit today, at this time of change and growth, to find the perfect career, personal workout, and creative outlet. Life is too short to let fear of change or fear of failure keep you from the life you deserve to live.

ADD VALUE

"The key to all of life is understanding how to add value to others."
– Jay Abraham

Adding value to the lives of others is a mindset and a choice. You woke up this morning determined to make it a great day. Will you choose to direct your efforts and energy to improving your own life or will you look for ways to add value and make a difference in the lives of others? Intentionally serving and putting others first cultivates friendships, strengthen relationships, and enriches lives, yours as well as theirs. Doing something for someone else improves and enhances the life of the giver.

Contributing without expectation of anything in return is a selfless, powerful action. Everyone has value. You nod to the security guard every morning on your way into work. Your mind is thinking ahead to the individuals you will interact with inside the building. Make today the day you take a moment to ask his name and, going forward, acknowledge and connect with him on a personal level.

Look for ways to make someone's day. The opportunities to make a difference are endless. Call a friend who's been sick to see if they need anything. Or take it one step further and drop off an unexpected care package. Smile and give a sincere compliment. Let people know you care. Ask questions and pay attention to the answers so you can really connect with them.

Surprise and delight someone with an extra touch to make them happy. Find ways to add value by anticipating needs they may not even recognize. Ask about the health and wellness of members of their family, send a card for a non-occasion, or bring a 'doggie' treat bag when visiting a pet lover. At the end of the day count the ways you added value and sleep well.

FIND YOUR VOICE

"The most courageous act is still to think for yourself. Aloud."
– Coco Chanel

Your opinion matters. Don't be afraid to share it, but don't be surprised when some people disagree with you. Their beliefs matter to them. Comparing views creates a healthy environment where open-minded individuals welcome opposing points of view so they can either justify or change their stance. Some people defend their personal opinion as if it is cast in stone, afraid that a change of mind will appear weak. It's not unusual for beliefs to change and grows as you do.

You may have believed children are better off raised by a stay-at-home parent until you were faced with balancing a promising career and a family. There's no shortage of opinions regarding the right way to parent. Everyone has different needs and should be able to decide what is right for their marriage and family. When the decision is made, own it. It's not necessary to rally support around your choice hoping for consensus. The only opinions that matter are the parents.

Once you listen to both, or many, sides of the story and have formed your own beliefs feel free to share them. Don't feel pressured to echo the attitudes of others to fit in. Find and use your own voice to share opinions formed based on your background, personal standards, and life experience.

If there's something you feel passionate about, let it be known. It might be just the information needed to change someone's mind and help them form a better, more educated decision. Share your knowledge, share your feelings, and be strong enough to stand up for your convictions. There will always be people who agree, as well as those who disagree, but in the end it's just a matter of opinion.

MAY THE FORCE BE WITH US ALL

"How lucky I am to have something that makes saying goodbye so hard"
– Winnie the Pooh/A. A. Milne

May the fourth be with you. This clever and fun play on words has gained popularity with Star Wars fans worldwide, making the fourth of May, unofficially, Star Wars Day. The original phrase "May the force be with you" is heard many times throughout the epic Star Wars series. It's a heartfelt farewell, meant to send someone on their way with good luck and hope for their safety. It's reminds us of the common thread in the celebration of the Catholic mass, "May the Lord be with you". Each time the priest intones the phrase the congregation replies, "And also with you." Is there a more perfect blessing?

You are excited to teach your baby to wave bye-bye. It's an important ritual and helps them understand that separation is a positive part of life and not something to fear. The custom of acknowledging leave-taking remains significant throughout life. Being fully present for a handshake, sincere hug, or a quick kiss and an 'I love you', will start the day on the right note. Offer the warm gesture and words that are appropriate for the relationship whenever you part. Wishing someone you care about good luck or safe travels is just the right send off.

There's no way to know what the day will bring, and a few kind words could be the perfect attitude adjustment needed to make it a good one. Don't miss an opportunity to wish your loved ones well every time you part ways. Send them off as if you are their personal goodwill ambassador, guiding and protecting. May the force be with you…today and every day.

NAMASTE

"If we are peaceful. If we are happy. We can smile and blossom like a flower. And everyone in our family, our entire society will benefit from our peace." – Thich Nhat Hanh

Namaste is a Sanskrit greeting that literally means 'I bow to you'. It is offered as a gracious welcome or farewell in India and Nepal but, thanks to the popularity of yoga, many people use it in a slightly different context. Some think of it as more of a spiritual gesture than a simple salutation. Either way it seems to center and calm the person offering namaste and is gratefully accepted as a demonstration of peace, honor, and respect by the recipient.

Our world can quickly become a pressure cooker and when it does it's important to know how to deal with the stressors and let off a little steam. Namaste can help by spiritually connecting us to one another, creating a feeling of unity and balance. Put your hands together as if in prayer, holding your elbows out. Take a deep cleansing breathe, exhale slowly, and repeat. It's a simple ritual that makes a big difference. You will immediately feel your tension drain and muscles relax.

If you still feel overwhelmed, follow your breathing exercise with an activity that calms you. Call a friend or relative for a quick up-lifting chat. Write a few paragraphs in your journal. Take a walk outdoors and enjoy the fresh air. Close your eyes and meditate or take a short power nap. Laugh out loud. Read a few pages of an inspirational book. Count your blessings.

You might discover the simple process of focused breathing is the easiest way to get through the stresses of an average day. Inhale, exhale, repeat. It will help you more than anything.

TAKE A CHANCE ON LIFE

"Take a chance! All life is a chance. The man who goes farthest is generally the one who is willing to do and dare." – Dale Carnegie

There are no guarantees in life. If you wait until you are 100% sure things will work out, you will never take the first step. There is no shame in trying and failing as long as you learn from the experience. Taking calculated risks is the best way to prepare for the next opportunity that presents itself.

Interviewing is a good way to hone your skills in preparation for real life situations. The job application process polishes up interview skills which will be confidence boosting and help you make a stronger impression next time. The same holds true if you audition for a part in a play, choir, band, or sports team. Dating refines courting skills even if you don't get past the awkward first date. Consider each date an interview. Improve your banter, fine tune the art of flirting, and practice putting your best foot forward. Chances are he or she is not 'the one' but you will have refined your criteria and reinforced your standards.

Weigh the risk verses the reward. It's more prudent to risk everything on a new business venture or investment opportunity early in life rather than later when there is less time to recover if it doesn't work out. Taking a few responsible risks might be necessary on your way to success. Responsible, not reckless.

I dare you to have the courage to take an educated, well considered risk today. Step out of the comfort zone and accept the challenge. What have you got to lose? vs. What could you gain? If you don't take a chance, you don't stand a chance.

DISCONNECT TO CONNECT

"Turn off your email; turn off your phone; disconnect from the Internet; figure out a way to set limits so you can concentrate when you need to, and disengage when you need to. Technology is a good servant but a bad master." – Gretchen Rubin

Too many people are hopelessly tangled in the web. Technology is vital, but the value lies in how effectively you use it to your advantage. The tradeoff to spending too much time in the cloud, instead of outdoors enjoying the clouds, is information overload, persistent preoccupation, and separation anxiety that grips us the minute we are offline.

Social media ups the game every day offering endless possibilities to engage, connect, and empower. That's a good thing if it impacts your life in a positive way. It's fun to share and tempting to overshare. You can post it and regret it, but you cannot take it back. Privacy is a precious commodity. The less people know about you the less they can judge you. And vice versa. So, tune in/connect/comment/like and then log out and live your life in real time.

It's exciting to capture that perfect moment in a photo. But it's a shame to miss it live and in color because you were viewing it through the lens of your smart phone. Your life might be richer if you were fully present and saw things with your own eyes, making lovely memories. Just for yourself.

Technology, electronic devices, and social media are here to stay. They will continue to influence your life, but, as with anything, moderation is key. Make a commitment to silence your phone during meals or when in the company of others. Some time-out will allow you to unwind, focus on conversations without distractions, or enjoy a little solitude. Unplug and connect, even if it's just for a short time.

MAY IS FOR MOTHERS

"The most important thing she'd learned over the years was that there was no way to be a perfect mother and a million ways to be a good one."
– Jill Churchill, Author, Grime and Punishment

It's a fact. Moms are the glue holding families together. The perfectly imperfect nurturers, teachers, and role-models who assure you that reaching the stars or the moon is a real possibility. They are able to convince you it's possible to single-handedly conquer the world. At least your little corner of it.

When you share your hopes and dreams, no matter how improbable, Mom will support you. She will pave the way, open doors, and protect you from adversity, standing up to bullies and naysayers, like it or not. Moms are the world's biggest influencers and most enthusiastic cheerleaders, seeing beyond your faults and unfailingly filling you with self-confidence, security, and hope.

Moms have eyes in the back of their head, accompanied by an uncanny maternal intuition that allows them to tap into even your deepest thoughts. They say the hard words to make their children better people and then lie awake at night worrying that they could have and should have done more. Mom is a selfless powerhouse celebrating every milestone, empowering you to achieve and accomplish more. She inspires you to reach your full potential and if she feels you're falling short will dish out tough love like no one else and then wrap you in the warmest hug ever.

Not everyone is gifted with a positive maternal experience. Many have lost their mothers, others wanted to be a mother, but it was not to be. Whatever the circumstances, seek out and thank the mother figures in your life for whatever part they played. If you are a mother give yourself a pat on the back for being a good one in a million ways.

TRY SOMETHING NEW

"Move out of your comfort zone. You can only grow if you are willing to feel awkward and uncomfortable when you try something new."
– Brian Tracy

Do you remember when you were a kid and you were stuck in a rut? No, of course not. The only ruts you encountered claimed your bike tire, not you. And the only one trapped on a hamster wheel was your hamster. Kids are little sponges soaking in all that life has to offer. They are willing to try anything and sometimes learn the hard way, but either way, learning happens. Take a moment and channel your inner kid back when every day brought new adventure. You constantly tried new things, pushed boundaries, and tempted fate.

Every day was a day of firsts. First time on a two-wheeler, first time the yo-yo magically travelled back up the string, first time you hit the ball. Followed by first date, first kiss, first day of college - life was new and exciting every day. Until one day you grew up, stopped living with reckless abandon, and settled into your comfort zone, where life is comforting but you don't stretch and grow.

Routines and rituals bring order to otherwise chaotic days, but if left unexamined will stifle your creativity and growth. Step out of the safe zone and get a little vulnerable. Do that by trying new things. Start simple with new foods, new colors, or a new route. If you're living on auto pilot it's time to change things up, press the re-set button, and try something new.

Wear something today that doesn't look at all like what you wore yesterday. It might be fun to add ice cream to your granola, play hooky, skip, whistle, or smile just for the fun of it. And then do it again tomorrow with a new twist.

FIND YOUR PASSION

"I have to face life with a newly found passion. I must rediscover the irresistible will to learn, to live, and to love." – Andrea Bocelli

Find passion and stop putting off the life you are meant to live. Without passion, it's impossible to live up to your fullest potential. If your current career/personal/spiritual/intellectual world is not igniting passion, it's time to fire things up. Revise, reframe, and redefine the life you live until you are unstoppable.

Start by revisiting your childhood. What were the things that made your heart sing and so captivated your attention you were laser focused and lost in the process? What fascinated and held you fully in the moment? If real life has over-shadowed those dreams, it's time to find the way back. As you work through the exercise of soul searching, don't look too far. It's always best to play to personal strengths. The answer might be as simple as polishing natural skills and talents to perfection.

What a disappointment to have potential and not step up to meet it. Be brave. Identify your natural skills, nurture and perfect them and watch them grow. Start by listing interests, abilities, and projects that excite you. Set goals and benchmarks to track progress and focus on the results. You've threatened to write a book, someday. What's stopping you? Everyone has at least one story to tell. Write that book, climb a mountain, start the business you've been talking about for years. If the right direction is still unclear, ask a few friends. You might be too close to recognize what is very clear to the people on the outside looking in. Now is the time to find your passion and live up to your full potential.

TIME WARPS

"Work expands so as to fill the time available for its completion."
– Cyril Northcote Parkinson, Parkinson's Law: The Pursuit of
Progress

Have you noticed that if you schedule one hour to complete a job
it will take exactly one hour? And have you also noticed the same
task will be completed in thirty minutes if that's the time allotted?
You assign timeframes that are much longer than it would take
if you would just buckle down and get it done. Given additional
time you overthink and overcomplicate, instead of simply doing.

Deadlines are the answer. If you want to accomplish more, with
greater efficiency, give yourself tighter deadlines. It seems so simple. Time vampires, like social media and email, can and will,
waste many productive hours. If your teacher or employer gives
you an assignment with a deadline, you will probably complete it
in the final hours before it's due. You're convinced you work better
under pressure but look at all the time wasted anticipating and
worrying about it.

You will get more done, in less time, with far less stress by planning
ahead and assigning realistic timelines to all scheduled tasks. Consider setting an appointment with your tax preparer in February.
You will spend considerably less time gathering documents than if
you schedule an appointment in March. Waiting until April, like
so many people do, may require filing for an extension which will
provide several more months to 'work' on your taxes.

Test this theory by planning a trip. The 'vacation phenomenon' is
a powerful force and it works every time. The day before you leave
town your overflowing in-basket will miraculously be emptied,
laundry caught up, and bills paid. Setting deadlines creates free
time to do more or to relax and do less. The clock is ticking.

FOCUS ON ABUNDANCE

"Whatever the mind can conceive it can achieve."
– W. Clement Stone

The Law of Attraction is real and it's always working. Spend too much time thinking about what you don't have, or lack, will attract more of the same. Positive thoughts focused on what you do have, abundance, will attract more good into your life. It seems simple enough but sitting around thinking about what you want or don't want won't get the job done. Apply a little action and watch what happens.

No one escapes the times when everything seems to go wrong. It's difficult to maintain a positive outlook when faced with more than your share of negativity. Your inclination is to give up and give in. Disappointment saps strength and it takes a lot of positive energy to turn things around. It starts with you.

Adjust the lens and view the world as you want it to be, not as it is now. Give serious thought to your goals and a better life by visualizing yourself in that new position at work, fit and healthy, debt free, or enjoying a new relationship. Fill your thoughts with possible solutions and small incremental changes that, put into action, will turn the tide to positive.

You've dreamed it, now do it. Update your resume and let the decision makers know you are the perfect candidate for the job. Get to the gym and hire a trainer if accountability is needed. Create a manageable budget and live within it. Attract a new relationship by distancing yourself from the one currently holding you back. Focus all of your energy and actions on the positive, abundant life just ahead. You have the power to attract and manifest whatever is desired. You conceived it, go achieve it.

ACCEPT THE CHALLENGE

"There is nothing like a challenge to bring out the best in man."
– Sean Connery

Is there something you really want to achieve? Anything can be accomplished by committing to a 100 Day Challenge. It's a simple concept. The 100 Day Challenge requires choosing just one thing, in one area of life, and to perfect it by completing the chosen task today and taking that same action every day for the duration of the challenge. Whatever you choose to do, pledge to do it every day for 100 days. It requires steadfast commitment, focused vision, and unwavering determination. Practice makes perfect, builds momentum, and forms good habits. By the time you finish you will have created a powerful life habit that is as much a part of everyday as brushing your teeth or making the bed.

Give some serious thought to one thing you want to improve. You must truly want it, or you will not follow through successfully. Start with the end in mind by determining what you want to accomplish in 100 days. You might want to improve the health and fitness sector or incorporate reading or meditation into daily life. Thoughtfully consider what must be done to hold your interest for 100 days. What will you stop/start eating or drinking? What will amp up your workout schedule? How much or how long will you read or meditate? Revise and redefine until you find a manageable commitment. Every day is already full so the only way to sustain the action for three plus months is to make the daily obligation as practical as possible.

Once you have confirmed your objective it's time to take action. Accept the challenge today and make a commitment to be unstoppable beginning with the next 100 days of your life.

TAKE THE BURN OUT OF BURNOUT

"You don't burn out from going too fast. You burn out from going too slow and getting bored." – Cliff Burton, Metallica's second bassist

It's that time of year again. Your New Year's Resolutions went by the wayside months ago. You're tired of pulling yourself up by the bootstraps and tired of trying to improve your body and mind. Frankly, you're just tired. Think back to your early days in the workplace. You met each day with determined confidence and perhaps a little naïveté about what it would take to succeed long-term in the real world. Many very talented individuals enjoy mercurial career success only to crash and burn as soon as they achieve what they perceive as their personal pinnacle. What could have been a lifelong, successful profession becomes a short stop-over between careers.

Challenging yourself on a regular basis will help to avoid burnout. Burnout disguised as fatigue feels like 'been there, done that'. When the high is gone dissatisfaction sets in, you stop the actions that worked, become distracted, and concentrate on the wrong things. Eventually those diversions fail to fuel your fire and you look around for something newer still. Where exactly did that wonderful rush go and why can't you get it back? You feel let-down and tired of trying. The solution is to understand how to infuse challenge and joy into the process.

Reflect, reevaluate, and set new goals. Vision and planning are critical to long term success. Follow a consistent daily routine and revive the optimistic, and fun, you. Reward yourself and celebrate every success. Schedule a vacation or a play day. Take on a new hobby, contribute and make a difference. Diverse personal interests make you happier and more attractive to others. Decide to be happy every day. You are the only stimulant needed to avoid burnout.

CONSISTENCY IS KEY

"It's not what we do once in a while that shapes our lives. It's what we do consistently." – Tony Robbins

Habits, good and bad, are formed by consistently doing things a certain way. Following predictable set-and-forget routines allows you to mindlessly perform many daily tasks on autopilot. That is comforting until you're in self-improvement mode and want to create better habits. If your morning routine consists of coffee/shower/work and you decide to incorporate the gym into the mix intentional change is required. Your new earlier schedule will take you out of the comfort zone, and until a habit is formed, it will be necessary to deliberately follow through and hold yourself accountable. It requires mindfulness every day until the new workout becomes an integral part of the daily ritual.

The true key to success is not intelligence, timing, or persistence. It is doing the right things day in and day out. It requires commitment to long-term continuous actions and being accountable to the outcome. Consistency is about doing the same things over and over until you do them without thinking. Repetition brings positive, life improving changes that will become part of you. It takes dedication and willpower in the beginning but in time, 'habits of life' form and you are on your way to a less stressful, more successful, existence.

Make a decision right now to improve one small area of your life. Decide how/when/where/why you will implement the task. No excuses, no whining. It's up to you. This process takes time, but the effort will be worth it. Go all in and take full responsibility for your actions. Good habits will replace bad habits in time. They will define you and in the long term improve and enhance your life. What change will you commit to starting today?

SEIZE THE DAY

"If opportunity doesn't knock, build a door." – Milton Berle

The very words 'seize the day' make you want to go out and do something meaningful with your life. You're tired of the past holding you back and want to leave it where it belongs. In the past. History doesn't offer a do-over, so shake it off and move on. This is also not the time to worry about what the future may hold. Make this day count by savoring each moment.

Seize and savor are very exciting concepts, but before you race out blindly to fulfill your purpose you must decide what that purpose is. It's not about enthusiastically claiming every opportunity that comes your way. It's about recognizing and pursuing the ones that have your name on them. Take a moment to review your goals and values and be crystal clear about what owning this day means to you.

If spending more time with family is a top priority make it happen today. There's no need to plan a big over-complicated future event. Put a last minute, impromptu get-together in place to meet at the park, backyard, or the local pizza parlor. No one is grading the size and scope of the occasion. Make it about being together. Resist the urge to over-plan and over-think it. All you really need is something spontaneously ordinary.

Devote a few minutes every evening to a thoughtful review of your day. Reflect on what you did right and what you might do differently next time. Yesterday is gone, but tomorrow is filled with promise and possibility. If you truly want to make each day memorable, live life to its fullest potential and be open and honest about the things that count. Start today. Carpe diem.

SOME RAIN MUST FALL

"The way I see it, if you want the rainbow, you gotta put up with the rain." – Dolly Parton

Henry Wadsworth Longfellow penned his "Rainy Day" poem in the 1800's featuring the oft quoted line sent to the top of the charts by Ella Fitzgerald in 1944," Into each life some rain must fall". It's true, there are failures, disappointments, and unwelcome surprises popping up at the most inopportune times. That's life. Things happen.

Prepare for the worst but expect the best. Carry adequate insurance, lock your doors, and look both ways before crossing the street. Take precautions whenever possible and do your best to safeguard and protect your place in the world. Everyone faces adversity on their journey through life, and when bad things happen to you, a good person, deal with it. It's all about facing the rain with the right attitude.

Every event doesn't fall conveniently in the good or bad, black or white, category. There are many shades of gray. Don't wallow in the 'why or 'why me' of the situation. Rise above it, consider your options, and wait for the storm to pass. Life is an endless opportunity for growth and there are many lessons to be learned through adversity.

While you're mired in that rough patch take a moment for reflection, look for opportunities, and discover solutions. Self-analysis will lead to self-awareness and help you understand what went wrong and what can be done to prevent it from happening again. How can you fix this and minimize collateral damage? Is there a way to turn the negative into a positive and create something better? As you learn from your mistakes, you improve and grow. Embrace the process and don't let setbacks set you back. Now smile, enjoy the cleansing rain, and wait for the rainbow to follow.

COME TOGETHER

"Individually, we are one drop. Together, we are an ocean."
– Ryunosuke Satoro, Japanese Poet

One can easily rip a piece of paper in half but stacked as thick as a phone book it's nearly impossible to rend alone. Call on a few friends and through combined effort the book will be in shreds within minutes. Strength comes from unity and change happens when people come together for a common cause.

Confidence grows when people work together to succeed. If the thought of presenting your report in front of the whole team sends you into complete panic, join a public speaking group such as Toastmasters. The members understand the fear is not irrational and allow you to practice and overcome your anxiety in a safe setting and an empathetic audience.

Many people struggle with substance or activity addiction. It's almost impossible to go it alone when fighting alcohol, drugs, gambling or other dependencies. Once they join a recovery group and connect with people fighting the same demon the collective strength and determination has the ability to successfully conquer the evil that often eludes one person struggling alone.

If there is a movement that supports an issue you are passionate about get involved. Learn as much as you can about the group, and if their goals and purpose align with yours, add one more voice to the cause. Your ideas combined with other like-minded individuals can truly make a difference. Don't sit on the sidelines and watch the world go by. Show up and do your collaborative part.

Don't be afraid to ask for support when needed. One person's single prayer may not be heard, but spread the word, submit a request to a prayer chain, and make some noise. God will hear your prayers and answer them. Come together and make the difference.

GIVE A LITTLE

"Service to others is the rent you pay for your room here on earth."
– Muhammad Ali

When you feel a little down reach out and lend a hand to someone in need and your happiness quotient will soar. Contribute even a little time, money, or understanding and make a big difference in someone's life, as well as, your own. Giving back is as good for the giver as it is for the receiver, possibly even better. It provides purpose and living a purpose-driven life is gratifying.

Find a charity that reflects your values or supports a cause that is near and dear to your heart. If there's money to spare, donate to the cause. If you cannot gift money, give the gift of time. Look for opportunities to volunteer in your local community. Food banks need re-stocking year-round, not just during the holidays. Pare down your wardrobe and gather clothes to pass down or donate. Encourage friends and neighbors to do the same and offer to deliver the donations on their behalf.

We are a nation of extravagant and generous 'gifters'. Instead of the customary gifting ritual for birthdays or holiday exchanges, ask that donations be made to a favorite charity or for families in need. It feels good to do good and it's a fun way to teach kids how to make a difference.

Positive contribution can be made in many ways. Set a goal to smile at everyone you see. They will smile back and, hopefully, pass it on to the next person they see. Joy is wonderfully contagious. Commit to paying a sincere compliment to at least one person every day. It will make their day and add a bright spot to yours as well. Creating goodwill costs nothing and benefits everyone. Give generously, make a difference, and find happiness.

TIME VS. TASKS

"Don't say you don't have enough time. You have exactly the same number of hours per day that were given to Helen Keller, Pasteur, Michelangelo, Mother Teresa, Leonardo da Vinci, Thomas Jefferson, and Albert Einstein."
– H. Jackson Brown, Jr., Life's Little Instruction Book

No matter hard you work, at the end of the day your to-do list is still a mile long. It's frustrating to work so hard and just tread water. Try 'time blocking' and approach time management from a more practical and realistic angle. Time blocking organizes time by calendaring tasks in specific increments, at times when they are most likely to get done.

Time-blocking requires setting appointments with yourself to focus on specific planned tasks. It works best when the most important items are scheduled during high-energy hours. If you typically hit a slump mid-afternoon, calendar lighter 'housekeeping' items during those low energy hours. Not a morning person? Scheduling tough tasks before your morning coffee kicks in is destined to fail. When not operating at full strength you are more susceptible to interruptions that waste time. It's simple. Block time for items requiring the most focus when you operate at peak performance. Spend your low performance hours handling menial tasks requiring less skill and concentration.

A visit to the gym is a perpetual to-do list item, but fitness is frequently preempted by a myriad of daily distractions. Get the workout done by blocking time first thing in the morning. Without set boundaries it's tempting to fill your days with details and minutiae. Allocating sufficient uninterrupted time for your highest priorities will steadily move you closer to your goals. Set and protect boundaries to prevent time-wasters from frittering away precious minutes. The next time you hear 'got a minute?' refer to your all-important daily agenda and block that 'minute' during a low-priority time.

BUILD A STRONG FOUNDATION

"The foundation stones for a balanced success are honesty, character, integrity, faith, love, and loyalty." – Zig Ziglar

Core values form the infrastructure upon which you build your life. If you have a clear understanding of who you are and why you do what you do, your foundation will provide a bedrock of support through all of life's ups and downs. Before setting goals and springing into action, take some time to reflect and identify your vision and values. These are the 'stones' necessary to form a foundation strong enough to sustain a vibrant, adventurous life.

Commit to becoming the best you can be starting with personal health and wellness. Establish a fixed morning routine to jump start each day with energy and positivity. Eat right, rest well, and exercise regularly to remain agile, both physically and mentally. Reinforce your foundation by practicing consistent daily habits that align with your beliefs and take action that reflects your true character. Start with small self-improvement goals and build steadily from there.

Use a daily list and detailed weekly goals as an efficient and effective productivity system. Accountability and doing what you say you will do builds trust and strengthens the framework the foundation supports. Authenticity is a valuable commodity and an essential ingredient for maintaining a solid base. Let your actions reflect the real you. Communicate openly and honestly to build and maintain lasting relationships.

The process of self-improvement is a work in progress as goals evolve and life events re-focus attention. You may experience a crack in the foundation from time to time, but since it was built with integrity it will stand up to the stresses of life. Temporary patches will hold until new habits and systems are put in place to restore balance and structure.

THE BLAME GAME

"Blaming others for your problems is like blaming donuts for being fat. It wasn't the donut, it was the choice." – Jeff Gitmor

Life is filled with the 'someone must be to blame' people who habitually point a finger at everyone else for unsatisfactory circumstances, instead of taking responsibility themselves. They find it so much easier to hide behind this convenient defense mechanism than hold themselves accountable, hoping it distracts from their own flaws and shortcomings. Finger pointing keeps them out of the fray and offers the luxury of viewing the world through a rearview mirror with the benefit of hindsight's perfect vision.

Monday morning quarterbacks love to sit on the sidelines and let everyone else do the heavy lifting and, after the fact, weigh in with their opinion. They claim they wouldn't have done it that way, find fault, poke holes, and deflate the plan put in place through the efforts of others. When this happens give yourself permission to drop the penalty flag and point out the infraction.

No one wins the blame game. If you're the blamer, toss out your real or imagined list of offences and failings. Take a moment and turn your focus inward. Life and people are not perfect, so the next time you feel like criticizing find a way to put a positive spin on it, stop judging, and make an effort to help. If you're the focus of the negative interaction put your hurt on hold and honestly assess the negative interaction to see if there is any validity to it. If you recognize some truth, use it as an opportunity to learn and grow.

No matter which side you're on, assuming a victim mindset will not improve the situation. Play fair, make good choices, and accept full responsibility for the part you play.

GIVE YOURSELF PERMISSION

"Dream and give yourself permission to envision a You that you choose to be." – Joy Page

Growing up you were taught to seek permission from your parents, teachers, coaches, and caregivers to keep you safe and on track. As an adult you continue that tradition and look to others for direction in personal life decisions. Starting today give yourself permission to feel every emotion, enjoy success, risk failure, and live your own life without needing or wanting the consensus of anyone else.

You're all grown up and don't need to seek direction from others. If you feel strained and drained, enjoy a mental health day and binge watch the hot new series or a favorite rom-com. Stay out past bedtime on a work night, eat dessert first, and say 'no' to the people or things that demand your time and don't return the favor. Take risks, fail often, and come back stronger, no excuses or explanations necessary. It's your life and no one knows what's best better than you. Don't worry what people may think if you change careers, partners, direction, or your mind. Throw caution to the wind and open the flood gates of opportunity.

Give yourself permission to be authentically you with all those perfectly human flaws. It's exhausting to maintain a facade or try to live up to someone else's expectations. Be your true self and attract like-minded individuals who relate to the real you, not who they think you are.

Starting today, allow yourself to step outside the safety zone and stretch to your full potential. Don't give any credence to negative self-talk or well-intentioned cautionary tales from friends and family. Quiet those qualms, discover what you're really capable of, and give yourself permission to experience all life has to offer.

FISH OR CUT BAIT

"Gratitude and complaining cannot co-exist simultaneously. Choose the one that best serves you." – Hal Elrod

The phrase 'fish or cut bait' can be interpreted in several ways. Should you cut up the fish you have and use it as bait to continue fishing or should you cut the fishing line and give up? It's a provincial call to action that suggests one stop complaining and make a choice - commit or quit.

If you are employed in a position that frustrates you or work for an organization whose values are not aligned with yours, it's time to make a decision. Either choose to stay and embrace the differences or look elsewhere for employment. Those are the options. Incessant complaining to anyone within earshot may be tempting, but it's not a constructive solution.

The same is true when a relationship presents challenges. If your partner is not living up to their commitment tell them, not everyone else. You can only bend an ear so far and the shoulder you cry on will eventually turn cold. If you have been expressing unhappiness about your current situation, ask this life-changing question: "What am I going to do about it?"

Start by honestly facing the problem. Why are you unhappy at work? If the job is unfulfilling or too stressful you might be able to make a few adjustments to solve the problem. If it's a negative work environment a new position might be best. Do you really want a better relationship or are you trying to justify a split by rallying others to your cause? Once you are clear about the change that's needed set a goal and work on a positive solution. Don't be disappointed if you don't get everyone's blessing or buy-in. It's your life and if change is necessary, fish/commit or cut bait/quit.

IT ALL BEGINS INSIDE

"If an egg is broken by outside force, life ends. If broken by inside force, life begins. Great things always begin from inside."
– Jim Kwik, Learning Expert

Real growth and lasting change can only come from within. There are legions of overweight individuals who say they want to lose weight, but fall short of wholly committing to a fit, healthy body. And then one day something snaps, and half-hearted wishes are replaced by a resolute long-range focus that nothing and no one can thwart. It could be a lifestyle change, a new inspiring regimen, a health scare, or the status quo is simply no longer acceptable.

If you want to improve your life, change your mind. Once you redirect your mindset, change can happen. Positive focused thoughts are very powerful forces that are able to transform life in long-term, sustainable ways. Use that power to unleash your full potential and make needed improvements, starting today.

Begin with honest introspection and self-examination. If you are a Type A, driven personality and you have no life outside the office, it might be high time to find some balance. 'Aha' moments like these plant the seeds that allow permanent changes to take root and grow. Decide exactly what steps must be taken to get from where you are now to where you want to be. Make a plan to take regular time off, book a vacation, or join a group that shares your interests. Schedule deadlines, set benchmarks and milestones to celebrate progress, and fully commit to living a balanced, joyful life.

Life can and should be an interesting journey of mindfulness and constant development. Dig deep and decide to change your life for the better. Conquer your Achilles heel and turn weakness into success, from the inside out.

FILL YOUR CUP

"Thou preparest a table before me in the presence of my enemies: thou anointest my head with oil; my cup runneth over." – King David, King James Version of the Bible

The 23rd Psalm assures us that with God all things are possible. As long as you have Him in your life you "shall not want". He will protect, provide for you, and bless you with health, wealth, family, friends, and success in every area of your life. Think of the full cup in this psalm as an analogy for God's blessings and you will never again be tempted to consider the glass half empty. Fill your mind with optimism and let your cup overflow with peace, joy, and love.

Start each day with a cup of positivity. As you prepare your brimming, but not overflowing, morning coffee or cuppa tea consider the opportunities the day offers. Adopt the famous line from New Year's heartfelt anthem, Auld Lang Syne, "We'll take a cup of kindness yet". Pledge to pay kindness from the past forward to the future. As you give back and treat others with compassion and understanding, blessings will come back to you tenfold and spill from your cup.

The cup is your destiny. Here's the question that only you can answer: Is my cup empty, half full, or brimming over? The choice is yours. Fill your cup to overflowing with confident, happy thoughts. This doesn't happen automatically. It requires that you live with purpose every day. Don't let life get in the way of positive direction or it will drain you of those good intentions. Control your thoughts and focus on exactly what you want. Live with an attitude of abundance and let your cup run over and fill your life with all the good it has to offer.

MAKE A LIST, CHECK IT TWICE

"Checklists seem able to defend anyone, even the experienced, against failure in many more tasks than we realized... They catch mental flaws inherent in all of us – flaws of memory and attention and thoroughness. And because they do, they raise wide, unexpected possibilities." – Atul Gawande, The Checklist Manifesto: How to Get Things Right

Every day is filled to overflowing with endless loose ends and countless details. How will you get your arms around it all to prevent important bits and pieces from falling through the cracks? Checklists are the answer. They bring order to the day, chronicle your actions, and calm the chaotic thoughts swirling through your mind.

The architect, Ludwig Mies van der Rohe said, "God is in the details" in reference to the buildings he designed. The same can be said of most anything worth doing. The little things in life make an occasion memorable or a project successful. Overlook important details and what could have been extraordinary suddenly becomes ordinary. When faced with an overwhelming day or special event take the time to list the particulars, both essential and trivial. This will free your mind of the many distracting thoughts ricocheting in your head. Once the demands of the day are memorialized on a list the constantly moving parts come into focus and become manageable. It reduces the risk that something will be overlooked or forgotten and provides clarity, direction, and motivation.

Checklists inspire you to do more. It's very satisfying to check an item off a list. In fact, one check encourages the next until it's time to scratch one page and start another. At the end of the day there's an accurate account of numerous accomplishments. Progress fuels momentum to the point you're tempted to list additional tasks just for the sheer pleasure of crossing them off, and therein lies the magic and power of the checklist.

FIND SOME MIDDLE GROUND

"Learn the wisdom of compromise, for it is better to bend a little than to break." – Jane Wells

There's rarely just one correct way to do something or one perfect solution to a problem. Even when you're sure your way is the right way, it's important to realize the opinions of others aren't necessarily wrong, just because they differ from yours.

Life works best when you strive for balance and allow a little ebb and flow in your relationships. Compromise sometimes asks everyone to give a little bit until a happy medium is reached. Your daughter has been asked out by the BMOC (big man on campus). Her curfew is usually ten o'clock, but this is a special evening and she asks to stay out until midnight. After some discussion everyone agrees that eleven o'clock is manageable middle ground.

Sometimes it takes more than a little give and take to find a resolution, making alternative workarounds necessary. You love romantic comedies and your partner prefers science fiction thrillers. There isn't a genre that incorporates both, so you might consider alternating movies of choice to keep it fair. If that's the solution one person will be bored when it's time for a rom-com and the other horrified during the sci-fi screening. A compromise in this case might involve a different technique. Divide and conquer. Find friends who share your interest and feed each passion separately. It might not feel like the perfect answer, but it may be the best one.

Making concessions doesn't mean you are weak. Compromise keeps life fair and balanced. If each side concedes a small amount in the course of daily life there's less chance anyone feels put upon or resentful. Peace and harmony reign and in the big picture of life, what could be better than that?

THE NEED TO NATTER

"Great minds discuss ideas; average minds discuss events; small minds discuss people." – Eleanor Roosevelt

Spreading unfounded rumors about others is generally frowned upon and definitely very poor form. If you become aware of a scandalous or juicy tidbit, hold your tongue. There's always a chance it's not true and regardless of the facts you don't want to be the person to damage another's reputation. Hurtful news doesn't need to be repeated, period. True and newsworthy information should be shared; however, it may not be your story to tell. Use yourself as the litmus test. Before you pssst or post ask yourself if you would want your friends or family to hear the news from anyone other than you.

Being the subject of whispered conversations might have been your biggest fear in middle school. Its sole purpose was to demean or embarrass a classmate. It was tempting to be on the gossip girl side to ensure the spotlight was shining on anyone other than you. That was then, and this is now, and thankfully most people outgrow that mean pastime as adults. Occasionally you will cross paths with a rumormonger who seems to have a need to find fault in others. Understand they do it to make themselves look better and put up a protective barrier to conceal their obvious insecurity.

If you don't have something nice to say don't say anything at all. That is excellent advice. If you do have something nice to say, shout it from the rooftops. Serve a higher purpose by inspiring and encouraging people around you. If you catch someone doing something right feel free to broadcast the news. Share stories that motivate, offer support, and focus on the positive side of humanity. That's constructive conversation, or good gossip, and always worth sharing.

LIVE FOR POSSIBILITIES, NOT PROBABILITIES

"If you so choose, even the unexpected setbacks can bring new and positive possibilities. If you so choose, you can find value and fulfillment in every circumstance." – Ralph Marston

Just because something is possible doesn't mean it's probable. There's a possibility it will rain, even on the sunniest day. The weather pundits announce a zero percent probability of rain and a small cell surprises everyone with a passing shower. Possibility gives us hope that an event will occur, and probability measures the chance that it will actually happen. One keeps us optimistic and the other dampens our prospects with statistical reality. Just because it can doesn't mean it will, so live your life and don't worry about what you can't control.

Bad things do happen, and the world will most likely end one day, but no good comes from incessant worrying about the likelihood of your worries coming to fruition. Think about how shallow and unfulfilled your life would be if you lived in fear of low probability occurrences. Lightning rarely strikes so there's no need to stay indoors and out of harm's way whenever there's a storm in the forecast. Speaking of lightening, you are more than 20,000 times more likely to be struck by lightning than win a lottery jackpot. It is possible, which is why millions of people regularly buy tickets and dream of being the big winner, but with such improbably low odds your money would be better spent on almost anything else. Spend your time and resources in the realm of possibility and don't let needless concern of unpredictable situations hold you back. Thomas Edison said, "When you have exhausted all possibilities, remember this: you haven't."

LET GO OF GUILT

"Guilt: The gift that keeps on giving." – Erma Bombeck

I was raised Catholic which means I memorized my catechism and tried my best not to sin. On Saturday afternoon my father took us to church to confess said sins. We were taught that, thanks to Adam and Eve, humans are imperfect sinners. The only way to save our soul was to confess to a priest in a stuffy, scary confessional. I spent a lot of time worrying about sinning and how to avoid it. Apparently, even having a 'bad thought' is a sin, but as an elementary school kid I didn't know what constituted a bad thought. Apparently, humans sinned weekly, so I searched for something to confess to the priest. I was a little bossy to my younger siblings, but beyond that I was harmless. I figured that asking for forgiveness for disobeying my mother (never) and fighting with my brothers and sisters (rarely) would cover a multitude of sins. My childhood involved large doses of 'Catholic guilt' which left me terrified of the consequences if I continued in my supposed evil ways. I was a good, but guilt-ridden, little girl.

If you feel guilty when you're working because you should be home with your family, or vice versa, it's time to decide. Enjoy a career and teach your children the value of a solid work ethic or stay home and confidently raise them. Either choice is admirable, but only one is best for you.

The moral of the story is: guilt is a wasted emotion. It holds you back and nothing good ever comes from it. Give yourself a break. If you exercise good judgment, and choose right over wrong, you will be able to live your life with a guilt-free clear conscience.

JUNE BLOOMS

"June is the gateway to summer." – Jean Hersey

Welcome June - a month long celebration of life! Students escape the confines of school and look forward to lazy, unencumbered days ahead. Everyone seems to have at least one graduation ceremony to attend in the month of June. Commencement ceremonies start as early as pre-school and kindergarten, as if it's not a given the child will advance to first grade. The pomp and circumstance continue from grade school through college. No matter what level they have conquered we smile broadly, pose for pics, and host celebratory parties dedicated to honoring their amazing accomplishments. The grads confidently walk across the stage, shake hands as rehearsed, proudly accept their diploma, and move on to the next chapter of their young life, which we will happily celebrate with new enthusiasm.

We dedicate the third Sunday in June to the celebration of the important father figures in our lives. Set up the deck chairs, fire up the grill, and raise a glass to the men who protect and influence us year in and year out. They deserve a day of R & R and a lot of love.

Traditionally, June has been a favorite month to tie the knot. In ancient Roman times June 1st marked the festival of the deity Juno and his wife Jupiter, the goddess of marriage and childbirth making it an auspicious time to wed. For practical reasons it didn't hurt that the ladies would have recently enjoyed their annual (yes, annual) bath and flowers were readily available to conceal any lingering odors. Those reasons apply today, but the combination of lovely weather, kids out of school, and available vacation days, it remains an opportune time to plan a wedding.

All things considered, this is a good day to decide to make June a great month, one exciting celebration at a time.

NOTE TO SELF

"The best way to predict your future is to create it."
– Abraham Lincoln

You can dream about it, believe in horoscopes, or consult a psychic, but trying to successfully foresee what fate has in store is pure speculation. The best way to create the life you want to live is to manifest your best future self by thoughtful and intentional design.

Sit down and write a comprehensive letter to your future self. Envision where you will be next year, or in five, ten, or more years. It's your story so make it good. Define life in as much detail as possible. Describe your family and rate personal relationships. How are they going? Are there children, grandchildren? If so, what are they like? Is your current career satisfactory or have you gone down a different path? Has travel played a part? Are you healthy, happy?

You are creating the future version of you. Identify the end goal and the changes that need to happen now will become clear. If your future self is trim and healthy start eating better now, join a gym, or take up tennis. If your future self is well traveled and you have yet to leave the state, get the map out. The sky's the limit, but don't expect to conjure up the impossible. If your vision included college education for the kids you might need to put the brakes on exotic trips and make plans involving a tent, the open highway, and a robust savings plan.

What needs to happen to turn your vision into reality? Work backwards and put a plan in place that takes you down the road to success. It's possible to live the life of your dreams if you commit today to stop dreaming and start doing.

THE LIVIN IS EASY

"It's a smile, it's a kiss, it's a sip of wine … it's summertime!"
– Kenny Chesney

The languorous days of summer lie ahead, queued up for summer fun. How will you eke the most fun out of the best days? You might have lots of ideas and a few vague concepts, but you really need a Plan with a capital P. Summer days will unfurl in an endless loop of sunshine and sunsets, lost forever unless you claim them as your own. It's time to make a list and fill those days with wonderfully memorable life experiences.

Start your list by jotting down whatever activities come to mind and don't overthink or refine the thought. Will you head to the water? List beach, pool, waterpark, or lake outings. Activities around water might include boating, water or jet skiing, fishing, surfing, or swimming laps. You can't let a summer go by without a trip to the ballpark, hot dog included. Think about the fun to be found in day hikes, evenings around the campfire, and cookouts with s'mores melting over the glowing coals. If you have planned a vacation add those anticipated experiences to your growing list. The vacation isn't complete until you have checked off your priorities and have derived as much fun as possible from the getaway.

If a staycation is in store look around, the options will surprise and delight. Ask yourself what someone would do if they were tourists in your town. Most of us have never properly explored our own back yard. Discover museums, art galleries, notable restaurants, and natural points of interest. Plan day trips, picnics, or treat yourself to a much-deserved spa treatment.

Share your Summer Plan with friends and keep the list close at hand. Wondering what to do with a few uncommitted hours? Consult the Plan with a capital P and make some memories.

STAY PROPERLY HYDRATED

"Drinking water is like washing out your insides. The water will cleanse the system, fill you up, decrease your colonic load, and improve the function of all your tissues." – Kevin R. Stone M.D., Physician, Orthopedic surgeon, Researcher

Water is hands down the most important nutrient needed to fortify your body. When you are consistently dehydrated your thirst mechanism diminishes, and it takes longer to realize you are thirsty. Once hydrated your body triggers thirst much sooner, alerting you to drink up.

Studies show the eight glass per day rule may have been overstated or misunderstood. The equivalent of eight glasses of water can come from food and other beverages along with a healthy dose of plain old H2O. Water is the main component of our bodies (60%), and regular consumption will prevent body and brains from becoming parched. Like the rest of our organs thirsty brains don't function properly and can actually shrink in size if they become too dry. The visual of your brain drying out might cause you to take the importance of hydrating around the clock more seriously.

Here is an easy to follow system that is equally easy to build a habit around. It's as simple as drinking a glass of water before bed and during the night if you wake up. This will feed your brain and organs over the long night. Drink when you wake prior to enjoying that dehydrating cup of coffee, when you brush your teeth, morning and night and throughout the day. Enjoy water with every meal and whenever someone offers it. Consider water your drink of choice. Go quench your thirst right now. It does a body good.

STAY IN CURIOUS MODE

"You can teach a student a lesson for a day; but if you can teach him to learn by creating curiosity, he will continue the learning process as long as he lives." – Clay P. Bedford, American Industrialist

Be a lifelong learner by remaining open to new ideas at all times. There is something very empowering about the act of learning. It broadens horizons, provides more opportunities for advancement, and generally enhances your understanding and enjoyment of the world. Life is so much more fascinating when you remain curious and committed to personal growth.

The world is moving so fast that if you become complacent for even a short while, it might pass you by. Sign up for the interesting class that caught your attention. Research the latest developments in your area of expertise. Make your passions known and become the go-to person for information in that arena. Knowledge is indeed power. The more you know the more you are valued.

Learning for the sake of learning builds confidence and self-esteem. Even a basic understanding of a subject will allow you to strike up a conversation with someone who is an expert in the field. Knowing the right questions to ask will let them know you are interested in hearing what they have to say. It gives you common ground to connect with people and is a wonderful way to strengthen friendships and initiate professional relationships.

Staying ahead of the curve is not easy. It is, however, vital to remain relevant. Keep an open mind and delight in new and thought-provoking ideas. Be patient when you suffer 'growing pains' and stay strong when you feel vulnerable. Understanding new concepts and philosophies will make you more interesting and a valuable influence on those around you. Don't go through life with your cell phone blocking your view. Stay in the moment, wide eyed and aware there's still so much to learn.

LIVE ON PURPOSE

"The person without a purpose is like a ship without a rudder."
– Thomas Carlyle

Life's purpose is not just about figuring out who you are and what you do. It's about figuring out why you do it and who you do it for. In short, purpose is your reason for living. Once you identify who you are at the very core your passion will appear. Passionate people put their heart into everything they do and are eager to share their joy with the world. Living life on purpose is about waking up in the morning guided clearly by your personal core beliefs. When day to day actions reflect those values and priorities, you are unstoppable.

The best way to live on purpose is to serve. It's really quite simple: To be happier, make others happy. To be successful, help others to succeed. Lead by example, live an exemplary life, and be a positive role model. Make it your purpose to have a meaningful impact on the lives of others. Delight in giving without expectation of personal gain, and you will enjoy a rich, fulfilling life.

Are you in business for the sole purpose of making money or do you sincerely want to help people live a better life through your product or service? It isn't necessary to focus on money to make money. Take your influence and contribution to the next level and focus on making a difference and genuinely helping others. Do this and the money will follow, along with satisfaction and peace of mind.

Give to receive. The more you give the more you will receive. Give generously from your heart and live up to your true purpose from a truly purposeful position of strength.

THIN THINGS

"We fritter away our energy and creativity…we get bogged down in the thick of thin things." – Henry David Thoreau

We write our goals, make grand plans, and then life gets in the way. We wake up inspired, determined to conquer the world, but somehow the hours are eaten up by insignificant and mundane things. Our lives would be so much richer, and we could make such a difference, if only it wasn't so easy to waste precious time on trivial things that in the big picture just do not matter.

Many of our daily conversations are perfect examples of getting 'bogged down in the thick of thin things'. The discussion might include a complete account of who did what to whom and what label they were wearing at the time. Perhaps it's embellished with details like the speaker's opinion of an event, a description of material possessions involved, and an editorial on the latest political/Hollywood scandal. In other words, nothing noteworthy or important communicated other than thin, superficial patter.

From now on commit to making the conversation count by asking good questions and showing genuine interest in the answers. Go a little deeper. Ask about important life situations, really listen to the answers, and then share your thoughts and possible solutions. Take the conversation where it matters and where it can make a difference.

Don't worry about how you look or what you own. Look for ways to layer more significance into your daily life at every opportunity. Raise the bar and add depth to the conversation by sharing ideas and thoughtful ways to improve and enrich the lives you touch. Skip the shallow end and jump right into the deep end of the pool. Instead of draining your energy, your creative juices will flow once you're in the thick of it.

BFF'S

"Friendship is the only cement that will ever hold the world together."
– Woodrow T. Wilson

Today is the day to celebrate friendship and show appreciation for your best friend, or if you're very lucky, friends. You are blessed if you have one or two people in your lifetime who would answer your call and come to your rescue in the middle of the night, no questions asked. You're comfortable hanging out in sweat pant and slippers, come as you are, with no particular plan or agenda. They are the same individuals you stay connected with even as careers and relationships change, and cross-country moves prevent day to day contact. They are true friends.

Best friends understand you, deal with your quirks and idiosyncrasies, and accept you unconditionally. When you call to discuss a problem or simply need a sounding board there's no need to fill in the tedious background details. They know your history. They are privy to inside jokes, deepest secrets, regrettable decisions, and poor choices. But don't worry, anything shared remains forever in the 'vault', no judgment. They have seen your worst and will always believe in your best. Good friends encourage you to stretch, grow, and become the best you can possibly be.

Friends might say what you want to hear, but best friends will not varnish or skirt the truth. When asked what they think of your new dress or hairstyle, they give you the straight no-holds-barred truth. You may not like it, but might need to hear, "It's not a flattering style", or "the color doesn't work". Thank goodness for true best friends. Pick up the phone today and let them know how important they are and how much richer life is with them in it.

START WITH A SMILE

"Sometimes your joy is the source of your smile, but sometimes your smile can be the source of your joy." – Thich Nhat Hanh

Here's a simple truth that probably won't surprise you: When you smile you feel better. Smiles relax and calm your nerves. It's a natural precursor to laughter, aka the best medicine, which is even more therapeutic. A good laugh, even a forced one, sends restorative oxygen to the brain increasing energy and making everything a little brighter. Why not smile more and jump start a cycle of positivity?

Life's not perfect and things don't always go your way. It's difficult to find humor in every situation. So, fake it, if you must, until your brain gets the message and improves your mood. Paste on a smile, even when you don't feel like it, and start a ripple effect that reduces stress and redirects your thoughts from negative to positive. A simple smile could become the pivotal moment that turns your whole day around.

People are naturally drawn to people who look happy. They feel comfortable striking up a conversation with someone who appears friendly and cheerful. A smile communicates joy and sends out welcoming 'talk to me' vibes. A sunny expression opens doors when you want to appear approachable and attract new friends or business prospects.

Make a commitment to smile at everyone you see today. The people you touch will be inspired to smile back and, hopefully, pass it on to the next person they see. Smiles are wonderfully contagious. Just think about how many attitudes you can change for the good, resulting in more productive, happier days. On a grander scale one sincere smile from you could impact a life today and make a difference in yours as well.

HAVE A GOOD DAY

"Not every day can be an easy one, nor every day fully happy; but even a day of tough going and difficulty can be a good day."
– Norman Vincent Peale

We want every day to be a great one, but outside influences and life events are out of our control, and often negative. No matter how much good stuff we try to put in our heads, bad stuff happens and must be processed. We can't avoid unforeseen disappointments and heartbreaks, but we can learn to cope with them when life deals us a low blow.

Some days are simply bad days. It's all part of the life experience, but something good comes from everything. Bad days make us stronger, the hard way. Through sadness we recognize happiness and appreciate good days. Rather than dwell on your problems look for something positive to focus on. It's easier said than done, but it's the first step to getting through it. Surround yourself with people and things that will uplift and raise your spirits. Positive distractions will infuse a little hope into even the darkest day and transform the endless loop of self-criticism and coulda/woulda/shoulda recrimination to acceptance of reality of the situation.

When life is good, enjoy it fully. When life is challenging, remember that nothing lasts forever, and better times are on the horizon. Just as we take care of ourselves when we're physically ill, it's important to guard and protect our mental and emotional well-being. Give in and experience the full range of your emotions instead of trying to hold them in. Take responsibility if you screwed up. Release allows healing to begin. There's some good in every day that, in some small way, can make things better. Some days you just might need to look a little harder.

NATURES GIFTS

"Smell is a potent wizard that transports us across thousands of miles and all the years we have lived." – Helen Keller

The aroma of fresh baked bread will have memories of your six-year-old self in Grandma's kitchen flooding back. A whiff of after shave and you're sitting behind your dad as he ferries the family to Sunday church. Many scents evoke emotional and very vivid childhood memories. It makes sense scientifically because smells are routed through the olfactory region of the brain which is closely connected to the areas that manage memory and emotion.

The sense of smell is more powerful than the other senses and the use of essential oils extracted from plants can help to reduce stress, lift moods, and ease a number of chronic conditions. Aromatherapy uses herbal and floral fragrances effectively to stimulate the brain and awaken emotions that boost well-being in body and mind.

Aromatherapy used for medicinal purposes has been practiced for centuries. It's natural, inexpensive, and inhaling or rubbing it into the skin is harmless, with no worrisome side effects. If you are struggling in any area of your life, investigate the healing properties associated with various essentials oils and find one that relieves the problem. Options are plentiful and fascinating.

Trouble sleeping can be remedied by the scent of lavender. Smooth on scented lotion before bed or spray a little scent on your pillow. Treating the kids to a lavender scented bath will soothe them and make bedtime easier. Strengthen your immune system with oregano or eucalyptus oil. Headaches can be relieved with peppermint or rosemary aromatherapy and, if they are stress related, other options will help to relax and unwind, reducing their frequency and intensity. Start today and increase energy, change your outlook, and cure what ails you.

START SMALL

"It's the little details that are vital. Little things make big things happen."
– John Wooden

Small changes add up to big results, both personally and professionally. It's not necessary to move the whole mountain. It's just as effective and much easier to move it one stone at a time. When you find yourself overwhelmed by goals or tasks break them down into manageable steps. Start with one small, confidence building step and when that is complete give yourself a pat on the back for making it happen. Now take one more baby step in the direction of your goals and feel the momentum build.

When was the last time a fad diet worked? You're guaranteed to lose excess weight quickly by drastically cutting calories, fats, or carbs. Eat bananas at every meal, fast, juice, cleanse. Those strict regimens don't work long term. Within two days you feel light-headed, short-tempered, and resentful. You throw in the towel on day three and overindulge in your favorite comfort food, adding back what you lost plus a little more. Small lifestyle changes and regulating eating habits, over time, are necessary to lose weight and keep it off.

Success breeds success. Committing to big change can be intimidating and tough to tackle. Small, incremental changes are not only possible, but forward progress in any amount is motivating and leads to lasting change.

Everyone fights a few frustrating weaknesses and traits. You want to be more organized/active/thoughtful/timely, but you're unable to override your natural tendencies. Identify one small thing you would like to improve and set intentions around the change you will make. Consistently focus on that one little area until a new, better habit is formed. Then pick another one and watch the changes add up. Small minor adjustments will eventually bring dramatic results.

BACKUP PLANS

"Success in life is not how well we execute Plan A; it's how smoothly we cope with Plan B."
– Sarah Ban Breathnach, Author Simple Abundance

There are two schools of thought when it comes to following your passion. Some people believe there should be one unconditional, cast in stone option that is pursued with singular purpose until success is achieved. The more pragmatic among us expect the unexpected, recognize there are always factors out of our control and prudently set up a Plan B, C, and possibly even a Plan D. A fallback plan is a good thing unless it's used as an excuse to give up prematurely, stop striving, or settle.

Having a contingency plan doesn't mean you expect to fall short of your hopes and dreams. It means no matter how well thought out Plan A is and no matter how prepared you are to execute, life sometimes gets in the way. Even the most thoroughly researched and detailed strategies are subject to the whims of life events. If your vision involves discretionary spending or starting a new business just as a recession hits, it might be wise to keep your day job until the economy improves. There's no need to give up completely, just take a step back and postpone launching until the time is right.

Hold your currently uninspiring job until the time is right, but don't get too comfortable. It's tempting to settle in, lose sight of your heart's desire, and allow your backup plan to backfire and take center stage as a poor substitute for your original goal.

Have backup, alternative, and contingency plans in place as a safety net, but never let go of your dreams. Stay focused on your primary objective, maintain realistic expectations, and exhaust every avenue before considering other options.

CELEBRATE DADS

"I can't think of any need in childhood as strong as the need for a Father's protection." – Sigmund Freud

Not long ago expectant fathers could be found pacing the hospital halls while their wives labored in childbirth, accompanied only by hospital staff. Today's dads take an active role in the delivery, as well as, the all-important bonding ritual immediately following birth. That same nervously pacing dad just added to the responsibility and stress of supporting a family while mom tended hearth and home.

These days the men pitch in at every level; volunteering at school, helping with homework, participating in household chores, and changing more than just lightbulbs. They do their part even if they are the primary wage earner. Although, it's not unusual to find the wife as breadwinner, bringing home the bacon, and the husband as stay-at-home caregiver, cooking and serving it. There are so many more options and possibilities for today's young families. Everyone benefits from the talent and passion of both parents without any limiting beliefs dictating what those areas of strength should be.

Men are doing parenthood right. They have stepped up, rolled up their sleeves, and just like moms, learn as they go. No handbook or 'how-to' can prepare one for parenting. There's no choice but to jump in underprepared, ask questions, and through trial and error manage to nurture kids through childhood. With a little luck they will do more than survive, they'll thrive.

Raise a glass to the father figures in your life, regardless of blood ties, marital status, age, or stage. If they were involved, inspired you to be your best, and led by example let them know how much you appreciate the difference they made. Recognize and reward them with a few heartfelt words of gratitude, "Thanks, Dad."

STEP INTO GROWTH

"In any given moment we have two options: to step forward into growth or to step back into safety." – Abraham H. Maslow, Author, A Theory of Human Motivation

Your comfort zone is a comfy place to be, unless you get too comfortable and complacency sets in. If you're hiding in the safety zone, it's time to step forward and take a chance. Move away from comfort where nothing grows and venture into that oh-so-scary growth zone. You evolve and develop by challenging yourself to try new things and go where you have never gone before. Doing this requires changing your current behavior and shaking up tried and true routines. What's stopping you?

Invest a little time in necessary self-discovery. Dig deep and explore your personal interests and natural talents. Ask yourself a few thought-provoking questions to help reveal clues leading to personal growth: What would you do if you won the lottery? What activities and skills do you want to master? What would happen if you weren't afraid to try?

Think of one thing you can do right now that will make life more interesting. Now list the steps necessary to make it happen. Don't let fear of failure hold you back. Step confidently out of survival mode and look for ways to move forward. Be open to new experiences, take calculated risks, and create a more rewarding life. Challenge yourself to consider all possibilities and fill your days with adventure, purpose, and continuous growth.

Change and growth enhances self-esteem, allows you to experience genuine joy, and flushes out your true purpose. Scare yourself today by taking one small step forward. Go for it. Tempt fate and use your imagination to seek new heights, chase more dreams, and live your best life.

LIFE IS IN THE DETAILS

"The difference between something good and something great is attention to detail." – Charles R. Swindoll

Details can be tedious and deflate or even derail your big-picture ideas. There's nothing better than dreaming larger than life scenarios and visualizing the success that will surely follow. It's less exciting to strategize and put tangible plans in place to breathe life into those dreams. If you're not a detail person tending to endless minutiae might feel as if it's holding you back when, in fact, it's the only way to move forward. Little things make big things happen. One without the other just won't work.

The details associated with relationships can be tricky. The 'honeymoon' period features clear blue skies, but eventually a few clouds may appear on the horizon. Patience, kind words, and expressing appreciation during everyday interactions will hold those clouds at bay. A healthy relationship requires awareness of your connection and actually relating to your partner. Head-in-the-clouds romanticism won't hold a real-world bond together long term.

Life happens somewhere in the balance. You think big thoughts and imagine changing your life from ordinary to extraordinary but dreams alone aren't enough to get you to the goal. Successful people pay close attention to the tiniest details and that is what sets them apart. Every vision needs a plan of action, time line, benchmarks, and checklists. If you're not a detail-oriented person by nature this can be challenging, but not impossible.

Continue dreaming big things, but remember dreaming is one thing and successfully nurturing an idea to reality is something very different. Once you visualize it, make a plan that consists of the many smaller actions that, once accomplished, will create one big, beautifully detailed, success story.

FAIR AND BALANCED

"I know the world isn't fair, but why isn't it ever unfair in my favor?"
– Bill Watterson

Some people always seem to be in the right place at the right time. Opportunity knocks, doors open, and blessings fall from the sky. Do you compare yourself to those born wealthy/gorgeous/athletic and feel like you can never catch a break? If, so, it's time to stop weighing and balancing. The key is to believe in yourself, do your best every day, and give up the 'us vs. them' comparison. We aren't privy to what goes on behind closed doors and there may be more to the story than meets the eye. One doesn't have to look too far to be reminded that some of the richest, most beautiful people in the world live very unhappy lives. It's quite possible the lucky descendant who inherited the family business had a different career path in mind and isn't completely thrilled with the windfall.

Focus on the goal and not the daily ups and downs. It's easier to stay centered and less emotional if you think long-term. Line graphs used to demonstrate continuing improvement typically indicate a number of declines on the way to eventual success.

You can do your best and still not completely insulate yourself from glitches and difficulties. If you are struggling in one area of your life focus on others; loving relationships, good health, or any other strengths. Let go of the past and don't try to predict the future. Think about the positive in the here and now. Do what needs to be done today followed by what needs to be done tomorrow. Life will never be absolutely fair and balanced. It's a process, not a race. Soften your perspective, celebrate the good, and cherish the life you have.

MAXIMIZE YOUR PRODUCTIVITY

"There are risks and costs to action. But they are far less than the long range risks of comfortable inaction." – John F. Kennedy

When faced with a large or overwhelming task it's sometimes difficult to get started. And if you do start it's next to impossible to stay on course. You allow distractions in, procrastinate, and end up in total frustration.

It's time to embrace, and eventually master, The Pomodoro Technique, one of the most popular and successful time management tools used today. This simple system was developed by Francisco Cirillo, an entrepreneur and author, in the late 1980's in an effort to train his brain to stay on task and in productivity mode until his job was done. He found that most people can learn to concentrate uninterrupted for 25 minutes and, if rewarded with a short break of 5-10 minutes, be creatively refreshed and ready for another 25-minute period. Simply tally each focused work session, or 'Pomodoro', (named after the tomato shaped timer Cirillo used), with an X. After you have completed four sessions treat yourself to a longer break of 15-30 minutes and watch your productivity skyrocket.

You have so much to do and so many interests vying for attention that you are sometimes 'poisoned by possibilities' and fail to complete anything. Looming deadlines have a way of spurring you on by releasing the energy and creativity needed to complete projects. Facing a deadlines every twenty-five minutes holds you accountable, helps push through projects and tasks, and maintains consistency. Over time you will train your brain and improve your powers of concentration which keeps your mind fresh and gets more done.

Choose one task that you have been putting off completing. Break through the inertia by testing this simple system and start today to get more done in less time.

PACK YOUR OWN CHUTE

"Hold yourself responsible for a higher standard than anybody expects of you. Never excuse yourself." – Henry Ward Beecher

It's up to you to take control of your life and accept full responsibility for it. Life is filled with opportunities, some decidedly better than others. It's your job to make good choices, face reality, and hold yourself accountable for the outcome. Aim for progress, not perfection. Consistent action will result in constant improvement, and little by little, a better you.

Many adults blame their shortcomings and flaws on their upbringing. It's true that not every child enjoys an idyllic childhood, and many parents do fall short, but once we leave the nest it's up to us to fly. It does no good to fault the economy, your career, or which way the wind is blowing. It's quite possible your parents did the very best they could. It's also possible your rear-view mirror is reflecting a slightly distorted image of reality. It's all about perception and at some point, we must grow up and own up. No excuses.

Frank Zappa said, "A mind is like a parachute. It doesn't work if it isn't open." Your mind-set can be the biggest obstacle to success and one sure way to invite failure. Eliminate negative self-talk and instead of looking for someone or something to blame, look for solutions. Keep an open mind, find the positive in every situation, and stop rationalizing problems and justifying your current situation with yesterday's news.

Starting today commit to overcoming your own limiting beliefs, set standards that reflect your true potential, and never settle for anything less than your best. If, and when, you come up a little short of the goal, look inward for answers, and commit to the best solution.

OVERCOMING FOMO

"That fear of missing out on things makes you miss out on everything."
– Etty Hillesum

Fear Of Missing Out. When I was in the third grade I had a legitimate case of FOMO. One of my classmates invited my friends for a sleepover, and I was left out. I was devastated, but in the absence of social media I was spared the hilarious pillow fights and ice cream sundae building that would look so festive and inviting online. I also missed the tears that inevitably flowed when a dozen overtired, overstimulated eight-year olds started melting down. The point is social media shares the highlight reel, but there' usually more to the story.

It's never fun to log-on and see your friends in the right places, at the right times, with all the right people, when you weren't even aware of the events. The truth is, everyone can't be invited to every party and maybe your best friends ended up at the concert, or on the cruise/at the award ceremony/restaurant, because they happened to run into the organizers just in time to grab the last two available tickets. Be happy for people who are enjoying their life while you take pleasure in your own life, your own way.

One person's fear is another one's pleasure. It feels good to be included, but how often, when asked, do you opt out? Maybe you don't have the time or energy to participate, or your budget is stretched to the max. It's time to embrace JOMO, The Joy Of Missing Out. If there's something you want to do, the timing is right, and you can afford it, make plans to do it. Be the organizer and invite a few friends to join you. Of course, you won't be able to include everyone, so let's hope the ones that miss out are happy for you.

SUMMER DAZE

"In early June the world of leaf and blade and flowers explodes, and every sunset is different." – John Steinbeck, The Winter of Our Discontent

Today we officially welcome summer in all of its sunshine and blue-sky glory. The summer equinox marks the longest day of the year, gifting us with additional hours of restorative daylight. We can look forward to weeks of sizzling days leading to intense sunsets and extended twilit evenings. It's a time to be a little more relaxed and casual - in a summer state of mind.

Before you immerse yourself in the joys of summer reflect for a moment on the passage through the past season and how it parallels your life. The sun has been reaching a little higher and staying a little longer each day for months. Have you been stretching yourself and mirroring that growth? Did you test your wings and leave the nest of your comfort zone? Are you living an intentional, balanced life and getting stronger and more confident with the passing seasons?

If you really want to take advantage of the season, make a list of things you want to try and accomplish before fall. Be clear about your intentions for growth and self-improvement. Will you get up at dawn, go for a run, and greet each day with joy and enthusiasm? Or take time to visit a museum, plant a garden, dust off your library card and make a dent in your reading list?

Summer is the season to open your eyes and your mind and truly appreciate the wealth of treasures the world holds. It's okay to indulge in a little summer down time, but then go out and take advantage of the long, glorious days to explore, learn, and expand your horizons.

WONDERMENT

"Youth is happy because it has the capacity to see beauty. Anyone who keeps the ability to see beauty never grows old." – Franz Kafka

I wonder when we stop wondering. I still don't know why the sky is blue or what makes wind, but somewhere along the way I stopped wondering about it. As we grow up we realize there are scientific explanations for the phenomena we loved to question so we leave the wondering to capable others.

Children are curious about the world and eagerly, and loudly, wonder about everything. They question and marvel at the amazing world unfolding before them every day. Much to the embarrassment of their parents they do it without filters or volume control. Kids unselfconsciously sing at the top of their lungs and expect parents and friends to be the audience as they produce endless plays and 'choreographed' dance routines. All without a thought or care about whether they were blessed with even an ounce of talent. Children are spontaneous, uncensored, and candid. They not only dress up like princesses and super-heroes, they become them. They believe.

It's been said that youth is wasted on the young. If you knew then what you know now, your life might have taken a different path. You would have been better prepared for what you faced and able to make educated decisions instead of posing with fingers crossed, hoping for the best, when taking those leaps of faith.

What's stopping you from experiencing wonderment at this stage of your life? Age doesn't matter. Embrace every opportunity to find beauty, experience joy, question, and yes, wonder. Tap into childhood memories and re-live the best moments. Channel your inner child and acknowledge, accept, and empower your youthful side. Take time to act silly, giggle uncontrollably, and treat yourself to a little uninhibited fun.

JUST A MINUTE

"If we take care of the moments, the years will take care of themselves."
– Maria Edgeworth, Anglo-Irish Author

Pay attention to the minutes and the hours will shape up nicely. Chipping away at tasks and life a few minutes at a time will get you to the goal one way or another. Some projects gain momentum as they progress and are completed on time, to great fanfare. More challenging circumstances require focused commitment in short, but consistent, intervals until the job is finally complete. The first scenario offers more enjoyment of the process and pride in the execution, but the second one gets the job done, too.

Where in your impossibly busy schedule can you find extra minutes? Start by getting up fifteen minutes earlier in the morning. Step outside and walk a mile, write a few personal notes, or pack a healthy lunch. Productively use those precious minutes to get to the office before the workday, with all of its distractions, officially begins. Limit social media interaction and casual web surfing to fifteen minutes. Log-on, like, comment, post, log-out. Don't waste time micromanaging your team or family. Trust that everyone is aware of their responsibilities and performs in a timely manner. Let go of unnecessary 'helicoptering' and free up additional time to move your own projects forward.

Setting a timer will help you focus, work efficiently, and bring tasks in on time. Anything that will take longer than fifteen minutes can be broken down into two or more smaller 'bites'. Without a deadline it could easily take twice as long, or longer.

What can you accomplish in a few extra minutes? Make a list of ways to carve out a little time and reallocate it more productively. Counting your minutes will make them count for you.

DO THE HOKEY POKEY

"Opportunity dances with those on the dance floor." – Anonymous

If something is worth doing, put your whole self in and give it all you've got. I love that dance tune from childhood, the Hokey Pokey, and the life lessons found in the lyrics. The song calls for you to 'put your whole self in'. Stop dabbling and commit. You're tempted to sit timidly on the sidelines, unsure of your next move, waiting for someone to come along and validate your decision. What if you jumped in with both feet and totally owned it? That's the best way to find out if it's a good move or not.

What's the worst thing that could happen? If the worst thing isn't life-changing give it a try. Once you're in motion it's so much easier to tweak things a little to find the perfect fit. Identify what is holding you back in any area of your life and find a way to fully commit to success by putting your whole self in.

The Hokey Pokey has another great line that works like a charm every time. You must admit even if your life is great, not every day is seamless. And certainly, every minute of every day will never be perfect. When you find yourself in a funk, call on the Hokey Pokey to get you through it. It's simple. Just "do the Hokey Pokey and turn yourself around". It will put a smile on your face and change your attitude for the better. It doesn't take much to set things straight if you just make the effort. Have a little fun next time you need an attitude adjustment. Get out there and take some risks. Seriously, what if the Hokey Pokey is what it's all about?

RISE UP

"The greatest accomplishment is not in never falling, but in rising again after you fall." – Vince Lombardi

You try to do the right thing, but you're human and make mistakes. You really want to do things right, so you feel badly when there are slip-ups. There's nothing wrong with that, but what about the people who make themselves feel better by pointing out the mistakes of others? They think that if they shine a light on what someone else has done no one will look too closely at them.

Some days it feels like it would be easier to sit life out rather than show up and risk human error, attracting unwanted attention and finger pointing. The MVP on your favorite baseball team plays a stellar game until the end when he misses the ball and he alone is blamed for losing the game. No one remembers the blunders and errors made by both sides over the course of nine innings. The final missed catch is all anyone is talking about. A true champion will rise up with confidence and quite possibly make the winning catch in the next game. If we let fear of failure stop us they win, and we lose. Trying and failing should not be the final answer. Failing and getting up to try again is what moves the needle and makes all the difference.

Most mistakes are not fatal. Trial and error is a practical, proven way to find the best solution for a problem. You'll never know if your great idea is truly great unless you float it out there. So what if it sinks? Make adjustments or approach it from a new angle and launch it again. Or simply put aside your ego and admit you made a mistake. The sun is guaranteed to rise tomorrow, along with you.

CASCADE OF EVENTS

"All human actions have one or more of these seven causes: chance, nature, compulsions, habit, reason, passion, desire." – Aristotle

Aeronautics giant, Lockheed Martin, is known for its forward-thinking development of a high-level division known as "Skunk Works". From behind closed doors this team successfully shaped some of the most influential advances in aviation history, as well as investigating and determining the cause when airplanes crashed. They found there was never just one reason for a crash, but a series or 'cascade' of events that caused it. Pilot errors alone can be corrected, and planes fly safely in bad weather every day, but the consequence of a pilot erring in stormy conditions, combined with any number of possible variables, can be disastrous.

Life events are much the same. They usually occur as the result of multiple actions leading to the event in question. Stop beating yourself up with 'what if?' when things go wrong. Maybe you thought you were the ideal candidate for a recent promotion but were passed over and the new kid was offered 'your' job. How could that possibly have happened?

Go back and re-visit the sequence of events prior to the unsatisfactory outcome. What if you hadn't invited him to join your team? What if you had stayed ahead of change by continuing education in your field as he did? What if his report at the last meeting wasn't quite so spot on? A single event can have multiple causes, but not all of them are in your control.

Pay close attention to what happens when you become more intentional about conditions in your life that you can control. A few thoughtful changes involving less negativity and more affirmative action will create a cascade of events that will impact and positively improve your world.

FIRST IMPRESSIONS MATTER

"You cannot climb the ladder of success dressed in the costume of failure." – Zig Ziglar

You get up every morning, shower, dress for success, put your best foot forward, and prepare to own the day. That sounds like a common-sense approach but look around and you quickly realize it is a morning ritual not always heeded. A clear majority have lowered their clothing and hygiene standards to the point that bedhead is acceptable all day.

Do you remember when travelers put on their Sunday best to board an airplane? Today's passengers are more likely to don pajama bottoms, sweatshirt, and slippers before heading to the airport. It is more comfortable for the wearer, but not the best way to present oneself to the world.

Many initial employment interviews are conducted via telephone and escalate to face-to-face meetings once the field thins. Statistics show when prospects dress better, they perform better, whether in person or out of sight. Suiting up for every business situation will bolster your confidence and composure. It only takes a few seconds to make a memorable first impression. Don't make the mistake of underestimating the importance of appearance and body language in those vital few seconds. Conclusions are drawn before negotiations begin so make sure your clothing communicates who you are, and what you are capable of. Even if relaxed dress is acceptable in your environment, careless is not. Business casual is buttoned-down, clean, and presentable. Before you leave the house confirm you're sending the right message and look together, smart, and clearly represent the business professional or (your title here) you are meant to be.

ONE GOOD TURN

"There is one word which may serve as a rule of practice for all one's life – reciprocity." – Confucius

Life is a balancing act requiring a great deal of give and take. You can tip the scales in your favor by implementing the Law of Reciprocity. Test the theory of reciprocity, or one good turn deserves another, by doing something helpful for someone else. When you do something nice for someone they feel obliged to reciprocate and do something nice for you. Maybe even nicer. It's pretty simple: If you want more, give more.

Try this. Make a commitment and then over-deliver on your promise. Offer that rare wow factor and the payback will be huge. Help someone without any expectation of compensation and the return on your investment of time or talent will increase many times. Take a page from Google's playbook and dispense help/information/knowledge for free. Identify areas where you can offer value and make a difference. Others will want to give back by sharing their information and before you know it the combined data or concept is exactly what you both needed to move forward.

Tit for tat. I'll scratch your back. Period. Not 'if you'll scratch mine'. You *will* scratch mine because that's what human nature compels us to do. You create positive reciprocity by performing good deeds without expecting anything in return. Good deeds are rewards in and of themselves. It really is better to give than to receive. If you need help, offer help to others and they will feel compelled to rush to your aid. Bank a few good deeds in advance and when you need something there will be a number of donors eager to step up and return the favor.

CONQUER FEAR

"Inaction breeds doubt and fear. Action breeds confidence and courage. If you want to conquer fear, do not sit home and think about it. Go out and get busy." – Dale Carnegie

Is fear holding you back? Are there demons that frighten you, stifle growth, and prevent you from reaching your goals? It's time to identify exactly what you're afraid of and take your life back. You feel safe in your comfort zone, now bravely step out of it. Confront your fears and face them head on. Go out and meet them with courage and confidence.

Some fear is rational and keeps you from taking unnecessary risks and out of trouble. The garden needs watering, but a large spider is suspended from the spigot, causing rising panic, clammy hands, and racing heart. The anxiety will subside when the threat scuttles away, but how do you overcome fears that don't go away? Acknowledge, confront, and work through them.

It's tempting to play it safe and avoid opportunities or situations where embarrassment, rejection, or failure are possible outcomes. Go ahead, take the plunge. Ask questions, try harder, and push your limits. What's the worst thing that will happen if you don't get the job or date? Interviews and first dates are daunting, but a few 'practice' runs will relax and improve the presentation until you fall comfortably into an acceptable conversation. Growth starts where the comfort zone ends.

It's okay to be fearful, but not if it stops you from being the best you can be. Challenge yourself to do the things that scare you. Be positive. Don't breathe life or energy into it and the fear will diminish. You have the power to overcome any obstacle and become the conquering hero you were destined to be.

REVIEW AND REVISE

"However beautiful the strategy, you should occasionally look at the results." – Sir Winston Churchill

Today marks the halfway point of the new year which means you're well on your way to achieving your annual goals. No? Goals are not 'set and forget'. It's important to review them regularly and revise as needed. Consistently measuring progress will take the surprise, or disappointment, out of the results. Make time daily/weekly/monthly to confirm the actions you're taking are moving you in the right direction. Rate progress and make any changes necessary to push yourself to your full potential.

Review and evaluate benchmarks and timelines in all areas of life. Evaluation is necessary because it shines a light on the results of your efforts, or lack thereof. It will reveal weaknesses or unrealistic expectations which can be demotivating. Once you understand what is working you will be inspired to keep going.

Did you make great progress in some sectors and stall in others? Just one small change might make all the difference in the outcome. If you gave yourself a high mark in relationships, but went backwards financially, could it be that you have been spending too much money trying to impress a certain someone? Be honest and assess the situation from a practical standpoint. If this person is important to you, full disclosure will earn their respect and further strengthen the relationship.

Commit to and be fully accountable to the outcome. Ask clarifying questions. Are daily actions moving you in the right direction? Do your goals need adjusting or updating? What areas need more attention? What will you accomplish in the next six months? The goals are yours to revise and replace, as needed. Be clear and fully commit.

HANDLING CONFLICT

"Peace is not absence of conflict, it is the ability to handle conflict by peaceful means." – Ronald Reagan

The head-in-the-sand-hope-it-blows-over approach may be tempting, but it's not an effective strategy for handling conflict resolution. If clashes aren't dealt with quickly and decisively they will continue to intensify until situations that could have been small bumps in the road explode into full blown battles not easily fixed.

Consider the company misfit, the guy with the dicey reputation who's unprofessional and flirts at the edge of 'gray area' ethics. You're not particularly proud to have him on your team, but it's tempting to keep him in status quo rather than deal with the unknowns of a new hire. By making the decision to cut him loose, you will send out a strong message about maintaining company standards, welcome news to one and all.

Don't try to avoid problems, praying they will go away. Confront them head on, clearly communicate what is, and what is not, tolerated and attach consequences to inappropriate actions. It's best to curtail escalation of conflicts by speaking immediately to the people involved before everyone else weighs in, chooses sides, and accelerates the problem. Addressing conflict in a straightforward, productive fashion is empowering to everyone concerned.

Positive reinforcement will keep competitive egos at bay. Approach the situation from a position of support and show empathy and understanding. Conflict resolution offers a learning opportunity but be aware you will rarely be able to make all parties happy. Let them know you care and make decisions in the best interest of the entire group. Take the high road, wave a white flag to clear the air, and begin soothing any egos that may have been bruised in the process.

WANDERLUST

"The world is a book, and those who don't travel read only a page."
– St. Augustine

There are few things in life that inspire possibilities and stretch limits more than travel. Your daily routine is comforting, but the anticipation of time away, diverse cultures, exotic food, and the thrill of adventure is life changing. The infinite prospects that present themselves when you step out of your element will transform you.

Traveling teaches us about ourselves, as well as the world. We learn to be patient. Some things are worth waiting in long lines, or travelling miles, to see. We learn to be flexible as our flight is cancelled, the weather is uncooperative, or we arrive at our destination to find out the locals are celebrating a religious holiday and stores and restaurants will be closed…for the remainder of our visit. The trivial details that fill our routine days are forgotten in light of the awe-inspiring beauty of natural spectacles and manmade wonders. We have a fresh perspective and make the most of every moment.

It isn't necessary to travel halfway around the world to experience the joy of travel. If time and budget limitations restrict travel to faraway lands, become a tourist at home. Every city has history, culture, diversity, and works of art. Every state boasts national treasures and natural splendor. Look around with eyes wide open, explore locally, and discover the secrets that have been hiding in plain sight.

Create a bucket list of places to visit and set up a travel fund to make it happen. The excitement begins in the planning stages so feed your wanderlust by always having something on the calendar to look forward to. Whether you venture far and wide or rediscover the land of your childhood, the journey to discovery is fulfilling and fun.

RE-FRAME IT

"When you change the way you look at things, the things you look at change." – Brian Tracy

Isn't it fascinating to listen to two people talk about the same event and hear very different accounts? There are at least two sides to every story. He said, she said. You view the world through your own personal lens while others see another version from their perspective. You make assumptions, jump to conclusions, and create your own truth based on emotion, expectation, and experience. The facts don't change, but by highlighting some words and downplaying others you frame the story to make it yours. It's not wrong, it's your reality.

When faced with a problem try taking a step back and re-framing your response by looking at the situation from a new angle. Your first impression might be negative but viewing it through a new lens will offer a fresh frame of reference making opportunities and solutions suddenly clear. The same technique applies to objection handling. Overcoming objections is nothing more than re-framing the positives to give the customer/spouse/child a new path forward.

A perfect example of two sides to the same story is evident in daily news reporting. Listen to the top story on one station and then switch channels. The facts are the same, but with a little nuance and a lot of finesse it sounds like a different story. Take another look at the easily overlooked introvert at the office. He's suddenly popular and surprisingly cool because he attended the holiday party with a stunning date. He didn't change, he's just being seen in a new light.

Try to look at the world differently. One way is not necessarily the right way or more valid than another. It just might be a little easier to understand the other side if you take the time to see it through their eyes.

THOUGHTS ON FREEDOM

"May we think of freedom, not as the right to do as we please, but as the opportunity to do what is right." – Peter Marshall

On this day in 1776 the members of the Continental Congress signed the Declaration of Independence, announcing the birth of a nation and America's symbol of freedom. The Liberty Bell was rung, and fireworks exploded in the sky to celebrate the momentous occasion. Perhaps the most quoted line in American history can be found in the Declaration of Independence: "We hold these Truths to be self-evident, that all Men are created equal, that they are endowed by their Creator with certain unalienable Rights that among these are Life, Liberty, and the Pursuit of Happiness."

The word 'pursuit' had a different meaning several centuries back. Our founding fathers were referring to one's occupation or daily habits. For example, a doctor was in the pursuit of medicine. The original intent was that Americans had the right to fill their lives with activities or pursuits that provided a good life for themselves, including good health and peace of mind, but also participate in the happiness of their fellow Americans.

In other words, it's not our right to take without giving back. It is our responsibility to replace our divots, be grateful to those who fought for, and fight for, our freedom. Many people devoted their lives to making this country a land of unlimited opportunity. Thank them by showing respect to others. Pay it forward, learn to compromise, find some middle ground and make the world a better place for the next generation.

These days we gather with our families and friends, wave flags along parade routes, and enjoy barbecues, picnics and pools. At the end of the day fireworks still explode in the sky. Enjoy the festivities and take a moment to reflect on the contribution you can make to continue to let freedom ring.

MAKE SOME LAUGH LINES

"Hearty laughter is a good way to jog internally without having to go outdoors." – Norman Cousins

Did you know that letting go and dissolving into a fit of giggles can lower your blood pressure, which will reduce the risk of a stroke or heart attack? A good laugh has healing power, will improve your health and keep you in great shape both physically and mentally. It relaxes and centers you while protecting you from the damaging side effects of stress.

Laughter can also substitute as a mini cardio workout, especially for those who are incapable of actual physical activity due to injury or illness. When you laugh out loud, the muscles in your stomach benefit from an enjoyable little workout. Your stomach hurts when you laugh too hard the same way it does when you work on your abs, only a lot more fun. Don't use it as an excuse to skip the gym, but as the quote above suggests, laughter gets your heart pumping and studies have shown that through humor you can burn off a few extra calories.

If that's not enough, laughter dispels anger and eases pain by releasing endorphins which are the body's natural painkillers. It lifts your spirits and makes it impossible to stay mad. Give in, act like a kid and laugh for no reason at all. It will give you a warm rosy glow and a positive outlook. Laughter really is contagious. Soon the whole world will be laughing with you. At least that's the goal. Laughter truly is the best medicine. Start now to infuse your life with joy and laugh your way to health. The prescription is fun, free, and fast working.

Warning: Side effects may include addiction and the appearance of annoying little laugh lines around your eyes and mouth.

FOCUS ON THE PROCESS

"Shutting off the thought process is not rejuvenating; the mind is like a car battery – it recharges by running." – Bill Watterson

You've set a goal to lose ten pounds before your upcoming cruise and are steadfast in your determination to meet the goal. It's a S.M.A.R.T. goal: specific, measurable, attainable, relevant, and timely. You post a note on your refrigerator door as a visual reminder of the 'Big Sexy Goal' but thinking about it makes you hungry. Ten pounds is a lot to lose in such a short time and you begin to obsess about the uphill battle you face. Doubt creeps in to sabotage your best laid plans. If this scenario sounds all too familiar, stop focusing on the goal and focus on the process.

Process thinkers focus on the steps to the goal rather than the goal itself. What must you do today to move you in the right direction? Progress is made one baby step at a time. Enjoy the process and give yourself a pat on the back when you eat half your meal and save the rest, choose cottage cheese over fries, or pass on dessert. If you're truly committed to the goal, break it down and commit to consistent daily action to achieve it.

The idea of consistent effort to reach the desired outcome is applicable in every area of life. Goals provide the motivation necessary to get started, but an effective process is required to move forward incrementally until you reach the destination. Design a system and map out a clear way to redirect your focus to what you can control. Every action you take, no matter how small, affects the end result. Consider it a win if you lose less than ten pounds but develop healthier eating habits. It's not all or nothing. It's all about the process.

EMBRACE DIVERSITY

"Diversity is about all of us, and about us having to figure out how to walk through this world together." – Jacqueline Woodson

The world is rapidly becoming a fascinating fusion of race, religion, and gender. A variety of views and customs exist within each category, with new combinations forming every day. Interracial marriages are common now and each generation blends and blurs the world's color lines a bit more. Religions that have existed for centuries are seeing believers break away and establish new sects that continue to honor some accepted beliefs, but with a new twist. Not long ago we were limited to two genders, but today people choose to identify in a number of unique ways.

It's one thing to be tolerant of differences and another to learn from them. Every culture and walk of life include positive qualities that can be embraced by others without the need to completely assimilate. Being open to new experiences and people gives you a broader and more inclusive perspective and makes life infinitely more interesting.

Muslims around the world celebrate Ramadan every year. They dedicate themselves to thirty days of fasting - no food or water during the daylight hours. They worship, spend time in personal reflection, and offer acts of charity and community to bring them closer to God. Awareness of this commitment to religious conviction and strength of character goes a long way to foster understanding, respect, and acceptance.

Diversity goes so much deeper than just the surface aspects of race, religion, or gender. It encompasses all the qualities that make us unique, as individuals and communities. Recognition and appreciation of those qualities makes the world a better place. This Muslim saying beautifully describes the value of diversity: "A lot of different flowers make a bouquet."

THE ART OF PERSUASION

"Don't raise your voice, improve your argument."
– Desmond Tutu, Address at the Nelson Mandela Foundation in
Houghton, Johannesburg, South Africa, 23 November 2004

Some people are experts at influencing the opinions of others and
getting them to see things the way they do, in the nicest possible
way. That is the essence of persuasion. When people know you,
like you, and trust you, they will buy into a personal relationship
or buy what you are selling in a business relationship.

You are drawn to people who share your interests. It's important to find common ground and build rapport. When rapport is
established people are more open to persuasive suggestions and
more willing to do things in their own best interest. Things that,
by the way, will also benefit you.

If you need a lesson in the art of persuasion just watch a child in
action. Children are pros when it comes to influencing adults.
They are charming and likable, essential factors in getting to 'yes'.
Selling is a natural skill and unhampered by the limiting beliefs we
impose on our mature selves, kids excel as little salespeople. They
put it out there, unfiltered and uninhibited. Combine those qualities with absolutely no fear of failure and they are unstoppable.

Repetition is a major factor in getting and keeping someone's attention. Tell a child 'no' and you quickly realize no is not an option. They up their game and improve their argument, until they
have persuaded you to their way of thinking. You can't give up if
you want to become a master influencer. Go out and meet people
and put your best foot forward to raise your likability quotient. It's
a process. Once they like you, it will be possible to earn their trust,
the key that paves the way to acceptance and approval.

BOUNDARIES

No matter what the situation, remind yourself "I have a choice."
– Deepak Chopra

There are people in our lives who, left unchecked, take advantage of our good nature and overwhelm us physically, emotionally, or mentally. In some cases, it's an intentional invasion of our space, but many times people are unaware they have overstepped their bounds. Either way, it's up to us to let them know where we draw the line.

Happy and fulfilling relationships will only remain healthy if you identify behavior that is unacceptable and communicate your feelings to the people involved. Without a clear line indicating where your responsibility and participation ends, life becomes un-balanced, leaving you feeling resentful. There's nothing healthy about feeling frustrated and out of control because you have al-lowed people to invade your personal space. And there's no one to blame, but yourself.

If you have trouble protecting your limited amount of time and energy you are not alone. Many of us are eager to please and try to do whatever it takes to make everyone else happy. It's not pos-sible to successfully be all things to all people and truly enjoy life. If you are the go-to person for everyone's problems, it's time to check your boundaries and recognize the need to find balance and identify personal limits.

The sooner you put boundaries in place, the happier and more successful you will be. If you feel the need to soften your response, offer alternative solutions that will handle the situation comfort-ably without commitment from you. "No, I'm sorry I can't help you now. Can we schedule another time or is there someone else who can lend a hand?" Enjoy peace of mind and harmony by put-ting clear, guilt-free boundaries in place and surrounding yourself with people who are prepared to honor them.

GO THE EXTRA MILE

"You can start right where you stand and apply the habit of going the extra mile by rendering more service and better service than you are now being paid for." – Napoleon Hill

My kids grew up with the sage, grandfatherly advice, "You won't get paid for more than you do until you do more than you're paid for." That's another way of saying success comes when you under promise and over deliver. You exceed expectations, stand out in the crowd, and earn respect when you buckle down and get the job done...plus a little more.

Unfortunately, we don't see enough determined overachievement in today's world. Many people wouldn't think of offering to collaborate on an associate's project without an official assignment or the promise of their name on the byline. Make the choice. Do the minimum and get by or look for opportunities to be of greater service and increase your value.

When you're running errands ask if you can help someone check a few things off their list at the same time. Double your recipe and take a meal to a sick friend. Offer to stay after work to help colleagues finish a project they've been wrestling with, even if it's not your responsibility. Lend a hand whenever possible, especially when it's least expected. Surprise someone by going out of your way to do something beyond the job description, just because. Generosity of time and expertise will keep your name at the top of the list when accolades are given, and promotions are being considered.

Look around today and identify ways you can make a difference. Go the extra mile to serve the needs of others. Your positive example will attract just the right attention as you strengthen and promote the much needed 'above and beyond' habit.

FAMILY FIRST

"Family is not an important thing. It's everything." – Michael J. Fox

No one knows you like family, and families love unconditionally despite more than a few questionable choices and regrettable decisions. Relatives share laughs about embarrassing moments and somehow, it's okay. They have seen you at your worst, they know your strengths and weaknesses, and through it all still love you. Because you're family.

Todays 'modern' families vary widely in makeup. They come in all shapes, sizes, and configurations. Some have a single parent, some have two, and others have two parents of the same gender. Throw a few blended and multi-generational households into the mix and let the fun begin. I am blessed with many quirky, wonderful relatives. Together we present a united front, us against the world. We enjoy celebrating birthdays and holidays, creating traditions and lasting memories. Any way you look at it, families are the best thing ever.

Blood truly is thicker than water, but sometimes bloodlines are not enough. Relationships are complicated and occasionally a branch of the family tree is damaged or broken. If it's possible to repair the relationship do whatever it takes to make it whole again. It might be prudent to enlist the help of others who understand the situation to initiate a reconciliation. If all your well-intentioned efforts fail, it's time to respect their desire to break away and cherish the ones who remain intact.

Change is inevitable. We grow, try out new careers, change our looks and locations, but through it all family is the constant force. They're always available to offer support, a shoulder to cry on, or a helping hand. Reach out today to your Mom, a sibling, or a distant cousin and keep your biggest cheerleaders close to your heart.

LIVE DRAMA FREE

"Let go of the people who dull your shine, poison your spirit, and bring you drama. Cancel your subscription to their issues."
– Steve Maraboli, Unapologetically You: Reflections on Life and the Human Experience

Spend time with people who bring out the best in you, not the stress in you. People who are fueled by drama add unnecessary apprehension and anxiety to our lives. They thrive on the conflict cycle: initiate drama, revel in it, kiss and makeup, forgive and forget. This is an unnecessary and unproductive waste of time and energy. Disassociate yourself from drama and reduce stress, strengthen relationships, and enjoy a more pleasant and productive life.

Are yours the shoulders everyone cries on? Even if you don't create drama, you might invite it by sending encouraging signals. You can't help everyone, so be selective. People you are close to should feel comfortable sharing, but instead of letting them vent and walk away, ask them to discuss solutions. That will send a clear message you won't play a leading role in their drama, but you will help them stage the final scene.

It's exciting to be in a relationship where you are comfortable letting your guard down, until your partner misinterprets or makes assumptions about something you said or did. Now your time together is wasted squabbling instead of relaxing. Unlike school days where we recognized the drama divas, supposedly mature adults acting like children can blindside us. Some people never outgrow the need for trivial backbiting, and at any age find ways to breathe life into conflict. Clear communication is key to working through misunderstandings. Try not to overthink or read between the lines of every conversation. Most things can be taken at face value and if the flames aren't fanned, small fires will burn themselves out.

RESIST OVERSHARING

"The reason we struggle with insecurity is because we compare our behind-the-scenes with everyone else's highlight reel." – Steve Furtick

I maintained a journal as a teenager, fiercely protecting it from prying eyes as if I actually recorded anything of interest. The worst that would have happened was a parent or sibling getting a little chuckle at the harmless trivia on those hallowed pages. Today people seem comfortable posting their most private moments for the consumption of hundreds of social media 'friends' they may never meet in person.

Think before you share. There's a fine line between appropriate and unacceptable. It's okay to post your ideas, opinions, and photos, but make sure the news is positive, yours to share, and adds value to the conversation. No one wants to be tagged in an unflattering pose or compromising situation. If you're struggling to make sense of a cringe worthy scenario, pick up the phone and call a trusted friend. Keep it personal and confidential. Posting that same info on the Internet leaves you open to criticism. The less people know, the less they can judge.

Avoid comparing your life to the highlight reels found on social media. Check in any time, any day, and you're guaranteed to find something to discourage you. What has been a satisfactory life suddenly feels small and insignificant. Your daughter's wedding was a beautiful, intimate family affair. All the others seem to be larger-than-life extravaganzas. You camped locally, and they went to Bali. Love the life you have created. Your camping trip was just the stress free, low-cost getaway you needed to rejuvenate while your Facebook friends may very well arrive home exhausted and in debt. Savor the private moments and share the best parts of your life with those who matter.

BE AN ENCOURAGER

"A word of encouragement during a failure is worth more than an hour of praise after success." – Unknown

When my daughter was in college she told me, she hoped to open a specialty restaurant one day and described it to me in well-thought-out detail. Regretfully, and uncharacteristically, I responded with discouraging statistics about the low success rate of restaurants. She graciously replied, "When your children share their hopes and dreams, you should be more supportive."

Well said, and so very true. In my effort to protect her from the possibility of future disappointment I did my best to stifle her passion and enthusiasm. I re-thought my response and told her that successful restaurants require a consistently excellent menu, a good front of the house personality, and someone in charge with solid business sense. She was strong in all areas and would no doubt be successful. I learned from my mistake and now strive to always encourage, not discourage.

Well-deserved praise is welcomed after the goal is reached, but encouragement is needed to empower, reassure, and build confidence on the long road to victory when it means the most. Ask questions about dreams, unearth fears, and offer solutions. Lend a hand by locating mentors or suggest classes to take or paths to follow to help them reach their goal. This will send a clear message you believe in them and will be in their corner, cheering them on for the entire journey.

Look for opportunities to boost morale, praise progress, and encourage the next difficult, but necessary, step forward. Think of the times in your life when just a little encouragement from the right person made all the difference between success and something less. A pat on the back or a few words of support is sometimes all it takes.

IT'S ABOUT TIME

"To have more peace, as well as more time, start by letting go of the notion that time can be manipulated. Then, let go of the idea that it confines you. Instead set out to use the time that is there for its true and best purpose – as the space within which you can live your life to the fullest."
– Michelle Passoff, Lighten Up: Free Yourself From Clutter

It is possible to balance a number of areas of life every day by making small incremental advances toward the achievement of your goals. Visualize a juggler balancing several spinning plates in the air. The first goal is to start them successfully spinning and the next is to keep them going so they maintain momentum and continue to spin. In the same way it's necessary to breathe life and energy into each area of life to continually move in the right direction.

No matter how hard you try to stop it, time marches on. You can't control it, but you can make it count by dedicating every minute to the highest and best use. Review your goals daily and allocate time to activities that will contribute to reaching them. Create a comprehensive 'daily accomplishment' list in order of priority. Once the most important ones are complete re-prioritize and commit to the best use of the time remaining.

Spend time on the right things. Keep your goals front and center and ask yourself if what you are doing at any given time is moving you closer to, or farther from, your goals. Exercise willpower until life-long habits are formed. Commit to this discipline and discover the key to living life to the fullest. That is the simple answer to the not-so-simple concept of time management.

MAKE GOOD CHOICES

"Life is about choices. Some we regret, some we're proud of. Some will haunt us forever. The message: we are what we choose to be."
– Graham Brown

Life offers a variety of choices and it's up to you to decide which ones are right. The better choices you make the more fulfilled and happier your life will be. Make the first healthy choice of the day by passing up a sweet roll in favor of granola and another one by taking a brisk walk before heading to work. Do the right thing by spending time with individuals who lift your spirit and strengthen your confidence. Don't disappoint and settle for less. Surround yourself with people who encourage you to aim higher. Life offers several options for every move you make, so be aware of the possibilities and look before you leap.

Choose to be happy. Find a career where your contribution makes a difference. One that inspires you to continually stretch and grow. Use the same criteria when developing relationships. Commit to gratifying, mutually beneficial relationships only. Be good to yourself by keeping your self-talk loud, clear, and positive. Choose to be the best you can be.

When you come to a fork in the road, weigh your options, take a chance, and make the smartest choice possible considering the information available at the time. If you allow yourself to stay stuck in neutral, you will overthink the possibilities and risk ending up on the slippery slope of indecision. Failing to choose rarely results in the best outcome. Make the right decision as often as possible and learn from the wrong ones. The choices you make will add up to a life well lived or one of missed opportunities. Choose wisely.

SCHEDULE IT

"How we spend our days is, of course, how we spend our lives. What we do with this hour, and that one, is what we are doing. A schedule defends from chaos and whim. It is a net for catching days."
– Annie Dillard, The Writing Life

Purposefully planning each day is an essential key to maximizing the use of your time. There are many scheduling options available, but the right system is the one that works for you. Some methods are overly complex and cumbersome, not a recipe for success. Experiment until you find the right one and commit to use it, day in and day out, to organize the essentials of your life.

Intentional scheduling generates more free time and reduces stress. Spend a few minutes every evening and list everything you need or want to do the following day, in order of importance. Preserve balance by mentally reviewing and identifying tasks that will contribute to the accomplishment of goals in every area of your life. Review and reschedule non-essentials if they can wait until another day. When you take the time to do this you will wake up prepared and ready to execute without wasting more time questioning what to do first, planning your next move, or back-tracking for something you forgot. You will also eliminate the worry of missing deadlines and commitments. Finish one task and focus on the next important item until your schedule is complete.

The hardest thing about maintaining a schedule is sticking to it. The only way to stay on track is to handle the distractions as they come up and return to your schedule as soon as possible. Be realistic in your expectations. Not everything will be completed every day, but thanks to your schedule, the important ones will.

LEAD WITH YOUR STRENGTHS

"Each person's greatest room for growth is in the areas of his or her greatest strength." – Donald O. Clifton, Now, Discover Your Strengths

We all have weaknesses, but we are also blessed with individual strengths. Acknowledge your shortcomings and do what you can to improve them, but if you really want to make an impact, play to your strengths. Figure out what you do well and work on cultivating those areas. It's much easier to do a superior job when flexing 'talent' muscles, and the process is so much more enjoyable. When you do what you love satisfaction and confidence will shine through. People prefer to interact with people who have real passion, so concentrate on what you do best and delegate the rest.

What makes your soul happy and your heart sing? What do you get so involved in you lose track of time? Consider what steps could be put into place to parlay your avocation into a vocation. If you're known as an organizational guru start a side business to help others who lack the neatness gene or if you're a party planner extraordinaire offer a lifeline to help apprehensive hosts overcome anxiety. Optimizing your talents sets you up to perform at high levels of efficiency and effectiveness and increases overall happiness dramatically. Everything seems to fall effortlessly into place. Go back to the basics and put your best foot forward. It's that simple.

Discover what makes you unique and tap into those natural gifts. Immerse yourself in becoming the best you can be in those arenas and share the enthusiasm with everyone you meet. Take a strength-based approach to life and become known as the go-to virtuoso in your specialty or forte. Do this and you will enjoy a vibrant, productive, and happy life.

IF NOT NOW, WHEN?

"One of the most tragic things I know about human nature is that all of us tend to put off living. We dream of some magical rose garden over the horizon - instead of enjoying the roses that are blooming outside our window today." – Dale Carnegie

Is there something you have always wanted to do, but the time has never been right? You devoted decades to your career in hopes of retiring at a reasonable age to begin travelling and enjoying hobbies. That's an admirable plan, but what if the corporation you dedicated yourself to was sold and you were displaced before you were prepared to retire? What if you don't live to see retirement? A life well lived is enjoyed every step of the way, not just at the finish line.

Challenge yourself today and every day to learn something new, share what you learn, serve others, and make a difference. Sign up for the salsa lessons you've been talking about for years. Apply for your pilot's license, plant a garden, and stretch your mind and body. Do something that enhances someone else's life and yours will be enhanced as well. New opportunities will open up like Pandora's Box once you express willingness and are open to life. Seize the day, smell the roses, and recognize beauty all around you. Stop simply existing and postponing really living until some nebulous future date.

Make the cliché 'today is the first day of the rest of your life' a personal mantra. Don't put off until tomorrow what can be done today because no one is promised a tomorrow. Make today and everyday count. The time will never be perfect, the ducks may never be in a row, but do it anyway. Start living today.

BECAUSE YOU SAID YOU WOULD

"You are what you do, not what you say you'll do." – Carl G. Jung

It's disappointing to be let down by someone who assured you they would do something and didn't. You signed the landscape contract after the contractor assured you the job would be completed in a timely manner, and then failed to show up as scheduled. Your new website is weeks overdue and no one is returning your calls. In retrospect, it's easy to see those promises were made solely for the purpose of sealing the deal. People often overpromise and under deliver, but that doesn't make it okay.

Honoring your word builds trust. People respect people who hold themselves accountable and do what they say they are going to do. Your part of the project is complete and with a sense of satisfaction you check it off your list. Days later you realize someone dropped the ball and the assignment is stuck in limbo, overdue, and your personal credibility is in question. Don't be the ball dropper. Commit, walk your talk, and do what you say you will do. Become a trusted person of your word. If you made a promise, keep it. If you said you would do it, do it.

Think about the times you have distractedly agreed to do something with someone, someday. "I'll call, we'll do lunch." "Yes, we'll go camping one day soon." Mentally review off-the-cuff remarks made about things you would do and never did, or commitments made in the enthusiasm of the moment that remain undone. It's not too late to schedule that lunch or outings the kids crave that never seemed to make it to the calendar. Up your credibility quotient and build lasting memories by doing what you said you would. It's a s simple as that.

IT JUST TAKES ONE

"Take up one idea. Make that one idea your life – think of it, dream of it, live on that idea. Let the brain, muscles, nerves, every part of your body, be full of that idea, and just leave every other idea alone. This is the way to success." – Swami Vivekananda

There are so many great ideas floating around it's difficult to focus on just one long enough to make it work. You think you have discovered the Big One and then are distracted by another shiny object and your attention is diverted. Given too many choices you freeze up, become overwhelmed, and stop short of success. You fall into the age-old procrastination trap before ever tasting success.

You are an excellent cook and quite passionate about providing healthy, delicious meals for family and friends. You create new recipes and offer taste tests to friends who marvel at your talent and encourage you to sell to local restaurants. That's a great idea, but it might also make sense to build a website to process online orders which would require the use of a commercial kitchen, a staff, a marketing plan, business license, oh my. It started as a fun, interesting idea and snowballed out of control. It's clearly too much work so you abandon the idea and begin the search for a new creative outlet.

There's no shortage of inspiration, but time and resources are limited. It's not possible to do it all and many interesting opportunities appear at an inopportune time. Choose wisely. Commit to one thing you are truly passionate about and fan the flame until you have a controlled bonfire. Stay focused on that one thing. Live, breathe, and nurture your amazing idea until you find success.

SPENDING PLANS

"A budget is telling your money where to go instead of wondering where it went." – Dave Ramsey

The term 'velocity of money' measures the rate at which people spend money. When you think about how long it takes to earn a substantial nest egg verses how long it takes to spend it, the speed or velocity at which money runs through your fingers will take your breath away. If you dread the idea of creating and sticking to a budget, reframe it in a positive light and think of it as a personal spending plan. It's important to have a strategy in place to shine a light on your financial practices, good, bad, and ugly.

It's no fun looking forward to time off work only to discover there's not enough money to do the things you hoped to do. A solid spending plan will take the guesswork out of life. You will sleep better knowing where your money is going instead of constantly worrying about the unknown. Take control of cash flow through counting and accountability. You may not be consciously indulging in retail 'therapy' during stressful times, but a quick look at your closet or your credit card statement will confirm what you probably already suspect.

Keep tabs on expenditures over the next few months to get a real time snapshot of what's going on. How often do you eat out and how much would be saved if you dined at home? What must-haves are you purchasing that aren't really needed? Review your credit card and bank statement and create a list to track the daily outlay of cash. Take a tally of unnecessary expenditures. With a few adjustments it might be possible to calendar that much anticipated vacation. When you control your money, you control your life.

PRESS THE RESET BUTTON

"I have always been delighted at the prospect of a new day, a fresh try, one more start, with perhaps a bit of magic waiting somewhere behind the morning." – J. B. Priestly

Do you sometimes catch yourself going through the motions of life, navigating on autopilot? If so, it's time to hit the reset button and readjust, refocus, and reboot. If your schedule is full and every minute is accounted for there's no time to reflect on what's working and what's not. Day in and day out the alarm clock signals the start of the daily race. Morning rituals, workout, office, groceries, dinner, evening rituals, blessed sleep. If constant deadlines and commitments prevent you from just 'being' put yourself in time-out and regroup.

Evaluate your life and rate your happiness quotient. Are you chasing goals that are no longer important? Is it really necessary to join every committee and attend every event or are you stuck in 'please the masses' mode? Take some time to zero in on what makes you happy today. Passions change and it's important to adjust priorities to fit each new stage of life. When raising children, a community of women going through the same daily trials builds confidence and provides a much-needed support group. Once the everyday job of parenting is behind you a little alone time might be just what you need.

When was the last time you read a book cover to cover, uninterrupted? Or spent a quiet afternoon puttering in the garden, lost in thought? Schedule a sabbatical, field trip, or a little breather. Call your manager and ask for a 'mental health day'. Stop what you're doing and reconnect to what and who you hold dear. Reset your life around the essentials – the people and things that put the magic into your daily routine.

MIND THE GAP

"Your problem is to bridge the gap which exists between where you are now and the goal you intend to reach." – Earl Nightingale

The London Underground is famous for its continuous loop message reminding passengers to avoid the dangerous gap between the platform and the train. Life presents many situations requiring us to be mindful to avoid making fateful mistakes. If you don't 'mind the gap' and pay close attention you can easily lose track and take a regrettable misstep. You do your best, put meaningful goals in place, and then face the difficult task of staying on course while you bridge the gap between where you are currently to where you want to be.

It's becoming increasingly more popular for graduating high school students to spend a 'gap' year focused on self-discovery and globe-trotting before jumping into college. It saves time and money pursuing the wrong career by directing them down the appropriate path from the beginning. They consider it valuable time spent soul-searching, exploring options, and clarifying direction.

Take a lesson from those students and indulge in a little introspection. The 'gap' experience isn't limited to eighteen-year old's and doesn't need to last a year. Schedule some 'you' time, even if it's just a few days. Use this time to stretch your limits, explore new ideas, gain a new skill, or improve an old one. Discover who you are and what you want out of life. Examine and compare opportunities to confirm the direction you're headed in aligns with your dreams. If you have strayed off-course, now is the time to change direction. When you are convinced you're on the right track commit completely and adjust your plan to successfully bridge the gap between where you are presently and the goals you intend to reach.

SET THE STAGE

"We are all actors, set on the stage of the world, as the curtains open we put on our best performance to this audience of life."
– Anthony Liccione

The tone of the day is established in the first few minutes. When you wake up with clear purpose about your intentions and what must be accomplished you set the stage for a successful day. Establishing a positive tone requires solid morning rituals. Wake up every morning at the same time, do not hit the snooze button, and do not immediately grab your smartphone to check emails or the latest social media posts. Take a moment to breathe, stretch, and gather your thoughts while your mind is fresh, before the onset of interruptions or distractions.

This is a perfect time to count your blessings. Look around, appreciate what you see, and give thanks. Starting the day from a position of gratitude will enhance mental clarity, increase spiritual well-being, and center you. Use the morning 'power' hour to exercise or take a brisk walk. Some of the best ideas come to light when oxygen-rich blood is pumped to your brain.

Everyday life will go smoother if you maintain a 'staging' area in your home and office to keep things running like a well-oiled machine. Items heading out can be placed in a convenient area near the door. When you leave, pick up what you've gathered and move them forward. This ensures you always have the book to return, clothes for the cleaners, packages to be mailed, and unwanted purchases to be returned. It relieves the frustration of being near the vicinity, but unable to complete the task. Focus on efficient routines and avoid the mad scramble that leaves you playing catch-up. Good beginnings heighten your effectiveness and set the stage for a good day.

BE PREPARED

"Today's preparation determines tomorrow's achievement."
– Unknown

The Boy Scouts got it right with their succinct motto, "Be Prepared". Without a trusty crystal ball, it's impossible to see what's coming around the bend, but with a little planning and forward thinking we can anticipate and prepare for some of life's certainties, emergencies, and daily activities. It's time to get your house in order, literally and figuratively.

When facing a change such as a new career, a move, or retirement, put a plan in place with action steps to smooth the transition. Set a deadline and work backwards with calendared benchmarks to chart progress and ensure you stay on track. Look for possible obstacles and, if necessary, put contingency plans in place to reroute the path to the goal.

Acts of God strike without warning and life has a habit of throwing us curveballs. You know they are coming and can count on them at the most inopportune time. Earthquakes rock and roll and storms knock out power for days. At a minimum you should have a supply of water, working flashlights, and ready to eat, high energy food to sustain you until things are powered up.

Sleep well at night by planning for unexpected expenses such as replacement tires, appliances, and big-ticket items. There's a 'baby needs a new pair of shoes' situations around every corner. A rainy-day fund will give you peace of mind and take the financial related worry out of the 'what-if' scenarios of life.

It's impossible to prepare for every unforeseen event. Life doesn't provide instruction manuals, so do your best to plan ahead and trust everything will work out in the end. In the meantime, live life to the fullest every day without stressing over unknowns that are out of your control.

REPLACE YOUR DIVOTS

"Clean up your own mess." – Robert Fulghum, Author

In golf, a 'divot' is the chunk of turf and soil that is gouged out during a solid swing. Golf etiquette requires a repair of the scuffed area by replacing the dislodged turf or sprinkling in sand and seed. In other words, cleaning up the mess you made in the process of playing the game. We should all be aware of our footprint on this earth and take responsibility to clean up any mess we make.

Your parents replaced your divots for you, using each messy situation as a lesson for learning. Growing up expectations changed, and it became your responsibility to clean up spills and keep your little area of the world neat and tidy. When your own household is humming along it's time to reach out and extend a hand to the community to keep it clean and beautiful. Help your neighbor and add a little fresh color outside of your own property lines.

A generation ago our attention was drawn to the problem of littering and fines were levied on offenders. Gum wrappers and trash no longer clutter our roadsides and the world is a better place as a result. The next big undertaking was clean air which we tackled by successfully curtailing auto emissions. Since that time recycling has become an established practice which decreases the consumption of raw materials and reduces pollution caused by waste. And globally we have become more mindful of 'ocean dumping' which protects our seas from harmful waste that can adversely affect the fine balance the marine environment requires. Commit to cleaning up after yourself and replacing the divots on your own home turf. Let's work together to keep planet earth pollution-free and safe for generations to come.

KEEP SHORT ACCOUNTS

Once a woman has forgiven her man, she must not reheat his sins for breakfast." – Marlene Dietrich

In simpler times you could send one of the kids to the neighborhood market for a carton of milk and the Mom or Pop proprietor would graciously add the charge to your account. It was more about friends helping friends than a business transaction, so it was poor form to allow your account to get too 'long'. People settled up on payday and began the next week with a clean slate.

We now live in more complicated times. Kids don't go anywhere alone, the 'corner' store is a chain supermarket in the center of town, and credit cards have eliminated the need for those neighborly IOU's. Individual customer accounts may no longer be relevant but maintaining current accounts relationship-wise is more important than ever. Sustain healthy relationships by clearing the air regularly instead of allowing a list of infractions and disappointments to pile up and overwhelm even the most solid partnerships. It's bad enough to be called out for a single misstep, but add a list of every past offense and resentment seeps in.

To foster open, trusting relationships face awkward issues right away, discuss the 'elephant in the room', and resolve misunderstandings or misinterpretations as they happen. Dealing with it in real time avoids pouring the fuel of past experiences onto the current fire.

Relationships hit rough patches from time to time but working through them and settling disputes quickly will keep your relational account balanced. Relegate the past to the past and don't hold grudges. Communicate clearly, find ways to reconcile, and be the first to humbly offer an olive branch. Keeping short accounts with people you love will bring happiness and harmony to the important relationships in your life.

CAN I BE CANDID WITH YOU?

"Lack of candor blocks smart ideas, fast action, and good people contributing all the stuff they've got. It's a killer." – Jack Welch

Some people talk in circles leaving you puzzled and confused. Others freely give compliments or criticism and then add an afterthought to temper their comments leaving you wondering if you should be pleased or offended. It's refreshing to speak with people who communicate openly and use their words to send a clear message.

Being upfront and truthful avoids misunderstandings. No one enjoys delivering bad news so instead of being candid we hide behind euphemisms. The words, "You're fired!" will most likely only be heard on reality TV. In real life the employee being cut might be told the company is 're-structuring and eliminating the position' or simply 'letting them go'. It sounds kinder and gentler, but no matter how it's sugar-coated they have been fired.

Direct talk minimizes problems by anticipating possible pitfalls and challenges. Discuss what is expected and who is responsible before things begin to go sideways. Straight talk isn't meant to be harsh. It's setting clear rules with your teenage driver before they borrow the car. No friends in the car, radio off, no phone use of any kind, drive from A to B and home again. Period.

When you avoid conflict and sweep uncomfortable topics under the rug, they fester. Minor problems add up and become big, unsolvable problems. A few well-chosen words will start a positive conversation, remove barriers, and create the connection needed to break the tension before things get out of hand. Speak up and let individuals you live or work with know what is acceptable and what isn't. People appreciate guidelines and clear boundaries. Encourage their input and participation and they will welcome your candor.

CIRCLE OF LIFE

"Life is a circle. The end of one journey is the beginning of the next."
– Joseph M. Marshall III, Author The Journey of Crazy Horse: A Lakota History

Life is not a straight line from birth to death. It's more like a meandering trail and there are a number of ways to make the most of life's journey. The choices you make are in direct proportion to the quality of the life you live. Individuals constantly learn, change, and grow. When you know you've come full circle in a career, project, or relationship, it might be time to walk away.

If you feel like you're running in circles career wise you may actually be on track and statistically relevant. The average person will take on a new career 5-7 times during their working life, according to career change statistics, and the number is rising. There are many more options today than in past generations, minimizing the need to continue working an unfulfilling or unchallenging job.

Likewise, not all relationships are meant to last forever. Ending a relationship can leave you feeling crushed. It's difficult to accept that someone who was a significant part of your life is suddenly part of the past. As you mature you outgrow more than romantic relationships. Some friends last forever, and others are relevant for one of life's passages and then move on. Learn from the connection and welcome the next friendship with a better understanding of what you need and what you have to offer.

Stake your place in the circle of life. There are endless choices available to us during our lives, some small and some life-changing. If you are to live your life to the fullest enjoy each journey and then move on with hope and joy.

THE FIXER

"I do not fix problems. I fix my thinking. Then problems fix themselves."
– Louise L. Hay

Are you someone who sends out vibes that make others feel comfortable confiding every secret and sharing every personal problem with you, unsolicited? You might not be aware, but if total strangers trust you with relationship problems, financial worries, insecurities and anxieties the first time you meet, they recognize you as a fixer.

You can't ignore someone who needs help, but once they dump their cares and worries in your lap they feel lighter and you are weighed down by the load. Everyone needs someone they can trust, but it doesn't always have to be you.

Fixers tend to be well-meaning, unselfish helpers who like to be needed. They rescue stray people as often and effortlessly as stray cats. They are drawn into relationships with individuals who are damaged in some way, happy to be their knight in shining armor. Many prospective partners are wonderful in almost every way and fixing whatever is holding them back becomes a fixers 'raison de vivre'. It's not your responsibility to fix or change people, as tempting as it is to try.

Stop trying to heal the world and focus on caring for yourself. Change your thinking and develop symbiotic relationships, mutually beneficial to both sides. No one is perfect so why work so hard to save, support, and comfort people who are perfectly capable of taking care of themselves? Build relationships with people whose quirks and shortcomings you find endearing and embrace them for their vulnerability and individuality.

You can't change others, but you can fix and change your attitude and how you approach problems. Focus on your own strengths, accept the flaws and imperfections, and let the problems of others work themselves out.

THANKS MOM AND DAD

"There are two things children should get from their parents: roots and wings." – Johann Wolfgang von Goethe

Parents are by far the most influential forces in our formative years, and therefore, the most impactful and important people in our lives. They deserve respect for stepping up and taking on the daunting task of nurturing young lives to and through adulthood. Parents don't have the luxury of taking sick days or desperately needed 'mental health days' from parenting. There's no such thing as a leave of absence. Parents are in it for the long haul and for that, and many other reasons, they deserve respect.

My daughter pointed out to me when she was in her teens that as a youngster she thought her dad and I could do no wrong. As she matured she was quite surprised to find we weren't perfect. (I was sure she was referring to her father.) There is no job description, handbook, or parenting class to fully prepare us for the daunting scope of the job. Even if we are lucky enough to navigate one child through the first few years without too much trauma, the next one arrives with a whole new set of needs and issues and the learning process starts all over again.

If you still have the opportunity, thank your parents for your life. They spent a lot of years doing a job that is often taken for granted. Reach out and include them as often as possible, listen to their views even if you don't share them. Communicate your love and respect for bringing you up the best way they knew how. If you are blessed with children, your folks will take great pleasure watching you experience 'payback'.

FAMILY FUN

"We didn't realize we were making memories, we just knew we were having fun." – Winnie The Pooh

August is 'Family Fun Month' so take a break from the daily grind, gather the family, and go outside to play. Spend time just hanging out with no fixed agenda or scheduled activities. Toss a Frisbee, ride bikes, break out the board games, or find someplace to stick your collective toes in the sand.

Some of our best memories happen unscripted, when we least expect them. Stretch out on blankets and watch the moon rise and the stars come out, one by one. Build a fire, roast s'mores, and tell stories. Hang a sheet and watch a movie under the summer sky. The size and significance of the event isn't important. Being together makes whatever you do, even the little things, important.

Twilight lasts for hours and it's far too nice to stay indoors. Take a walk, breathe, de-stress, and add in some fun. It's a perfect time to enjoy the friendly competition of an old-fashioned scavenger hunt. Divide family and friends into teams and set out in search of hidden treasure. The list of items to discover is as unlimited as your imagination. Look for natural wonders in flora and fauna or create clues to discover man-made gems like a specific make and year of car, street sign, or local landmark. Make sure each team is armed with a smart phone camera to document and confirm discoveries.

Be open to new ideas. Some will hit and some miss but keep them coming until family traditions are firmly in place. Who knows? Scavenger hunts might become the next family 'thing' with each team vying for bragging rights and ambitiously creating clues that test the best. Your family will bond, laugh, and in the process make memories to last a lifetime.

TALK IS CHEAP

"It isn't what we say or think that defines us, but what we do."
– Jane Austen, Sense and Sensibility

"You can trust me, I'm honest." Red flags fly the minute those words are spoken. We feel just as suspicious when someone claims to be a pillar of their church, caring humanitarian, or selfless mentor. If you really are what you say you are it will be verified by your actions. Just because you say it, doesn't make it true. Take people at their word and reserve judgement, unless at some point their actions contradict those words.

You have to wonder why some people feel compelled to disclose their income, net worth, and the market value of their 'things'. The numbers they share could be true, but it really doesn't matter how much they make. The only thing that matters is how much they keep. In 1996 Thomas Stanley and William Danko published an eye-opening book, The Millionaire Next Door. The book chronicles the results of extensive research conducted by the authors to identify traits shared by self-made millionaires.

They compared the behavior of Americans they call UAW's (under accumulators of wealth) and PAW's (prodigious accumulators of wealth). The very surprising results indicated there are significantly more millionaires in middle class and blue-collar neighborhoods than in higher end, white collar communities. The high-income UAW's like to flaunt their wealth and live above their means, incurring debt instead of accumulating assets. The actual millionaires, the PAW's, were lower wage earners, who enjoyed modest lifestyles typically well below their means. They were frugal, saved regularly, invested wisely, and didn't feel the need to talk about it. The prodigious accumulators of wealth became millionaires quietly, behind closed doors.

Start today to communicate loud and clear through actions, not words.

COMMIT TO EXCELLENCE

"We are what we repeatedly do. Excellence, then, is not an act but a habit." – Aristotle

Excellence means you demand more of yourself than others demand of you. It means doing the right things when no one is looking and doing the little things until they add up to big things. Strive for perfection but stop short of unrealistically expecting to reach it. Almost perfect is good enough. You are human with intrinsic flaws and limitations. Work on improving and strengthening those areas while focusing on your strengths.

There will always be someone younger, thinner, smarter, or more successful than you. Don't compare your own amazing self to anyone else. Comparing your life to the highlight reel of others, the part you see, will always disappoint. On the other hand, when you measure yourself against your own past performance you are motivated to improve bit by bit until you reach excellence. By tirelessly 'self-improving' you build on your accomplishments and raise not just personal standards, but the standards of everyone you come into contact with. Spend your days trying to be a better version of the person you were yesterday.

Your life is comprised of a series of days that become weeks and years. The days add up to a full life, but each one can be a stand-alone representative of the whole. It's a wonderful practice to rate your life at the end of the day. Ask yourself these questions: Did I make a difference? Live healthy? Make someone's day? How could the day have been better? How could I have been better? Refuse to settle for less than your best. Commit to taking small incremental steps towards a better you every day. There will always be room in yesterday's 'you' for improvement, growth, and, if not perfection, excellence.

YOUR REPUTATION DEFINES YOU

"It takes 20 years to build a reputation and five minutes to ruin it. If you think about that, you'll do things differently." – Warren Buffet

Your reputation is your brand. It sets expectations and validates your skills, experience, and credibility. It's not easy to maintain and it is easily tarnished. A good reputation defines who you are, creates demand, and becomes a bankable asset. Every time you make a move you validate the opinion of family, clients, and peers. Having a good reputation means you have maintained a high degree of credibility, are a positive influence on others, and hold yourself to higher standards.

Be cognizant of your reputation at all times. Show proper respect to everyone you meet. Smile and be courteous. Being respectful includes being a good listener. Be interested instead of interesting. Understand the position of others and respect them for it. Interact with people in a constructive way. Don't indulge in gossip by spreading, or even listening to, rumors. If you aren't open to it the gossipers won't feel comfortable sharing with you.

Here are six words that define a good reputation: *Honesty.* People expect and deserve honesty. Don't gloss over the process or the problem. *Trust.* Do what you say you will do. *Dependability.* Do what you say you will do, when you say you will do it. *Authenticity.* Get real. *Responsiveness.* Listen, understand, and respond to people's needs. *Communication.* Respond to people in a timely manner and by their preferred method of communication. Take responsibility for your actions or lack thereof. You will make mistakes, but when you do, admit them and make amends. Do the right thing and good things will come to you.

LEAD BY EXAMPLE

"What you are speaks so loudly, I can't hear what you are saying."
– Ralph Waldo Emerson

It has been said, and history has proven, the speed of the leader is the speed of the team. Your co-workers/family/friends are watching every move, prepared and eager to follow your lead. Raise the bar, hold yourself to a higher standard, and people will fall in line behind you.

People are thirsting for leadership and it is important to step up and be the leader you were meant to be. Send clear messages to those who look up to you by following your words with aligned action. Set the right example by striving for excellence in everything you do, and others will be inspired to follow in your footsteps.

Calling yourself a leader carries no weight. The only thing that works long term is actual leadership. Lead by example by being the first one in the office in the morning, the last one out at the end of the day, and the person who can be counted on to pitch in at every level. If you can do it, so can they. Show them how it's done, and they will proudly step up their game to meet yours.

When you send the message 'do as I say and not as I do' you lose credibility. Hypocrites say one thing and do another, but as the leader, you establish the rules, and you must follow those rules if you want to maintain any authority. Anything short of sincere collaboration will spark mutiny in your children, co-workers, teammates, and friends. Hypocrisy creates resentment and erodes respect and trust. Just because you claim fame doesn't mean it's true. What you do demonstrates your true intent and no amount of talk will out shout action.

EMBRACE IMPERFECTION

"That which does not kill us, makes us stronger." – Friedrich Nietzsche

The Japanese embrace the philosophy of kintsugi, a method that celebrates imperfection by highlighting flaws instead of hiding them. The goal is to repair or restore damaged goods instead of tossing and replacing them. The kintsugi technique creates unique works of art from cracked and broken objects by joining each distinctive fragment with precious metal giving the broken item a new, polished look. The Japanese believe damaged objects are still valuable and reveal a special kind of beauty. What the object lacks in perfection, it gains in character and history.

We are all faced with adversity during our lives. Painful and traumatic events often leave us scarred or changed in some way. Our natural instinct is to hide the imperfections, but there is a better way to cope with disappointment and loss. Tough times shape, strengthen, and teach us resilience, making it possible to adapt to change and recover from hardship. Repairs and adjustments transform us from one precious work of art to another as we write our own personal story. Live by the kintsugi philosophy by learning what you can from difficulty and wearing it as a badge of honor.

Life is far from perfect. You may feel as if you have fallen short in your career goals or failed at an important relationship. Should you walk away and replace it with something new or do you find a way to repair it to form something different, stronger, and more successful? Scars heal and will bring honor to you as the survivor you have proven to be. Look for the potential in every loss or failure and salvage what you can. Find ways to rebuild and repurpose rather than throwing away the broken pieces.

BIG ROCKS FIRST

"In today's environment, the key to true productivity is not to get more things done, but to get the right things done." – Adam Merrill, Co-Author, The 5 Choices to Extraordinary Productivity

Dr Stephen R. Covey, author of First Things First uses a simple fable to illustrate the importance of getting big things done rather than squandering time on minutiae. I'm sure you've heard the story, but it's worth repeating and might have more impact the second time.

A wise professor placed a number of rocks in a gallon container and asked his students if the container was full. The class confirmed it was indeed full. The professor added gravel and it settled into the areas between the rocks. The next time he posed the question the class caught on and agreed that it was still not full, so the professor scooped in a little sand and watched it sift down through the cracks...followed by water, which finally filled it to the brim.

The moral of the story is this: If you don't put the big rocks in first, there will never be room to add them later. Make time for the significant things before life sidetracks you with the never-ending small stuff. If you don't pay attention, daily life will distract you from relationships, projects, education, and causes that you were once so committed to.

Is there something big that you have been putting off while wasting time sifting gravel? It's not easy, but it is crucial to put plans and systems in place that address the big 'rocks' in your life. Schedule your time around personal goals and intentionally focus your attention on what is most important. At the end of the day you will revel in a feeling of accomplishment and in the process, clear out some of life's sand and debris.

HEALING POWER

"Health is life energy in abundance." – Julia H. Sun

We are alive because a 'life force energy' moves through our body, mind, and soul. It can't be seen, but it is the essence of our existence. From time to time this flow of energy becomes blocked or unbalanced and causes 'lack of ease', or disease. When this happens, it is possible to re-direct the flow through one of several types of energy therapies which reduce stress and realign us emotionally and, in some cases, physically. Alternative techniques used with traditional medicine have the ability to improve health and enhance quality of life.

Massage therapy is a lovely treatment involving a hands-on technique used to increase circulation and relieve tension, stress, and anxiety. Reiki and Therapeutic Touch are hands-off energy therapies that have the power to heal, reduce pain, and cure some ailments. Practitioners' of Reiki and Therapeutic Touch hold their hands over the body to raise energy and allow it to flow freely until it is balanced. Acupuncture and Chinese medicine are also believed to have real therapeutic benefits, both physical and emotional. Meditation, yoga, and tai chi are well known, self-healing techniques that are free and easy.

An easy way to alter energy and gain balance on your own is to write your problem on a piece of paper and hold it between both hands. Clearly set your intentions about the solution needed to bring about change. Try this several times throughout the day to focus on positive results and confirm your intentions. This form of self-improvement will send healing energy to any area needing a boost. Try one of these natural and safe methods whenever you want to feel relaxed, peaceful, and energized.

IT'S YOUR LIFE

"A man who wants to lead the orchestra must turn his back on the crowd." – Max Lucado

Most of us worry too much about what others think. We become inhibited, insecure, and risk missing out on opportunities that come our way. The truth is people are so wound up in their own lives that they don't have time to pay attention to what everyone else is doing. The part of your life that people see is just the tip of the iceberg. There are so many variables to consider when making life decisions that regardless of what your peers may think, they aren't qualified to judge. You are the only one privy to all the details requiring consideration and, therefore, you are the only one with enough information to make the right decision.

It takes courage to step out of your comfort zone and decide to go in a direction that might be frowned upon. You want people to like you and approve of your actions. But if you worry too much about the opinions of others you will remain stuck in neutral and never take the break-out steps necessary to get to the place you really want to be.

Live your life with confidence. When someone offers an opinion that would hold you back, it's possible they aren't aware of everything you considered when making the decision or maybe they don't have your best interest at heart. Either way, there's no need to explain. Thank them for their input and continue down the road you determined is best. Life is too short to waste time trying to please everyone. It's simply not possible. You are the priority and if the direction you're headed gets you closer to the ultimate goal, it's right for you.

BE STRONGER THAN YOUR EXCUSES

"He that is good for making excuses is seldom good for anything else."
– Benjamin Franklin

Have you fallen prey to the all too common practice of covering up your failures and limitations with an endless supply of excuses? If so, today is the day to break the pattern. Pointing fingers and placing blame is the coward's way out. It's time to stop rationalizing your failings or behavior and start living up to your true potential. Excuses, even good ones, demonstrate that you are looking for an easy out. They become a go-to part of your vocabulary, often becoming default answer.

"I didn't have time" is just one of many excuses we hear, and possibly use, every day. It is a popular defense that we're comfortable using because we all do keep very busy. What we're saying is that we didn't make time, or we didn't consider our priorities. Maybe we wasted the time we had by busying ourselves with the wrong things. It takes a little more planning to meet expectations and obligations in a timely manner but think about how much better it feels!

It is tempting to hide behind an excuse when faced with fear. Some fears are overwhelming like fear of failure (or success), and some are as simple as the fear of being caught embarrassingly unprepared. Admitting you need help and enlisting the support of others is the first step toward taking responsibility for your life. There is no shame in asking for help, but there is in selling yourself short and missing opportunities to advance. Challenge yourself today to get a little uncomfortable and recognize when you need to hold yourself accountable. Once you see where there's room for improvement identify ways to develop healthier, more productive habits. C'mon, get started…no excuses!

GET UNSTUCK

"As soon as you open your mind to doing things differently, the doors of opportunity practically fly off their hinges." – Jay Abraham

There are many situations in life when you feel frustrated and tired of the status quo, but no matter how bad you feel the idea of change feels worse. You might not be in a perfect place, but familiarity lulls and dulls you, with no threat of surprises or challenges. If you are currently feeling comfortable step out of the safe zone, embrace discomfort, and start living.

There comes a time when you realize your 'story' is getting a little frayed around the edges. You're not unhappy with your current situation until one day you realize you're celebrating yet another milestone birthday, and life is picking up speed as it passes you by. There's so much more to experience outside your comfort zone so stop taking the path of least resistance and start exploring some uncharted territory.

Say 'yes' to life. Don't put off what you can do today because today's opportunities might be gone tomorrow. The summer concert might be too long/loud/crowded, but it might also be a thoroughly entertaining evening under the stars. Get off the sofa and go fly a kite, learn to sail, or join a group with a shared passion. The risk pales in comparison to the reward.

When you're ready to thrive and grow, shake things up, change your routine, and actively discover new interests. It's okay to take it slow. If the deep end of the pool is too scary, wade cautiously into the shallow end and learn as you go. Every challenge you overcome builds self-confidence and attracts even more opportunities. You'll feel energized and inspired to tell a new story, guaranteed to be a riveting, can't-put-it-down, page turner.

BE MORE

"If you want to have more, you have to become more. For things to change, you have to change. For things to get better, you have to become better. If you improve, everything will improve for you. If you grow, your money will grow; your relationships, your health, your business and every external effect will mirror that growth in equal correlation."
– Jim Rohn

You want to live up to your full potential and be the best version of you, but it can be hard to recognize how to manifest your best life. Everyday life can be very distracting which makes it difficult to get things done. Consider a few simple changes to free up time for what really matters.

Simplify life. Eliminate excess stuff to create white space with room to grow and think. Get rid of energy vampires who drain you and replace them with inspiring, motivating individuals who share similar values. Learn to say 'no' to commitments that don't serve a positive purpose or move you closer to your goals. Fewer obligations means more time for the people and things you love and opportunities that pique your interest.

Break big goals into manageable projects and launch them as soon as possible. Conditions will never be perfect, and the time will never be exactly right. Act now and infuse positive energy into your life.

Get it right the first time. Pay attention, plan ahead, and stay single focused to minimize the risk of mistakes. Take pride in your work and strive for excellence in everything you do. A confident and optimistic mindset will pave the way to success and eliminate the need to go back and waste time, energy, and resources on tasks that could have been completed in one take. Be more through consistent growth and improvement in everything you do.

IMPULSIVE, IMPETUOUS, IMPROMPTU

"Be spontaneous, be creative, go out and have fun, let things happen naturally." – Conor McGregor

Make tonight's dinner delightful by serving dessert as the first course. It's okay to surprise your family with a little spontaneous treat now and then, when the whim hits. When was the last time you acted on an impulse, without overthinking or over planning? Short of a visit to a tattoo parlor or the Little White Wedding Chapel in Las Vegas, spontaneity makes life more interesting and a lot more fun.

Carve out a little unscripted white space in your calendar. Resist the urge to pre-plan every minute and simply follow your heart. If you love to cook open a cookbook to any page and invite a few friends for an impromptu meal featuring the recipe you randomly selected. If every vacation is spent with the same people at the same place, change things up. Select a different venue, invite new travel companions, or go in search of uncharted territory. Pile in the car for a spur-of-the-moment road trip with absolutely no agenda. Go jump in the lake for a skinny dip or dive in fully clothed. Take time to discover beauty in the unexpected and let your day unfold exactly as it should without any outside influence.

Rule-followers are fine, upstanding citizens who spend their lives trying to do what's right. It's an admirable way to handle life's big moments and important decisions. However, rigidly following the rules every minute requires sacrificing important things like creativity and fun. Life is about balance and a little 'me time, free time' is a key factor in a joy filled, healthy life. Give yourself permission to cut loose, 'waste' a little time on your hobbies and interests, or just go out and play today.

WHAT'S YOUR IKIGAI?

"Our ikigai is different for all of us, but one thing we have in common is that we are all searching for meaning."
– Hector Garcia Puigcerver, Ikigai, the Japanese Secret for a Long and Happy Life

The Japanese embrace a concept known as 'ikigai' (eye-ka-guy) which loosely translated means 'the reason you wake up in the morning'. It manifests itself in many ways including work, family, and self-actualization such as hobbies and interests. Ikigai represents the center of your life where four basic elements come together. It's uniquely personal and sometimes takes years to find a balance that brings joy and a clear sense of purpose.

Ask these questions: **What do you love to do** when your calendar is completely open, and no one is watching? List the activities that motivate or excite you. **What are you good at?** Have you been honored or recognized for your talents and skills? Do you have an aptitude for something that others struggle to grasp? **What does the world need from you?** How can you make a difference? Can you use what you're good at to give back? **What do you get paid for?** Make a list of things that you have been paid to do. Money doesn't necessarily lead to fulfilment, but actions you have been paid for make a difference.

Look for areas of overlap. You're passionate about music. You make it your mission to spread that love by teaching music to children. You're offered a job at the music academy and since the world needs music and you're paid to teach it, your profession becomes a vocation. When passion, mission, profession, and vocation are in balance you have found your ikigai, your true purpose.

THE DAFFODIL PRINCIPLE

"Be the change that you wish to see in the world." – Mahatma Gandhi

Every year in early spring five acres of land in Lake Arrowhead, California, bursts into glorious bloom. The acreage is known as 'The Daffodil Garden' and features fifty thousand bulbs in a breathtaking display of vibrant yellows and orange. One woman, Gene Bauer, created this magnificent vision by patiently planting one daffodil bulb at a time, beginning in 1958. The result forever changed the mountain top and brings beauty and joy to all who are lucky enough to witness it. In this way one woman significantly changed her world.

The Law of Accumulation says many small things, accumulated over time, will result in big things. Sticking to one single commitment requires discipline, persistence and constant attention to the desired outcome, for years. It's easy to lose interest in the beginning since small things are not very impactful, but eventually you will see and feel the difference which will fuel energy and momentum.

How will you contribute to the change you wish to see in the world? It's just as feasible to build a thriving business one client at a time or a solid nest egg one dollar at a time, as it is to transform a plot of land into an enchanted forest, one bulb at a time. Make it happen step by step, little by little, every day until the effort pays off. Enjoy the 'doing' and find happiness and satisfaction in the process. Don't waste a minute wishing you had started earlier. There's no better time than today to start creating a positive future. Make the commitment now and dedicate small increments of time and energy to the cause, again and again, until you successfully change your world for the better.

A MICROWAVE SOCIETY

"Achievers don't submit to instant gratification; they INVEST in the LONG-TERM payoff." – Darren Hardy

They say the attention span of a goldfish is a scant nine seconds, but according to a new study by Microsoft Corporation, humans top that. Today's distracting lifestyle has reduced people's ability to concentrate to a mere eight seconds. You may as well stop working on your thirty second elevator speech. The elevator ride still takes that long, but the purpose of the pitch is to gain a listener's interest and today's audience will tune you out before the descent begins.

We want it and we want it now. Since patience is no longer our strong suit, businesses accommodate by setting up drive thru lanes at fast food restaurants, pharmacies, banks, and coffee shops to grab a cafe macchiato to go. There are even drive-in ministries to provide spiritual connection and prayer support to busy people. All of your basic needs and wants can be met on your morning commute.

Perseverance is the best option. To fulfill the need for immediate gratification you stop short of the goal, settle for less, and pursue the next shiny object vying for your attention. Patience is a virtue but waiting makes you feel anxious and you settle what you have in the short term. Haste truly makes waste. Take your time and do things right. Incomplete or haphazard jobs often require more time and resources to make them right.

Look closely at the people you most admire. Did they really enjoy overnight success, or did they commit to doing what it takes, for as long as it takes, until they met their goal? Slow down and give yourself time to achieve your dreams. Believe that good things come to those who wait.

BEST DAY EVER

Write it on your heart that every day is the best day in the year."
– Ralph Waldo Emerson

Wouldn't it be wonderful if every day was a perfect day? We know that's unrealistic, but there's no reason we can't do our best to make it so. Start each day with gratitude for all that is good in your life. Make a list of the people who enrich your life and the things, no matter how basic, that enhance it.

Allow enough time to savor your morning ritual. Coffee or tea made just so, served in your favorite cup. Read something inspiring. Stretch. Go for a walk and let the fresh morning air clear your head as you soak in the beauty of nature. Think about your intentions for the day and the three most important things you will accomplish. When you're ready to put your best foot forward select a comfortable outfit that makes you feel terrific, enjoy a nourishing breakfast, and head out with purpose, focused on activities that bring value and meaning to your life.

Contact someone who inspires or motivates you and include them in your day. Make time to connect even if it's just for a few spirit lifting minutes. Be sure to let them know how much their presence in your life means to you. Pare down your to-do list by eliminating or re-scheduling low priority items. Schedule small pockets of time for pastimes and hobbies that bring you joy and fulfill creative desires. Simple pleasures purposely enjoyed throughout the day make all the difference.

Each person is unique and what makes one person happy might not mean anything to the next. The important thing is to string together a series of small meaningful moments to ensure the day is the best it can be. Find your own path to happiness and make each day the best day of the year.

STAY IN YOUR LANE

"We are not in a position in which we have nothing to work with. We already have capacities, talents, direction, missions, callings."
– Abraham Maslow

We are all blessed with natural gifts, talents, and skills that make each of us as individual as a fingerprint. It's up to us to identify our strengths and build a successful life around them. Pay attention to the things you do effortlessly that win compliments, kudos, and awards. Don't downplay your attributes or take them for granted. A closer look might reveal your true calling, the lane you are meant to drive in on the journey of life.

Once you recognize your passion, you have found your avocation, the thing you love to do that gives you joy and purpose. If you're good at it and it makes you happy, why not make it your life's work and turn your avocation into your vocation? People born with natural physical ability excel in organized sports in school, but the odds are very slim they will ever go pro. If your calling is sports, there are many opportunities to use your God-given talent by choosing a sports related career instead of changing lanes and settling for an unrelated job.

If you could spend the rest of your life doing one thing, what would it be? You have always been passionate about music/cooking/health/fitness and would love to dedicate your life to it in some way. If you don't know where to begin or how to make it happen ask for direction from someone you trust who would be willing to help. Consider the choices and strategically map out a plan to start moving in the right direction. Once you're on your way stay in your lane and enjoy every minute of the ride.

SHADES OF GREEN

"To cure jealousy is to see it for what it is, a dissatisfaction with self."
– Joan Didion, Author

Jealousy is a wasted emotion. Worrying that your partner is losing interest won't fix the problem if your hunch is true. In the event you are misreading the situation, nothing good will come by stressing over it. Letting a partner know you are jealous sends a signal you don't trust them, and a previously happy relationship can be soured by misunderstanding. If you feel the relationship is getting stale commit to self-improvement to rekindle awareness and solve the problem, whether real or imagined.

Professional jealousy is also a no-win. Sulking around the office because you feel the promotion should have been yours sheds a harsh light on your insecurity. It doesn't change anything, in fact it possibly confirms the right decision was made. It's natural to feel jealous from time to time in a competitive workplace, provided you shake off the negativity and put the energy to work in a positive, confident way. Take the high road, show your support for the team, and genuinely congratulate the victor on their success.

The next time you feel threatened, try to identify the basis for the fear and put a plan in place to deal with it. Moods are momentary, but reactions can cause permanent damage. Think before you act. Learn to deal with jealousy as the emotion it is and react to it logically. Jealousy is so powerful it can become a self-fulfilling prophecy. Project your fears onto someone else one too many times and you might just drive them into someone else's welcoming arms. Re-direct the irritation you feel at the associate who gets all the breaks and commit to creating a few breaks of your own.

ESTEEM FOR ELDERS

"By the time you're eighty years old you've learned everything. You only have to remember it." – George Burns

Our lives get busy and the days fly by, but it's not like that for seniors. Their days are long and can be lonely. If you have an elderly relative or friend you haven't connected with lately take time to schedule a visit. Let them know in advance you will be coming, and they will eagerly anticipate your visit. If you are local and able to see them often, establish a routine and give them something to look forward on a regular basis. They will appreciate a thoughtful call before you come to see if they need anything and to remind them you are on your way. If you're not local, a scheduled phone call might be the bright spot in their day.

Look at your life and what you've been through. Now multiply that by two or three and imagine how much they have experienced in their lifetime. They may not have much to add in the way of current events but asking them to share stories from their past will prompt a treasure trove of rich memories. Treat them with respect by slowing down, silencing your phone, and listening to what they have to say. Pay careful attention. Seniors are more than willing to offer valuable insight into the ups and downs of life.

These oldies but goodies may have trouble with short term memory, but they can often recall what happened fifty years ago like it was yesterday. Draw them out with a few thoughtful questions and let them reach back and reminisce. Pour a cup of coffee or tea and serve something sinfully sweet. This quality time with them could very well be the bright spot in your day.

SCARCITY VS ABUNDANCE

"The world is full of abundance and opportunity, but far too many people come to the fountain of life with a sieve instead of a tank car… a teaspoon instead of a steam shovel. They expect little and as a result they get little." – Ben Sweetland

Scarcity thinkers worry there will never be enough. They protect what they have, contribute a little less than their fair share to the lunch tab, and pinch pennies as a savings plan. A scarcity mentality doesn't easily offer kudos or congratulations when others succeed. They view any success, other than their own, as a threat. Team situations don't bring out the best in them because they prefer their own ideas, aren't interested in competing opinions, and have difficulty giving credit where it's due. If life was one big pie they would hoard it, fearing that once it's gone, it's gone.

Abundance thinkers believe there will always be another pie. They are team players who welcome new opinions and concepts. Big thinkers share ideas and welcome collaboration to foster learning, growth, and development. What's theirs is yours. There will always be more.

Steer clear of pessimistic mindsets. If you catch their attitude you will join them in a life of fear and insecurity. Gratitude is the hallmark of an attitude of abundance. If you want a life of joy and fulfillment don't worry about running out of all things good. Be thankful for what you have and genuinely happy for any success enjoyed by others. Abundance means there's plenty for everyone.

Make the choice to live with a grateful heart and maintain a positive, optimistic outlook. Look for opportunities to help, contribute what you can, and your life will be blessed with riches. Now wait for it. There's more where that came from.

ALL YOU NEED IS (SELF) LOVE

"Happiness follows a sincere effort at self-discovery. We cannot possibly be happy if we are strangers to ourselves. Self-understanding is the door to quietude." – Vernon Howard

We can't love another until we love ourselves, but we can't fully love ourselves until we understand who we really are. To fully accept yourself you must stop trying to change into someone you think you should be and start celebrating the real you. Evaluate your life from every angle. Go deeper than the scorecard in your head where you rack up the wins and losses. What characteristics describe the truly authentic you? What positive qualities do you want to be known for?

Make a list of personal attributes and refine it by drilling down to the few important characteristics that define you. Going forward, shore up your weaknesses wherever possible, but put more effort into cultivating and developing areas of strength. This exercise might demonstrate that who you think you are isn't really you at all. You are so much more than you give yourself credit for.

The good outweighs the not-so-good and your best foot forward is good enough. It's time to start practicing a little self-compassion. It's not necessary to cover up or make excuses for your short-comings. Start appreciating and embracing your perfectly imperfect self. When you accept yourself unconditionally you can enjoy a little self-love without the need of smoke and mirrors. Stop judging, blaming, and beating yourself up every time you fall short. Just because you spent years (and a small fortune) in one particular field, if it's not for you, make a change. Find humor in your quirks and idiosyncrasies. Forgive and forget disappointments, learn to laugh at your mistakes, and start living a life of genuine peace and happiness.

DO YOU MEASURE UP?

«If you can›t measure it, you can›t improve it.»
– Peter Drucker, Author

It's frustrating when you are diligently dieting, but inexplicably, not losing an ounce. Start counting daily consumption and the mystery will be solved. Calories, carbs, and fat grams add up quickly, therefore keeping track of portions is critical to successful weight loss. It might be low cal, low carb or fat free food, but too much of even the healthiest choices will thwart your best laid plans. Start tracking every bite and you might find you've consumed the daily allowance by noon. Armed with accurate information it's possible to adjust your eating habits and begin the exciting process of tracking and measuring lost pounds and inches.

It seems you're doing all the right things and spending time on what's important, but it is easy to overlook the occasional forbidden morsel or skipped gym day that keeps success just out of reach. When you're ready to embark on a self-improvement routine, plan a clear course to the goal. Show up, set benchmarks, and track positive progress and results.

The only way to know if you're making headway is to count, measure, and track your moves regularly. Without a performance measurement system in place there is no way to confirm all that effort is actually making a difference. Awareness is the number one key to success in every area. Measure what you want to improve and use the data as a starting point to implement sustainable growth and development. Keep a tally, count everything important, and set benchmarks along the way to celebrate success.

Measure to stretch yourself and to discover what you're really capable of accomplishing. When you pay attention, it becomes very clear where your priorities lie verses what you claim as priorities. You do what you measure, so what are you measuring today?

THIN THE HERD

"Surround yourself with people who make you happy. People who make you laugh, who help you when you're in need. People who genuinely care. They are the ones worth keeping in your life. Everyone else is just passing through." – Karl Marx

Jim Rohn, one of the world's foremost business philosophers said, "You are the average of the five people you spend most of your time with." If that's the case, carefully vet the people who surround you, both personally and professionally. The people closest to you greatly affect your attitude, motivation, and decisions. Interacting with positive, optimistic people who are dedicated to your success, and you to theirs, reduces stress and increases joy.

Do your colleagues and friends encourage you to set the bar higher and challenge you to live up to your full potential? If they don't share your values or quest for self-improvement it may be time to move on. Take a strategic approach to find and foster new relationships that will test your limits. Look for people who love to recommend books or share what they learned at last evening's seminar. Take advantage of networking opportunities that will broaden your horizons. Show sincere interest and purposely schedule time to get to know them. You won't be as comfortable as you were with the group who didn't push your limits, but you will improve.

Be selective and choose wisely. When you're surrounded by the right people you become dependable sounding boards and constant supporters determined to bring out the best in each other. Symbiotic relationships form as each party inspires and motivates the other. Seek out people who will enrich and bring joy to your life and do the same for them.

FACE YOUR FEAR

"F-E-A-R has two meanings: 'Forget Everything And Run' or 'Face Everything And Rise.' The choice is yours." – Zig Ziglar

It's your turn to stand and give the project update at the quarterly business meeting. You are overcome with anxiety, weak knees, and dry mouth. You reluctantly stand, give the report, and just like that, it's over. As your palms dry and heart rate returns to normal, a thoughts pops into your head. "That wasn't as bad as I thought it would be".

Facing your fears is the first step to overcoming them. Identify activities that cause the jitters and find ways to expose yourself to those anxiety provoking situations in small doses. Knowing that another presentation will be required at some future date, practice speaking up from the sidelines, when the spotlight isn't on you. Offer an opinion or add a comment during meetings. Make it a point to engage other attendees in conversation before the meeting begins as an ice breaking technique.

Eleanor Roosevelt encouraged individuals to "do one thing every day that scares you". It doesn't have to be something that instills sheer terror, like bungee jumping or skydiving. Seemingly insignificant worries can be blown way out of proportion given the chance. You have been feeling strangely fatigued lately for no apparent reason, so you google your symptoms to self-diagnose. Now you're not sure which is scarier – your fear of doctors or the frightening list of possible illnesses associated with the symptoms. Move past the fear and make an appointment.

A little healthy worry is a good thing. It helps us to recognize problems and 'puzzle out' the best solutions. It's not easy, but it is necessary, to find a balance between helpful apprehension and excessive worry that dictates every move. Face your enemy today and proudly say, "Now, that wasn't so bad, was it?"

TANGLED WEBS

"Some people create their own storms, then get upset when it rains…"
– Unknown

When asked a question that makes us uncomfortable, we withhold the unpleasant part of the story, or we side-step and give vague and ambiguous answers. Putting up walls in self-defense serve us well, especially when deflecting inappropriate questions about things that are no one's business. We do it to protect our privacy, but distorted truths and mixed messages often come back to haunt us.

Dating websites are perfect examples of seemingly harmless misinformation going unnoticed until two hopefuls meet and realize the posted photos were sadly out-of-date. Setting unreal expectations might result in barely concealed disappointment, but you asked for it by shaving eight years off your real age. Now the truth is out, and your date is wondering what other details may have been misrepresented.

It's easier to become tangled in a web of deception than to disentangle yourself after its spun. You filled out the job application with mostly true information and landed the job of your dreams. Unfortunately, HR followed up and exposed your attempt to conceal potentially embarrassing information. Chances are you would have been hired despite that youthful bad decision, but it's too late for transparency and now you must face the consequences.

Privacy matters. The less people know the less they can judge. It's okay to play your cards close to your chest. Provide information with discretion, and on your own terms but be aware that inaccuracies and half-truths will follow you. Once you decide whether to share or withhold information, proceed with caution. Life experiences change us from naïve 'tell-all's' to mature 'information processors'. Share wisely.

CREATURE COMFORTS

Don't get too comfortable with who you are at any given time - you may miss the opportunity to become who you want to be."
– Jon Bon Jovi

When you hear the expression 'creature comforts' you might think of material possessions and luxuries that comfort or possibly basics necessities like food and shelter come to mind. Comfort is in the eye of the beholder. No matter how you define it, when you're comfortable you are a content and happy creature.

It's all relative. Bhutan is a tiny country tucked in the shadow of the Himalayas. It has a population of 800,000 people who spend their days eking out a living that lacks even the most basic creature comforts. In the early 1970's the king of Bhutan introduced a radical philosophy and put his little nation on the map. He declared that "Gross National Happiness (GNH) is more important than Gross National Product (GNP)". He took the emphasis off traditional measures of success and focused on the happiness of his people. The collective well-being of that struggling nation is more than a concept. The goal of happiness has been incorporated into the constitution of Bhutan and has attracted the attention of nations worldwide.

What brings you comfort? Do you find peace and comfort on your own or are you at your best surrounded by lively friends and family? Some people are most comfortable lost in a book or alone with their thoughts and others are happiest living life a little louder. It's okay if you're a 'homebody' and consider your personal surroundings a center of comfort while the girl next door enthusiastically looks forward to the next party. There's no need to compare your happiness quotient to anyone else's. Carve out fifteen minutes a day, starting now, to do something you enjoy, where and with whom you enjoy it, in a state of comfort.

COMMIT TO SOMETHING

"The only limit to your impact is your imagination and commitment."
–Anthony Robbins

It doesn't matter what you commit to, it just matters that you commit. Anything less than dig-your-heals-in commitment will compromise the results. Success comes to those who are 'all in', focused on the goal, not relying on Plan B.

Still suffering from commitment phobia? A short walk down memory lane might snap you out of it. If you didn't commit to the first nervous young man who invited you to the junior prom in hopes your secret crush would ask you, it's too late for a do-over. Lack of commitment creates missed opportunities and stifles progress.

When you are in a committed relationship it's not necessary to agree on every issue. In fact, that would be a very dull existence. Two devoted individuals can remain happy together and disagree on fundamental issues, like religion and politics. It's possible to be committed to the relationship and to respectfully disagree on certain topics.

The same applies in the workplace. You weigh in on a change you would like to implement, but the rest of the team decides to go in a different direction. If you are truly committed to the organization, you fall in step with the majority. It doesn't mean you've changed your mind, it means you are part of a team that works for the good of the whole organization. Each case requires the buy-in of all parties. The more readily you can fully commit, the better chance the relationship, business or personal, has to succeed.

Commitment makes the difference between wishing for, and realizing, goals. Dreamers sit and hope, doers make things happen. Pledge your allegiance to something now. Jump in with both feet, hang on with everything you've got, and you will reach your goals.

LETTING GO

"Grief can't be shared. Everyone carries it alone. His own burden in his own way." – Anne Morrow Lindbergh

Losing a loved one is a sad, but natural passage, and grieving their loss is the pathway to healing. How we handle it is personal, private, and depends on the circumstances, our ability to cope, and our experience dealing with loss. The sudden, unexpected loss of someone in their prime can be more difficult than the slipping away of someone older who has enjoyed a full life. Both beloved, one loss inexplicable, the other inevitable.

If you are mourning the end of a relationship reflect on what was really lost. You might be lonely, but release from a contentious environment could be a better option. Possibly the grieving is for what could have been, instead of what really was. Focus on closure and in time you will move on, past the pain.

Pets become beloved members of the family, living long enough to find a place in our heart, but not long enough to outlive us. It is normal to feel devastated after the loss of a faithful companion, and the healing process can be very difficult. Unlike other losses the pain can be eased by finding a new pet to love.

There are no timetables for grieving, no guidelines, and no one-size-fits-all answer. You search for just the right words of comfort and always seem to come up short. It's impossible to know exactly how others are feeling, even if you have experienced a similar loss. Simply lend an ear or a shoulder to cry on, until they can face the new normal.

Part of life is loving, and part of loving is letting go. Hopefully, time will allow acceptance of the loss, and the love and memories will be kept alive.

COMPENSATION

"It is one of the most beautiful compensations of this life that no person can sincerely try to help another without helping him or herself. Serve and you shall be served. If you love and serve people, you cannot, by any hiding or stratagem, escape the remuneration."
– Ralph Waldo Emerson

You get what you give. You will be compensated commensurate to the level you contribute. If you give a lot, you get a lot, but beware, stingy efforts will result in a very meager harvest. Most of us willingly go out of our way to perform good deeds when opportunities present themselves. We do this without expectation of recognition or reward, but we benefit because the ebb and flow of the universe has a habit of compensating individuals who commit selfless acts of kindness.

Doing something nice for others makes us feel good which by itself is very rewarding. It is, however, a good idea to leave the door wide open to allow more positivity to come your way in return. The lucky recipients of our good deeds are usually quick to thank us. Typically, we respond to their gratitude by brushing it off with a quick, "no problem", "my pleasure", or the standard, "you're welcome". Since one good turn deserves another it would be smart to position yourself front and center to receive the next available courteous gesture. A gracious reply to their thanks might include any of the above phrases, but by simply adding a few more words, "I know you would do the same for me", we encourage them to return the favor.

Increase your compensation by increasing the significance of your contribution and giving a little more. Ask yourself what you can do to make a greater difference. Look for ideas, put them into action, and serve.

DECIDE TO BE DECISIVE

"On an important decision one rarely has 100% of the information needed for a good decision no matter how much one spends or how long one waits. And, if one waits too long, he has a different problem and has to start over. This is the terrible dilemma of the hesitant decision maker." – Robert K. Greenleaf, Servant as Leader

People who have trouble making decisions aren't necessarily re-sorting to the path of least resistance. They truly agonize about making the best decision possible but hesitate to pull the trigger in case it's wrong. Until they do, there's no way to be sure it was the right move or the wrong one. They are caught in a holding pattern, stuck in uncertainty, wasting time overthinking and second guessing. That's a real dilemma.

Too many options confuse and obscure the issue. Benjamin Franklin suggested a pro and con chart to help in the decision-making process. He drew two columns on a sheet of paper and in one column he listed all the pros associated with the decision he was wrestling with, and in the other column listed the cons. When you do this, a clear choice usually surfaces, but if you're still conflicted ask someone you trust to listen while you verbally weigh the alternatives and identify the best direction. Once the answer is clear, take action.

There are so many people who would love to take a chance and grab at least one brass ring on their journey through life, but for numerous reasons just can't make the move. There are no guarantees, but if something is important to you, calculated risks are worth taking. Decide today to take charge of your life. Do more and be more, and don't look back.

QUESTIONABLE DECISIONS

"It's not hard to make decisions when you know what your values are."
– Roy E. Disney

We tend to put off tough decisions on the pretext we need time to gather more information before we commit or, the real reason, hoping it will go away. Most problems aren't as bad as we think, practice makes perfect, and the process gets easier. If you find yourself obsessing over even the smallest decision start with just one and ask yourself these questions.

How will this impact my life? If you're having trouble deciding what shoes to wear, it's okay to make a bad choice. You can wear a more comfortable pair tomorrow. The decision will not have lasting impact on your life. If the result could be life changing, call for a lifeline from someone who puts your best interest first. Don't ask the opinion of just anyone and everyone. If they don't have a vested interest in your success/failure their opinion won't matter.

What's the worst possible outcome if the wrong decision is made? If the risks aren't high and the consequences are not life altering, you might be able to live with making a less than perfect decision long enough to make a few changes and adjust your direction.

What are the alternatives? The preferred solution might be a shade between the black and white, all or nothing, alternatives. A middle ground answer may offer an opportunity to hit pause until the time is right and the facts are clear.

Do you trust your 'gut'? Sometimes everything points in one direction, but it just doesn't feel quite right. Trust your instincts and wait until the direction is clear. The most important thing to remember is that your final decision must align with your core values. When it does, move forward with confidence.

DIAL IT BACK

"I'd like to dial it back 5% or 10% and try to have a vacation that's not just e-mail with a view." – Elon Musk

People love to celebrate and opportunities and reasons to party run rampant. Pre-wedding celebrations sometimes start years in advance with engagement parties, bridal showers, bachelor/bachelorette nights, and a wedding week with brunches, spa treatments, golf tournaments, and rehearsal dinners highlighted at some point by the actual wedding vows. When baby makes three another round of parties fills the calendar to celebrate the happy news, including, but not limited to, announcements, reveals, ladies' luncheons, and baby showers (plural). Finally, the wrapping paper settles and the stunned couple are left alone to face the reality of life without the limelight and the cheering crowds.

Companies fall prey to the same one-up mode at the annual holiday party or award banquet. Expectations are set a little higher each year until those bigger and better celebrations become a burden. It's all very fun and exciting, but also a little intimidating when every holiday is expected to eclipse the one before. There must be a way to simplify life and still share love, good wishes, kudos and accolades.

Dial it back. Re-adjust unrealistic expectations and re-confirm priorities by acknowledging what is truly important. Parties are fun but without a plan in place they can turn out to be expensive, wearing, and before you know it, unnecessarily excessive. Pare down the guest list, simplify refreshments and decorations, and prepare as much as a possible before the big event so you can enjoy the celebration along with the guests. You might be rewarded with a collective sigh of relief from all sides. Keep it easy, keep it real, and focus on the joy of the occasion.

KNOWLEDGE IS POWER

"I am still learning." – Michelangelo

Summer vacation is behind us, schools are back in session, and learning at the student level is once again underway. But learning doesn't stop at graduation. It should be fostered as a lifelong passion regardless of the level of education you completed or failed to complete. Enhance your quality of life, expand your mind, and inspire others by committing to learn something new every day.

It's easier to make good, educated decisions when armed with a deep well of information and facts to draw upon. Information provides options to help us deal with the inevitable changes we face in life. We adapt more easily to new situations with awareness and understanding.

Knowledge in general empowers you to speak with authority on an endless variety of subjects. It makes you more interesting and builds self-confidence. Committing to learning something new daily will foster interest in a wide range of issues, broaden your horizons, and open your eyes to a world you never would have known existed. Pique your interest with something completely foreign to you. It might trigger a healthy wanderlust and encourage you to plan a trip to investigate new places, people, and things. Exposure to new concepts forces you to think, inspires creativity, and encourages innovation.

Opportunities to learn are all around you. Pick up a book, tune into an educational program, question everyone, and google everything. Read a magazine focused on a topic you know nothing about. You will be excited to share what you learn and, in the process, become the sparkling conversationalist you've always wanted to be. Start today and enrich your life by committing to learn something new and interesting every day.

PURSUE HAPPINESS

"Happiness is when what you think, what you say, and what you do are in harmony." – Mahatma Gandhi

The Declaration of Independence doesn't guarantee happiness, it simply gives us the right to find it. It's up to us to identify our own happy place, but there are many unhappy, discontent people in the world who don't know how to achieve true, long-term happiness. The answer is complex and subjective. What makes one-person happy leaves the next one untouched. We've seen that money doesn't buy happiness, fame can isolate, and good health is often taken for granted. Disappointment and dissatisfaction set in when we devote our energy and most of our day to careers and relationships that are not aligned with our core values.

If you are unhappy with your job and have expressed this to others, it's time to stop idly complaining and take positive action. Make a list and put a plan in place to change frustration into joy. What career would challenge and bring out the best in you? Look for meaningful work that will encourage you to bring your best every day. There are many inspiring stories about employees who are happily fulfilled doing something as simple as serving lattes. Their satisfaction and joy is infectious, making every encounter a day changer for customers.

The next time a friend launches into the same tired rant about her deadbeat partner (or fill in the blank) ask this transformative question: "What are you going to do about it?" Ask yourself the same question in any area life has left you wanting.

If you want a happy life fill your days with activities that satisfy and fulfill you. Make time for the people and things that matter. Find a healthy work/life balance, sprinkle in a little fun every day, and find your happy.

CELEBRATE GRANDPARENTS

"Never have children, only grandchildren." – Gore Vidal

Nothing quite compares to the relationship between grandparents and grandchildren. Grandparents don't worry about spoiling the children, they revel in it. They conspire against the parents by letting the kids enjoy two helpings of dessert, stay up past their bedtime, and indulge or overindulge them in every possible way. In fact, the older generation has found this to be such an amazing relationship that it's been suggested parents avoid the trials and tribulations of raising their own family and hold out for the grandchildren. But that's not how it works.

Parenting years are a hectic flurry of days that run together. It feels as if you take two steps backward for every step forward. It's not easy to maintain a household, and in many cases, a career, while rearing responsible future citizens. You pack lunches, provide emotional support, save for college, and bandage scrapes. There are extracurricular activities involving sign-ups, fundraising, somewhat presentable uniforms, practice schedules, game times, and countless other details. Some days there's barely time to breathe.

Once your own children have flown the nest there's more time to relax and enjoy life. Cue the grandkids who entertain without even trying. They love you, and are loved back, unconditionally, spreading pure joy without the prickly responsibility of parenting.

If you are lucky enough to have grandparents, reach out to them today. Let them tell you how smart and good looking you are. If you are a grandparent yourself schedule some special time to spend with your partners in crime. Provide an audience of one to an endless supply of cheesy knock-knock jokes. Play hide-and-seek for hours. The key to the fun is to count slowly and take your time looking for them. The rules don't require you to find them right away.

LIFE'S PASSAGES

"You live like this, sheltered, in a delicate world, and you believe you are living. Then you read a book... or you take a trip... and you discover that you are not living, that you are hibernating."
– Anais Nin

In the first few decades of life our innocence insulates us from serious life situations. If we suffer a loss it is likely either someone elderly, and not completely unexpected, or the result of an unforeseen accident. There comes a time when we lose someone our own age due to natural causes and it sends shock waves through us. We understand it could have been us and the realization shakes us to our core. We can no longer convince ourselves we are bullet-proof or invincible. We are mere mortals, and facing that truth is one of life's passages.

The many things we planned to do 'someday' in life are suddenly front and center. We are forced to face reality and review our journey so far. The image may be uninspired and short on the exciting life experiences we have always planned to do but continue to put off until some future unknown date.

Let's re-define someday and call it today. Sign up now for the painting/cooking/dance class you have been talking about for years. Learn a new language and set up shop in a foreign country for a time. Change careers, start a side business, teach a class, or try out for a play. Catch a train and travel the country at ground level, a great way to enjoy the purple mountain majesty and fields of waving grain. Stop hibernating and start to live. It's high time to embark on a new passage that features a fulfilling, experience-rich life. It's time to give your dreams a deadline.

READ, LEARN, GROW

"I believe that the habit of constant reading of good books and scholarly periodicals and magazines in many disciplines is vital to give a larger perspective and to constantly sense the interdependent nature of life."
– Stephen Covey

Reading to young children every day is beneficial in many ways. It starts them on the road to success by introducing new concepts, building vocabulary, and encouraging reading 'readiness' as they begin to correlate the written word with the stories they hear. Daily reading should start in childhood, but not stop there.

If you aren't a reader by nature try to fit in five pages a day. This might require getting up a few minutes earlier in the morning or eliminating a little social media or television time, but it will be worth the effort. Introduce uplifting, interesting reading material into your day until the reading habit is formed. Once you're hooked you will look forward to one excellent book after another.

Audiobooks offer an efficient and effective alternative to the written word. Listen and learn while taking a walk, driving, before bed, or whenever you can carve out a few minutes. They are conveniently available on your phone, making educational entertainment easily accessible. Reading, or listening, to books as part of a daily routine will enhance life a few minutes at a time. Find a genre that interests you and start there. When you're ready, venture out of your comfort zone and discover fresh new topics and interests.

Reading develops a thirst for knowledge that is not easily quenched. Everything you need to know can be found in a book. The words convey wisdom, stimulate your mind, and force you to think. Reading enriches lives in countless ways and will dramatically open your eyes to a multifaceted world and all that it offers. Read = learn = grow.

LIFE-CHANGERS

"At times our own light goes out and is rekindled by a spark from another person. Each of us has cause to think with deep gratitude of those who have lighted the flame within us." – Albert Schweitzer

Think of those magic moments in life when someone demonstrated their belief in you, offered encouragement, or granted a timely leg up. Maybe it was a teacher who amazed you with an opportunity to feed your passion or a coach who recognized some hidden talent and dedicated time outside of normal practice to hone your skills. Possibly your manager took a chance and promoted you to a position that intimidated as much as it thrilled, but you rose to the challenge and launched a successful career.

Consider what life would have been like without your own personal cheerleaders, AKA parents. Dad patiently put you back on the bike when one spill too many threatened to end your cycling career at the tender age of five. It hurt him to do it, but Fathers know best and you're grateful for his patience and confidence that one day you would find balance and remain upright. Those same loving parents made you stick it out when the going got tough, until you eventually landed the coveted lead in the play, a position on the team, or a college degree.

Each scenario describes a life-changing event and you feel tremendous gratitude to those individuals who gave such generous support. It's never too late to reach out to them with a heartfelt 'thank you' for the role they played in shaping your life. Let them know you appreciate what they did for you and consider their help a true blessing. But don't stop there. Once you have thanked your mentors be sure to pay it forward and become a life-changer yourself. Opportunities to make a difference are everywhere.

LIVE YOUR DREAMS

"The future belongs to those who believe in the beauty of their dreams."
– Eleanor Roosevelt

The world is full of amazing inventions, discoveries, books, and structures that were conceived in vivid, creative dreams before they were brought to life. Walt Disney believed, "If you can dream it, you can do it". Evidence of his conviction is all around us, but the key to fulfillment requires 'doing', not just dreaming.

In your favorite daydream you imagine what it would feel like to cross the finish line of your first marathon. You see yourself flashing a radiate smile as the crowd cheers you on, and other than a bit of sweat you look as fresh as when you started. Unfortunately, that will never be any version of you if you continue to live in a dream world. Bring your vision to life by creating a plan, committing to a training schedule, and reaching each milestone that will eventually see you through 26.2 triumphant miles.

Unleash your imagination and build castles in the sky. Let the vision motivate, energize, and inspire action. If you dream of a more satisfying life, but you don't know how to get from where you are now to where you want to be, ask for help. There's always someone a step ahead willing to guide you. Start with one small step followed by another and turn your pipedream into reality.

What is your dream? Will you achieve it in your lifetime or will it always remain an elusive fantasy? If you know you want it and get excited just thinking about the possibilities, it's time to get your head out of the clouds, tap into your full potential, and pursue it relentlessly. Make today the day you take a step in the direction of your dreams.

NEVER FORGET

"If we learn nothing else from this tragedy, we learn that life is short and there is no time for hate." – Sandy Dahl, wife of Pilot Jason Dahl, Flight 93

The horrific events of September 11th, 2001 will forever be etched in our memories. It was a peaceful late-summer morning until all hell broke loose when four terrorist attacks changed America forever. We remember where we were when the carnage started, and our lives stood still. We will hold the 2977 innocent victims whose lives were lost that day in our hearts forever.

We will never forget the 265 souls onboard the four planes used as weapons of war, including the heroes on Flight 93 who gave their own lives to save countless others. We will never forget the sight of 414 first responders charging bravely into the inferno at the Twin Towers in an impossible attempt to save even one of the thousands of lives lost at The World Trade Center. We will never forget the 55 members of the military who lost their lives that day in the attack on the Pentagon. And we will never forget the many wounded, or the incalculable grief suffered by the families and friends of the victims. Lives across the world would never be the same.

We will never forget how we came together as a nation on that fateful morning. We were truly the United States of America. So many people gave blood The Red Cross suspended donations. American flags were completely sold out and could be seen waving from car windows and porches across the country. Drivers showed kindness to other drivers and everyone reached out to loved ones to give and receive comfort. It was a day of devastation met not with fear, but with strength, compassion, and an outpouring of love in honor of all that we lost. Take a moment today to remember and reconfirm that you will never forget.

THINK SMALL

"It's the little details that are vital. Little things make big things happen."
– John Wooden

Small things matter. Give thanks for all the little moments that comprise your day. Alone they may seem insignificant, but the combined energy they create can be momentous. Deliberate small steps in the right direction make all the difference.

Success rarely blesses you with one big win. It usually takes many small ones to get you to the goal. There's tremendous power in small wins when you string them together in a series. Taking action is vital if you intend to transform some area of your life, but it doesn't have to be massive action. Many small actions become a string of small wins and cause lasting change.

Big projects or events can be so daunting that we're tempted to give up without trying. You almost resigned when you were asked to direct the club's annual fundraiser. Just the thought of organizing an agenda, securing space and caterers, soliciting donors, and attracting attendees was enough to make you hyperventilate. Instead of looking at the big, overwhelming picture create a plan and put a detailed strategy in place. Enlist a talented team and through well thought out delegation divide the big list into manageable projects with qualified individuals responsible for each. It's possible to apply this model to any overly big venture and, by thinking small, successfully move mountains without breaking a sweat.

This might seem like an ordinary day but look a little closer and you might discover an opportunity to make it extraordinary. Adopt a 'no job too small' attitude and decide to make one minor moment notable by nurturing it into something major. The prospects are endless. Find one small thing you can do today, increase it little by little, and make a big difference.

WON'T POWER

"Willpower knows no obstacles. Find your greatness." – Nike

It takes real self-control to resist short-term temptations on your way to long-term goals. Why is willpower in such short supply? Even when you wake up fully charged, in control, with unwavering determination to win the day, your energy batteries and willpower batteries at some point begin to run low. When you're tired, resistance weakens, and it's easier and more gratifying to give in and say, 'I will' than 'I won't'.

You're determined to get into shape, but consistently hit the snooze button instead of rolling out of bed for the gym. You vow nothing will stop you from losing weight, but when asked to select a side with your sandwich, fries are the uncontested choice. How will you ever meet your goals and find your greatness if you continually let little things derail your best intentions?

You started today on the right foot by taking the stairs instead of the elevator and passed up the donuts in the coffee room. Fortified by those early victories it should be easy to stay on track all day, but the catered business lunch taunts you, and your present hungry self overrules your future svelte self, and your willpower dissolves. There's no room in your budget for discretionary spending, but you find a great sale and enjoy a little impulse buying spree you will soon regret. Log out and step away from the computer before you finalize the online purchase of more 'must haves' you don't need.

If you're short on self-control the best way to strengthen your resolve is to exercise it in small ways instead of depleting it completely. Flex your willpower muscle and don't give in to cravings and desires you will soon regret. Splurging will ultimately make you feel bad which will lead to more indulging, because you can. Exercise your 'won't power' and find your greatness today.

FIND YOUR NICHE

"You gotta keep trying to find your niche and trying to fit into whatever slot that's left for you or to make one of your own." – Dolly Parton

We can't be all things to all people although it is tempting to try. The problem with pleasing everyone is it spreads us too thin and dilutes what makes us special in the process. We must do our own 'thing'. Find it and perfect it, rather than trying to juggle a number of mediocre things to please the masses. Decide what you stand for, refocus on your unique value, and own it.

A niche might be described as a 'clearly defined narrow space' to securely hold a statue or, on a personal level, as the 'clearly defined narrow space' where you make a difference. Make a list of your interests and passions. Narrow the list by comparing one talent or skill with the next to determine where you fit in most securely and comfortably. Eventually one area of life will stand out. This is what you want to be known for and what you want people to think of when they think of you. Focus your energy on being the absolute best within your area of expertise.

You know you have found your niche when someone is looking for X and they positively associate you and the reputation you have built with that need. Congratulations, you found your 'thing'. What you stand for is top of mind, highly respected, and sought after. Now embrace and take full credit. You're one of the lucky ones who know who you are, what you do, and why you do it. Spread the word. Find like-minded people and organizations to pool resources, share knowledge, and continue to grow and refine your personal clearly defined narrow space and make a difference.

THE DEMOCRATIC WAY

"The ballot is stronger than the bullet." – President Abraham Lincoln, Speech, May 19, 1856

Democracy makes freedom ring. The majority rule system is at work at all levels of our government but stops short of the family level. Decisions concerning "What would you like for dinner?" or "What movie should we see?" can be settled by popular vote, but more important issues can be overruled by Mom and Dad who have the final say. Put democracy to work whenever possible. It's never too soon to instill democratic ideals in our youngest citizens.

In a democratic society there are many voices, all of whom need and deserve to be heard. Talking louder isn't the answer. Being firm in your commitment and standing by your beliefs counts. Don't let others shout you down because they disagree with you. As citizens we all take part and share equal rights "of the people, by the people, and for the people."

Know your rights and exercise them. We, the people, elect government officials. Voting is an important civic duty, but to choose wisely you must form your own opinions by listening to the views of potential candidates. If their beliefs align with yours, they earn your vote. But duty doesn't stop there. It's also important to hold those elected officials accountable and call them out if they don't live up to their campaign promises.

Stand tall when the national anthem plays in honor of the men and women who have given their life to protect freedom. Stand in solidarity as an American, not as supporters of rival sports teams or political parties, or because you identify as a certain gender/religion/culture/color. Proudly pledge your allegiance to the flag that flies over fifty great states. Red for valor, white for purity, and blue - justice for all.

UNDER THE INFLUENCE

"There are exceptional people out there who are capable of starting epidemics. All you have to do is find them."
– Malcolm Gladwell, The Tipping Point: How Little Things Can Make a Big Difference

Are your personal traits and characteristics a result of genetic influence or did the environment and experiences in your youth shape who you are today? That question has been debated forever with solid supporting evidence on both sides. Obviously, parental genes influence physical factors and parenting style dictates our early development, but once we're in our formative years many other powerful influencers contribute to our character.

We are who we are because of the many people who helped shape our lives. Teachers have a huge impact on who we become by encouraging and supporting our strengths and skills. It just takes one good teacher to instill a love of learning and positive sense of self that will last a lifetime.

Friends are tremendous influencers and should be chosen with care. We want to fit in and may be tempted to follow the crowd even when it undermines our values. The people we spend time with have an impact on our thinking and behavior. Follow the ones who are responsibly chasing big dreams and goals. Surround yourself with positive, inspiring individuals and you will be influenced to lead an inspired life.

There are certain areas of life you can't change, but awareness of the many factors influencing your feelings will help make better life decisions. Just because your parent's relationship was contentious doesn't mean you should avoid committing to a long-term relationship. Be cautious, but don't miss out on life because of outside negative influences. Weigh the factors and consciously shape your life around the ones that work for you.

FAIL TO LEARN

"The only real mistake is the one from which we learn nothing."
– John Powell

We live and learn. At least that's our goal. Humans err on a regular basis and no matter how hard we try to avoid mistakes they still happen. Regrettable words are spoken, and disappointing actions happen every day that cause some level of embarrassment or chagrin. They range from harmless faux pas like the annoying slip of your ex's name when addressing your current beaux, to a major foot-in-mouth blunder like innocently asking a woman not in the family way when her baby is due.

The deed is done, now what? You can beat yourself up or look for a solution. If it's possible to repair the damage put a plan in place to make that happen. Apologies should include changes you will make to avoid similar mistakes in the future, how you will use the experience to grow and learn, and a sincere 'I'm sorry' for your words or actions. If you are to learn from your mistakes you must step up and take responsibility and not shift the blame to someone else. What part did you play and what would you do differently, given the opportunity for a do-over? Being accountable empowers you as it clears the air.

It's not always easy to process, understand, or accept the situation, but you must to get past it. If necessary, enlist the help of a mentor or supportive friend to help you work through the error of your ways. A trusted friend's perspective will be more objective and perhaps more forgiving than your own. Shake off the guilt and remorse and get back in the game. Mistakes mean you're human and offer new opportunities to learn and grow.

TAKE A SOUL STROLL

"If you are seeking creative ideas, go out walking. Angels whisper to a man when he goes for a walk." – Raymond Inmon

It's an indisputable fact walking is good exercise and beneficial for our body. But beyond physical benefits, walking has been proven to be valuable in ways that are harder to measure. Walking opens your mind, lifts your spirit, and enhancing overall well-being. Take a brisk walk and start your heart pumping oxygen to muscles, organs, and most importantly, your brain. An influx of oxygen will clear your mind allowing fresh ideas to surface. You feel a sense of peace as you breathe the fresh air and take in the scenery. In addition to toning your muscles and burning off a few calories, walking relieves tension, boosts the immune system, sets you up for a better night's sleep, and feeds your soul.

It's easy to incorporate walking into your lifestyle. It's free, requires no expense for training or equipment, and can be enjoyed alone or in the company of friends. Start your day on the right foot by taking an early morning walk, unplugged and distraction free. It's a perfect opportunity to organize your thoughts and center yourself for the day ahead. A brisk walk in the middle of the day will refresh and energize you. When the afternoon slump hits, grab a friend and use the time to re-connect while you stroll. A leisurely walk in the evening allows you to unwind and prepare for a good night's sleep. Let your mind wander uninterrupted while you walk, anticipating sweet dreams ahead.

Make a commitment to put one foot in front of the other for twenty minutes a day for all the right reasons. Your body, mind, and spirit will thank you.

BE INTERESTED TO BE INTERESTING

"You can make more friends in two months by becoming interested in other people than you can in two years by trying to get other people interested in you." – Dale Carnegie, How to Win Friends and Influence People

If you want to be influential, personally and professionally, interact with interesting people. To do that it helps to become one yourself. It's simple. Identify something you enjoy, become knowledgeable on the subject, and share the information with other people you meet. Open the conversation with your interests and pass the baton to them. Ask thoughtful questions about their life. Pay attention to their answers and follow up with even more in-depth questions. Be curious and open to new ideas and experiences. Actively seek advice and knowledge that will change the way you look at things. You will be remembered as a person of substance not because of what you said, but because of what you let them say.

It's more fun to discuss things you find fascinating than things you find tedious. Make it your mission to know as much as you can about things that interest you. Open up, share your knowledge, and start a conversation. Be well versed enough to ask a few leading questions and let the discussion grow and flow from there. It's a natural transition that begins when you attract attention about a topic that excites you and then encourage others to participate and share their thoughts.

The best way to become more interesting is to become more interested in what other people have to say. It's a small world and often what you glean while paying attention one day serves a good purpose another day when the same subject comes up under different circumstances. You can be an interesting contributor simply because you showed an interest.

PHRASE IT AS A POSITIVE

"Accept everything about yourself – I mean everything. You are you and that is the beginning and the end – no apologies, no regrets."
– Henry Kissinger

We try our best to do the right thing and when we fall short we're quick to apologize. Friends step up and lend a sympathetic ear while we let off a little steam or when we need a shoulder to cry on. Once the vent is spent there's no need to apologize for your outburst. That's what friends are for. Thank them for listening and let them know how much you appreciate their support.

Some situations call for an apology but substituting 'Thank you' for 'I'm sorry' sends a positive rather than negative message. The word 'sorry' connotes regret while 'thanks' express appreciation. Say "Thank you for your patience" instead of "Sorry, I'm late", and the meeting will commence on a positive rather than negative note. Once you've offered thanks cross your fingers you will hear the positive and gracious response, 'you're welcome' and not today's popular negatively phrased expression, 'no problem'.

Rephrasing a request when you anticipate a negative reply will change the conversation as well as the results. "Don't play tag in the house" reworded as the less contentious "Please go play outside" invites cooperation. Rather than risk a 'no' by asking your sullen teenager to load the dishwasher, turn it around. "Is there any reason you can't help with the dishes?" The restatement sets you up for a win.

Feedback sounds less like criticism when good and bad are presented together. "Thank you for your contribution to the project, however, some of the work was completed by other team members. Better communication will lighten your workload in the future." Put a positive spin on everyday expressions by rephrasing your words and give thanks, not apologies.

FALL IS IN THE AIR

"Life starts all over again when it gets crisp in the fall."
– F. Scott Fitzgerald, The Great Gatsby

The days and nights are equal in length at the autumnal equinox and summer inevitably turns into fall. The change takes place seemingly overnight. Evenings cool down and even warm days feel a little less 'summery'. Our northeast regions erupt in glorious color as the leaves turn vibrant shades of red and gold. In the southwest the leaves simply dry and wait for the autumn winds to blow them away.

Sports fans are in their glory. The baseball season is coming to a head, with playoffs looming and hockey fans are gearing up for another grueling season. Football is in full swing, dominating the airwaves and filling the sports bars weeknights and weekends with loyal screaming fans.

Kids talk about Halloween costumes and daydream about the superpowers they will assume once disguised. The fun is in the planning, strategy, and design. Don't get started too early. You can count on them to change their minds more than a few times in the coming month.

Grocery stores are loading up their produce departments with pumpkins and gourds in all shapes and sizes to brighten our walkways and tables. Apples ripen and the crisp, clean flavor is celebrated in pies and cobblers, caramel-dipping or pressed apple cider. Combine that with the most noticeable harbinger of fall and prepare to be overwhelmed by the wonderful pumpkin spice aroma that permeates the air. Pumpkin spice lattes, pumpkin scones, all things pumpkin confirm the fact that fall is in the air.

So, cozy in, bring a sweater, sleep a few minutes later, turn the lights on a little earlier, and look forward in joyful anticipation of the Autumn season ahead.

PUT OTHERS FIRST

"Put others before yourself, unselfish love, do unto others as you would have done to you." – Jessica Chastain

We spend our early lives as selfish 'me first' children until we have children of our own and priorities change, putting family first. Parents everywhere are examples of selfless love. They lead by example and demonstrate the joy and satisfaction that comes from lending a helping hand and now it's up to us to rise to the occasion.

A cafeteria worker used the money she earned at her day job to feed nutritious meals to the homeless in San Diego. She used her time and her dime to bring hot food, empathy, and compassion to people in need. The community took note and thanked her by presenting her with a much newer and more reliable car to make her rounds. She was amazed to realize her purely altruistic efforts were praiseworthy. She considered her selfless actions a privilege, just grateful she could help.

Putting others first doesn't require grand gestures. It doesn't take much effort to hold the door for someone with their hands full or to slow down and make room for the driver next to you frantically indicating a lane change in time to make their turn. If someone steps up to the checkout counter at the same time you do, let them go first. Put yourself in their shoes and put their needs before your own. These small, but mighty, actions can make a big difference. Pay attention as you go through the day and you will see many opportunities to put the needs of others first, leaving them feeling grateful and you feeling gratified. What small, unselfish act will you do today to put the needs of others first?

FILL YOUR VICTORY BOX

"Memory is a way of holding onto the things you love, the things you are, the things you never want to lose." – The Wonder Years (ABC Television, 1988 through 1993)

A memory or 'victory' box is a powerful way to preserve positive memories by keeping them close at hand to revisit whenever your self-esteem needs a little boost. You won a sales contest and were awarded a certificate of excellence. Evidence of that victory is box worthy. Honors, recognition, and acknowledgement of jobs well done aren't given lightly and should make us proud. When you're feeling deflated nothing will lift your spirit faster than a review of what you've done right and words from the people who have taken notice.

Treat yourself to a trip down memory lane and reexamine some of the things you love. Many cards bring joy in the moment, but a select few will resonate in a special way and have lasting value. Thank you cards that express love and appreciation are always worth holding on to. Heartfelt words from special people can be read and re-read forever connecting you to happy memories.

Looking back and reminiscing about memories that make you smile feeds and soothes the soul. Someone you love surprised you with a gorgeous bouquet of flowers. Tucked inside was a little card with a heartfelt hand-written message. Every time you see the card you remember how happy you felt that day. Photos are a quick link to a lifetime of good memories. The ones that evoke positive emotion are definite keepers, not only in your phone, but in your victory box, always within arm's reach. Little mementos that connect you to successful events or make you feel happy, loved, or appreciated are definite keepers and should not be allowed to fade away.

WHEN TIMES ARE TOUGH

"The human capacity for burden is like bamboo- far more flexible than you'd ever believe at first glance." – Jodi Picoult

We all face difficult times, unwelcome change, and personal challenges. It's an unavoidable part of life. If we can stop resisting change and learn to be more flexible through unpleasant experiences, we will adapt and grow instead of becoming immobilized by every unexpected curveball headed our way. Resilience keeps us in balance which allows us to survive and eventually thrive in the face of adversity. The longer we live the more complicated our problems become. The process of growing older and wiser makes us more adept at working through complex life experiences and better equipped to handle setbacks.

We can choose to let circumstances get us down or we can decide to make the best of them. You were so sure you would be offered the job of your dreams that you didn't put a safety net or backup plan in place. Now you want to bury your head in the sand, but the truth is you need a job. Maintain a positive, solution-oriented attitude and focus on what you can learn from the situation. When times are tough, show resilience, take control, and commit to finding a better job.

There will be more tough times, but resiliency and learning to take life one day at a time will get you through them. When best laid plans don't work out, learn what you can from the disappointment and accept what you cannot change. There is a Japanese proverb that asserts "The bamboo that bends is stronger than the oak that resists." Life is not what happens to us, it's how we respond to it. Choose the best option and face the future with tenacity and optimistic confidence.

STAY GROUNDED

"Flying starts from the ground. The more grounded you are, the higher you fly." – J.R. Rim

When you're grounded you feel peaceful, present, and comfortable in your own skin. You've built a firm foundation, on solid ground. Life's ups and downs don't keep you off your game for long. When faced with a challenge, grounded individuals stay centered like a 'punch me' inflatable toy that springs upright after every swing. Maintain balance and stay connected to your core values and you'll make it through life intact and on your feet.

Social media provides a constant stream of photos, posts, and videos showcasing better dressed people, with better ideas, living 'better' lives. Or not. Too many distractions and constant stimulation make it tempting to follow the friends we are 'following' and make changes in our lives that are inconsistent with our personal goals and values. Grounded people don't base their happiness on other people's 'busyness' or business. They can be happy for others and content with the choices they have made in their own life.

If overstimulation leaves you feeling antsy or anxious head outside and commune with nature. Go out for a run, take a brisk walk, or ground yourself literally by digging in the garden or sprawling on the grass to study the sky. Breathe, count your blessings, and concentrate on the things that truly matter. Remember where you came from and respectfully honor your roots by remaining the person you have always been with consistent family/work/community ethics.

It's okay to have your head in the clouds as long as your feet are planted firmly on the ground. Chase big, bold dreams grounded in reality that encompass every aspect of your life. Stay humble, be true to yourself, and let well-grounded personal fulfillment be your reward of choice.

SILENCE IS GOLDEN

"Better to remain silent and be thought a fool than to speak out and remove all doubt." – Abraham Lincoln

Our parents raised us with the sage advice, "If you don't have something nice to say, don't say anything at all". The world would be a kinder, gentler place if more people listened to their parents. Every silence is not begging to be filled and all comments don't require a response. You have the right to remain silent. Feel free to exercise that right whenever it serves your needs.

When we were kids we were taught to respond to verbal taunting by chanting, 'sticks and stones will break my bones, but words will never hurt me'. The problem is, unkind words can and do hurt, no matter how much we hate to admit it. Some people thrive on conflict and will say things just to get under your skin. It takes great strength to remain silent, but if you hold your tongue and don't give them the satisfaction of a response you are in the power seat.

Many individuals aren't accustomed to silence and find it unsettling. When conversations appear to be winding down both sides are likely to fill in the blanks with incessant chatter in an effort to avoid a potentially awkward pause. The next time you run out of words, relax, savor the moment, and breathe.

There's something very peaceful about being alone with your thoughts, calm and undistracted. We're so conditioned to living in an atmosphere that constantly buzzes with 'white noise' that we fill opportunities for refreshing quiet time with background music, television, or idle talk. Treat yourself to a golden moment. Turn everything off and just sit and enjoy a few peaceful minutes of silence to quiet your mind and center your feelings. Invoke your right to silence.

DON'T LOOK BACK

"Renew, release, let go. Yesterday's gone. There's nothing you can do to bring it back. You can't "should've" done something. You can only DO something. Renew yourself. Release that attachment. Today is a new day!" – Steve Maraboli

You can't change the past, but you can make peace with it. Acknowledge and accept that you could have succeeded, if only you knew then what you know now. Don't dwell on 'should've or would've' or allow frustrating thoughts to hold you back. There are no rewind buttons to erase past mistakes and once opportunities are lost, they are lost forever. Instead of complaining about the road not taken or regrettable choices save your energy for the next round of new and possibly better options. If you truly regret the path you're on, do something about it starting today.

You reminisce about the good old days, forgetting they weren't all as rosy as your edited and filtered memories portray them. Last summer's vacation stands out in your mind as the best one ever, but when you look at the photos you see clear evidence of painful sunburn, swollen bug bites, and the annoying poison ivy rash that drove you crazy for weeks. Our minds are biased, leaving out some details and enhancing others. You're far better off looking forward to this year's escape with sunny optimism and sunscreen than trying to duplicate last year's fun, but imperfect, adventure.

Think of yesterday as 'been there, done that'. Stop harboring tired grudges, let go of time-worn disappointments and free yourself to accept all the wonders the future holds. Don't look back, you're not going that way. But every now and then, when you can't resist, take a quick look just to celebrate how far you've come.

LOYALTY

"Loyalty means I am down with you whether you are wrong or right, but I will tell you when you are wrong and help you get it right."
– Anonymous

Chicago Cubs fans are incredibly loyal. They steadfastly supported their team through a losing streak extending more than a century and never once considered turning their backs on their beloved team. Cub fan-atics faithfully show up to spring training and every game, eternally hopeful and doggedly committed to the team. They love the Cubs through rare 'thick' seasons and decades of 'thin' ones.

Take a page from their playbook when tempted to bail from a relationship that is inherently strong but has hit a rough patch. Most marriages and seasoned relationships face challenges along the way that threaten to break them. If you are able to work through the difficult times you strengthen the ties that bind, and the relationship is refreshed and fortified.

Dogs are man's best friend, primarily for their loyalty. They protect and love unconditionally. Count on your faithful companion to greet you with the same level of enthusiasm and pure unadulterated joy every time you walk through the door. No matter what happens they are simply happy to be with you. Unlike humans, they never provoke, dwell on problems, or work on an exit strategy. They are 'all in' for the long term and can teach us a lot in the way of lifelong commitment.

It's not always easy to put the needs of others before our own. Just as it's not always easy to be patient and understanding. Being loyal requires standing by and supporting people who are important to us even when we're not on the same page. Step up to the challenge and instead of looking for a way out, look for reasons to persevere.

FRUGAL IS THE NEW FANCY

"I'd like to live as a poor man with lots of money." – Pablo Picasso

I am a very frugal person which means I feel the need to get my money's worth out of anything I purchase. I don't enjoy shopping and rarely buy anything not on sale. It's easier to pay retail, but the real fun lies in finding hidden treasure through patience and perseverance.

My parents were raised when the severity of the great depression was fresh in everyone's memory. Nothing was wasted, including used tin foil, lunch bags, and household utilities. We turned off lights when we left the room and re-cycled everything before it became a responsible environmental practice. The budget was strictly followed and did not allow for extravagant or unnecessary consumption of any kind. It was a happy, modest upbringing.

Take a close look at your monthly expenses. If you order online there's a risk you signed up for on-going monthly debits without realizing it. You might be paying for subscriptions that you don't need or use, gym memberships long forgotten, association dues to groups you are no longer associated with, or phone plans that can be re-negotiated. Reduce your expenses and give yourself a raise. The money you save can be stashed away for a rainy day, an unexpected expense, or maybe even something a little frivolous.

Exercise good judgement and make well thought out decisions when managing your money. Wasteful habits can be changed. It's not always necessary to buy brand names or top of the line items. Its false economy, and not at all prudent, to postpone auto or home maintenance until faced with expensive repairs. Don't be tempted to overspend just because others do. Make frugality a game, a way of life, and you will end up with the gold.

LIVE UP TO YOUR TRUE POTENTIAL

"Find the place inside yourself where nothing is impossible."
– Deepak Chopra

The only potential you can fully live up to, is what you believe in your heart is possible. Others can tell you how fortunate you are to have such remarkable prospects, but you are the only one who must recognize and accept you have the ability and skill required to reach the level of success others imagine. Maybe you had no interest or lacked confidence when the door to your 'dream life' was open. Don't worry, it's possible to find another door.

You were on your way to a sports scholarship when an injury side-lined you, and the opportunity slipped away. But the talent and star quality that allowed you to excel in sports will serve well in other areas of life, it just needs to be re-directed to other opportunities. Leadership, a collaborative spirit, and the ability to make and act on quick decisions are skills many athletes exhibit. These assets, and many more, are critical components necessary to succeed in business and life. Fortunately, these valuable resources are transferable and when focused on new goals will make it possible for you to live your best life.

Living up to your full potential means realistically assessing your current situation and tapping into the wellspring of what could be, if only. Embrace your unique qualities, explore all options, and discover that the sky really is the limit. Create a detailed plan to get you from where you are today to where you know you can be, regardless of fear, naysayers, or past mistakes. No one can want it more than you. Make the choice today and take one small step in the direction of your dream. Do it again tomorrow and every day until you re-connect with and take ownership of your amazing full potential. Oh, yes you can.

SWEATER WEATHER

"I'm so glad I live in a world where there are Octobers."
– L. M. Montgomery, Author Anne of Green Gable

Soon we will say goodbye to the dog days of summer and enthusiastically welcome autumn with its crisp, fresh air and vibrant fall colors. Is it just me or are there a few others who won't miss those skimpy summer frocks with their sheer, dainty fabrics? Summer fashions definitely look best on people blessed with flawless skin and tanned, shapely limbs. For the rest of us (or just me), fall styles do a great job camouflaging and concealing imperfections.

No one can deny a long-sleeved shirt, layered with a cozy sweater and a wool scarf is a flattering look on any type of body. Layer up and once you're appropriately dressed, take a hike. Pull on a pair of good boots and hit the great outdoors. A brisk walk in bracing air does wonders to clear minds, uplift moods, and get hearts pumping. The pesky bugs have disappeared and no matter where you live the landscape is taking on a new look that should not be missed.

Take time to dust a little cinnamon in your coffee or indulge in the seasonal joy of a pumpkin spiced latte paired with a pumpkin flavored treat, the spicy scent that permeates the air and everything we eat in October. And speaking of pumpkin, a visit to the pumpkin patch is an essential fall ritual. Grab a sweater and go. The gourds provide seasonal décor until it's time to carve them into ghoulish jack-o-lanterns.

Make the most of every minute this month and cross your fingers that once you've 'sweatered up' and stored last summer's clothes, Indian summer won't preempt the classic fall weather you've waited so long to enjoy.

FEED YOUR SOUL

"The soul is often hungrier than the body…and no shop can sell it food."
– Henry Ward Beecher

It's understood we must eat well to fuel our bodies and keep them in optimum condition. We try to make healthy food choices by limiting junk food, sweets, and portions. An entire industry thrives on our lack of control in all of the above, but the diet and weight loss business continues to flourish because even though we know the importance of maintaining a healthy body we need constant hand holding to do it. How much and what we feed our body is necessary for survival, but it's not enough. We must also feed our soul.

What we put in our mind becomes food for our soul. Just as we avoid unhealthy physical food we should be mindful of unhealthy soul food - what we watch, who we listen to, and what we read. Television offers a smorgasbord of junk food starting with the news. It's important to stay abreast of current affairs, but most reporting deals with disaster and corruption, not exactly nutritious fodder. There's also no shortage of dark storylines in network or movie lineups. Be selective and discerning before you immerse yourself in an evening of cinema or a new book. In each case keep it light, fresh, and wholesome.

Feed your soul a diet of comfort food, rich in positivity and hope. Choose to listen to uplifting messages that motivate and encourage self-improvement. Read books that expand your mind and make you think. Avoid going down Internet rabbit holes wasting valuable time with nothing in return. Limit time on social media simply because enough is enough. Seek out blogs, books, and podcasts on personal development and achievement. Surround yourself with like-minded people who open your mind to endless possibilities. Listen to music that moves or inspires. Go outside, breathe fresh air and enjoy a centered, soul-full existence.

TAKE TEN

"Breathe. Let go. And remind yourself that this very moment is the only one you know you have for sure." – Oprah Winfrey

A popular parenting technique recommends removing an unruly or unhappy child from the fray for a little quiet time to improve their attitude and behavior. It helps center and calm children who aren't coping, and it will center and save your sanity, as well. When life becomes all work and no play, put yourself in timeout. Stop whatever you're doing, find a quiet place or walk outside, and breathe. Relax, gather your thoughts, and when you're ready, plug back in with a new, refreshed perspective.

Once you find a happy balance, you're properly equipped to run your life and business instead of letting it run you. Put one foot in front of the other and maintain a steady pace. No more scrambling to keep up just to stay in the race. Concentrate on one task or activity at a time, in order of importance. Be aware that activity does not necessarily equate to progress. Stop running in circles before you run amok by committing to actions that move you closer to your personal goals.

When you're clearly in the driver's seat you won't be tempted to cave and say 'yes' to yet another responsibility that doesn't align with your values and objectives. Focus with renewed energy on new opportunities instead of automatically passing because your plate is too full. Make thoughtful decisions after carefully weighing the options. If you feel overwhelmed, take ten and recharge you brain so you can fully concentrate on the project at hand.

Treat yourself to well-deserved breaks on a regular basis and don't come back until your attitude is refreshed and renewed. A few well spent minutes might be all it takes to turn your day, or your life, around.

THINK BEFORE YOU SPEAK

"Speak only if it improves upon the silence." – Mahatma Gandhi

Do you sometimes find yourself prattling on in an effort to avoid an awkward silence? Next time you're tempted to fill in the gaps with incessant small talk take a deep breath, compose your thoughts, and enjoy a quiet moment or two. Slowing down gives you the opportunity to thoughtfully choose the right words before communicating the message.

It's important to THINK before you speak. Use this acronym to help soften or stifle the words before you form them into sentences. T - Ask yourself if what you are about to say is **T**rue. If it's questionable don't risk spreading a baseless rumor. H – Will what you want to share be **H**elpful? Will your words add good or useful **I**nformation to the conversation? I - Will what you have to say **I**nspire or influence something positive or creative? N – Is it **N**ecessary to voice your thoughts? Sometimes what we say makes a lot of noise without providing any real value. Be mindful. Just because you think it, doesn't mean you have to share it. K - And finally, is what you want to say **K**ind? If the words in your head are spiteful or mean keep them to yourself or re-frame them. Some conversations are hard, but necessary. No one likes to deliver bad news but adding a little positive reinforcement will soften the message and spare personal feelings.

The next time a (possibly) brilliant thought pops into your head exercise some restraint and refrain from immediately blurting it out. Your intentions might be good, and you certainly never intend to offend or hurt feelings but speaking without thinking often results in regrettable foot-in-mouth gaffes. Some things are better left unsaid and sometimes a little silence is golden.

EXPERIENCES ARE THE NEW BRAG

"A mind that is stretched by a new experience can never go back to its old dimensions." – Oliver Wendell Holmes, Jr.

There was a time when what you owned defined you as a person. Cars, homes, jewelry, or the 'it' brand of jeans were viewed as status symbols. Assumptions were made about the kind of person you were by a quick perusal of your possessions. People were willing to go into debt for the latest shiny object, but the minute they owned it they set their sights on the next 'must have'. More was better until it just became more.

What is important to us materially changes throughout our life, but experiences stay with us forever. Today's 'brag' or status symbol has shifted toward experiences rather than material things. Great moments and adventurous getaways are much more fun to hear about and share on social media. Enjoying a fresh and tasty meal on the patio, hiking in the local hills, a concert in the park, or a visit to an art gallery with friends are post worthy ventures. The good news is, the incredible things to see and life-changing experiences to enjoy in this wide, wonderful world are limitless.

You develop and grow through life experiences. When you follow your passions in search of what you love, you learn valuable life lessons in the process. Live your best life by trying new things and in the process gain a clear understanding of who you really are and what truly makes you happy.

A rich life is all about finding and enjoying as many priceless experiences as possible. Commit to discovering simple ways to feel fulfilled and alive. Dream, strive, discover, and along the way recognize that the journey was more valuable than the destination.

MODERATION IN ALL THINGS

"Moderation. Small helpings. Sample a little bit of everything. These are the secrets of happiness and good health." – Julia Child

If only we could control the weather. We suffer through years of drought, followed by excessive rain, which leads to dense under-growth. The vegetation withers and becomes an arsenal of dry fuel, the perfect food for raging wildfires. Fires strip the landscape, and next seasons epic mudslides complete the perfect storm. Un-fortunately, temperate weather is beyond our jurisdiction. The best we can do is take refuge from the storm and relate the need for moderation to our own life, which we can control.

Living to extremes is stressful and draining. Eating too much can be unhealthy, as can eating too little. The same goes for drinking, drugs, sleeping, working, sugar, salt, and everything else in life that affects your body or mind. Regular exercise is admirable and a wonderful thing unless it's taken too far. Over-exercising can contribute to chronic health problems and an increased risk of injury. Fast food can be convenient and acceptable in small doses, but too much contributes to health worries by overloading your body with calories, salt, and preservatives. A little goes a long way.

It's fun to stay in touch with friends and family via social media, until you get hooked and waste precious hours living vicariously through their posts instead of actually living. Try a little some-thing new and post it for others to enjoy. Then move on to an-other activity that gratifies and satisfies. Become a dabbler and see how much more rewarding a well-rounded life can be.

It's essential to recognize and limit excess in your own life to main-tain a healthy lifestyle. Too much of even a good thing, is too much. Strive for a comfortable balance in every area and enjoy a long, happy, moderate life.

HYGGE HELPS (pronounced hue-guh)

"The whole world is a series of miracles, but we're so used to them we call them ordinary things." – Hans Christian Andersen

Denmark consistently ranks at the top of the list of the world's happiest countries for a good reason. The Danes embrace the key to happiness and they call it 'hygge'. It's a simple concept that anyone and everyone can easily incorporate into their lives. The premise is positivity and finding joy in the simple things. The Danish word hygge doesn't have a corresponding word in English. It takes several words to capture the essence, but simple, cozy, content, and comfy are all part of the feeling.

Hygge happens when you enjoy a special moment, either alone or with friends, and take time to acknowledge and savor the moment as a joyful or comforting experience. There are no rules, no set expectations and no right or wrong way to enjoy hygge as long as you keep it simple and real. Think candles, cozy sweatpants worn with thick socks or your favorite slippers, and maybe a good friend or two and no agenda. Add hot tea, cocoa, or a glass of red wine and you're in hygge heaven.

It's easy to bring hygge into your life any time of year, but it's especially fun in the chilly winter months. Slow down, bake some cookies or your favorite comfort food. Soups, casseroles, and pot pies make wonderful hygge meals especially if you enjoy them in a casual candlelit atmosphere or in front of a cozy fire.

What are the simple things in life that make your heart sing? Bundle up and take a walk, drop in on friends for potluck and a favorite movie. If you crave quiet curl up alone with a good book. You know you are there when you sigh with contentment...or with hygge.

MAKE THE CONNECTION

"Humans are social beings, and we are happier, and better, when connected to others." – Paul Bloom

There is a commonly recognized theory that claims every person on the planet is connected if you follow the chain of people through six contacts or less. When you hear "a friend of a friend knows someone who knows someone" it could very well be just the person you need to know. Connect the dots whenever you can make a valuable introduction that will benefit others. If you know of a service person who is timely, talented, and reasonably priced let others know. Word of mouth advertising is priceless. A good job deserves to be rewarded with a positive testimonial and people in need will be grateful to you for the introduction which will also enhance your value.

Humans require connection for support and happiness. The world is a complicated place and it's easy to become isolated and lonely. It's necessary and neighborly to feel comfortable relying on friends and family when an egg or cup of sugar is needed in the middle of a baking moment, a computer glitch requires knowledge above your pay grade, or ginger ale and flu meds would save the day when you're under the weather. Look for ways to reach out to people in your sphere and make a difference. If you suddenly realize you haven't seen or heard from someone in a while check in to see if they are okay.

Join a group with similar interests and commit to meeting as many members as possible. You won't connect with everyone, but a few like-minded individuals in your life will make a big difference. Eat meals as a family as often as schedules permit, volunteer, chat with the person next in line, and stay well connected.

BE A MAGNET

"Optimism is a happiness magnet. If you stay positive, good things and good people will be drawn to you." – Mary Lou Retton

Some people are blessed with magnetic personalities and own the room the minute they enter. They are charming, charismatic, and naturally garner attention wherever they go. Others are money magnets and everything they touch seems to turn to gold. Opportunities are abundant because they are known and sought after as individuals who make things happen. If they can do it, so can you.

Be approachable. The wallflower staring intently at their phone will not likely draw a crowd. Take a deep breath and enter the room with confidence, an expectant smile, and a friendly demeanor. You are guaranteed to be noticed. Make eye contact, start a conversation and discover common interests to create a bond. Introduce topics and pose questions that are interesting, relevant, and require an answer more involved than a simple 'yes' or 'no'. Become known as a problem solver. Others will be drawn to you for answers or because they believe you know someone, who knows someone, who can help.

People will respond to you if you are happy and exhibit an optimistic attitude. Find joy and spread it around. A sullen countenance will have everyone rushing in the opposite direction, but a welcoming sunny disposition will act as a magnet to draw them in. You don't need to be the class clown or life of the party. A good sense of humor and a positive outlook are all you need to create a dynamic magnetic field.

Put your best foot forward, be knowledgeable, personable, and real. Know what you want, believe you can achieve it, and it won't be long before you become a powerful magnet attracting and manifesting your hopes and dreams.

DISORDERLY CONDUCT

"Let today be the day you stop living within the confines of how others define or judge you." – Steve Maraboli

The goal of World Mental Health Day is to start frank, open conversations about mental illness and the way it touches so many lives. Mental health struggles are real, and they are rampant worldwide. With one in five people annually suffering from depression, anxiety, addiction, PTSD, and personality and eating disorders, it's high time to take the stigma out of it and acknowledge the severity of the problem. Education brings awareness and understanding. With understanding comes much-deserved empathy for the daily struggle faced by those fighting mental illness in its' many forms.

Depression is an illness that can range from mild to debilitating. Positive thinking alone won't turn it around. Proper treatment and support will. The same can be said for every other mental health issue. People with eating disorders aren't just refusing to eat, they can't eat, and deep breathing exercises won't always relieve an anxiety attack. Educate yourself and understand the severity of the problem. Do your part to eliminate the hurtful stereotyping and judgmental attitude that can cause so much pain and shame.

Mental illness has been treated as something to hide or avoid but that is changing. When someone is physically ill we send flowers and wishes for a fast recovery. Those same best wishes should be conveyed regarding all forms of illness. Everyone deserves to be treated with respect, especially someone who faces each day expending enormous energy just to be on par with the rest of the world.

Starting today make the decision to offer a helping hand, a kind word, or a little human compassion to someone in need. Commit to learning the real facts and then pass them on. Keep the conversation going.

ASK BETTER QUESTIONS

"A wise man can learn more from a foolish question than a fool can learn from a wise answer." – Bruce Lee

Toddlers question everything, incessantly. Children instinctively understand asking questions is the best way to learn and unself-consciously ask a litany of 'whys' to understand what makes wind, the sky blue, or anything else that piques their wide-eyed interest. Adults sometimes fear that questions make them look unprepared or incompetent, when the opposite is true. Don't be afraid to ask good questions. They show you are engaged and interested in learning more about what the speaker has to say.

The goal is clear and concise communication. Asking good questions is the most efficient and effective way to ensure the message you intend to convey is received correctly. Often, you say one thing, and others hear something entirely different. Unnecessary mistakes happen when you assume everyone is on the same page. It's prudent to have the listener repeat the message for validation and confirmation.

Questions are critical when gathering data to form your own opinion. Sergeant Joe Friday, of Dragnet fame, said it best. When questioning someone who became too wordy he cut them short with, "Just the facts, Ma'am." He focused on the evidence and factual data to come to his own educated, reality-based conclusion.

Questions are also necessary when soliciting the opinion of others. "How do I look in this dress?" is risky on many levels and may not elicit a helpful response. Re-frame it as a better question and you will be more likely to get insightful, constructive answers. Changing the query to "Is this dress appropriate for my body?" or "… the occasion?" offers the respondent several safe and sincere answers that will not personally offend. Ask better questions and get better answers.

DON'T MERELY SURVIVE, THRIVE

"Live life as if everything is rigged in your favor." – Rumi

Barely keeping your head above water day after day provides a tiring and discouraging existence. If you commit to implementing a few small, but critical changes, the energy generated will immediately transform your existence from floundering to flourishing.

Do more. Give up expectations of perfection and just do it. Try something completely new and challenging. Read directions, ask for guidance, watch a YouTube video, and tackle the project you've been threatening to take on for far too long. Surprise yourself with new found abilities and watch your confidence soar. Even a small measure of success will inspire you enough to take the next step and do something you never thought you could accomplish.

Be more. Smile at strangers, compliment often, and avoid eye-rolling judgement. Contribute, encourage, and uplift people around you. Wake up every day with a positive agenda, committed to your goals and don't stop until you reach them.

Be yourself. You can't live up to everyone else's expectations, so stop trying. Be clear about who you are and what you want. Set your own bar high and strive for what is important to you. Thoughts are things. Give the boot to limiting beliefs that hold you back. Fill your mind with positive, 'sky's the limit' thoughts and dedicate yourself to conquering YOUR world.

Laugh more. Don't take life, or yourself, too seriously. Find humor instead of censure in daily life. Learn to laugh at your mistakes and forgive them just as quickly. Allow the healing properties of a good laugh to ease tension and improve your overall well-being. Happiness is contagious, catch some today and go from simply surviving to thriving.

FIND YOUR WHY

"The two most important days in your life are the day you are born and the day you find out why." – Mark Twain

People who spend their life watching the clock, content to simply mark time, aren't leading a very inspired life. If this sounds familiar it's time to focus on your true purpose and take ownership of the 'thing' that lights your fire and fills you with take no prisoners resolve. We all have it, even though it may require the scale of an archaeological excavation to find it. Start digging and discover your purpose. When you do, re-ignite and re-direct your energy to the things that matter...to you.

You might be the life of the party, but what do you actually bring to the party? Committing to fully live the life you were meant to live involves taking inspired action. What's your purpose and where do you add value to others? Take stock of your strengths and passions. If you were blessed with a natural gift or talent don't take it for granted. Look for opportunities to succeed and career paths calling your name.

Once you are clear about who you are and why you're here, live it, breathe it, own it, and make your 'why', a priority. Individuals who enjoy life from a purposeful spirit of contribution feel a sense of accomplishment that continually fuels their fire. Create space in your day to nurture your true purpose and don't give an inch when work, family, friends, or life in general, tries to intrude on that sacred time.

When you tap into your purpose, you tap into an energy flow of no resistance. Connect with your passion and begin making a difference. The new focused, influential YOU will inspire others and make a lasting impact.

DOUSE THE FLAMES

"People who spend most of their time putting out fires are usually also the arsonists." – Dan Sullivan

Some people fan the flames of controversy and confrontation because they thrive on the drama of 'fire-fighter' syndrome. If you find that a good part of every day is spent putting out fires, consider a proactive approach and douse the sparks before they flare. Pay attention, anticipate problems on the horizon, and find solutions before the fires break out.

Many fires will burn themselves out before they hijack your day, but others will smolder on a back burner until they eventually burst into flame. Conflicts arise due to unclear or unaligned expectations. You said you would deliver the project next week. The client hears 'next week' and hopes for delivery on Monday. You have it calendared for Friday which meets the promised time frame, but not the expectation. Any breach of trust, no matter how innocent, is guaranteed to lead to dissatisfaction and disenchantment.

Communication often falls prey to 'he said, she said' gaps in understanding. Everyone hears what they want to hear and two parties to a conversation often come away with a very different message. Set expectations properly by clarifying what will happen and when it will happen. Ask questions until you are sure both parties share the same clearly defined, mutually agreed upon expectation.

When you avoid sharing bad news hoping the problem goes away, you are usually rewarded with a bigger problem. Today's society is impatient and wants instant gratification when, in reality, more time may be needed. Face the music, say the hard words, and get everyone on the same page from the beginning. They might be disappointed, but once the message is clear you can stop playing fire-fighter and concentrate on solutions and getting things done.

SEASONS OF LIFE

"For everything there is a season, and a time for every purpose under heaven." – Ecclesiastes 3:1-8

Just as we experience changing seasons through the calendar year, we enjoy seasonal fluctuations during our lives. We start in the innocent carefree season of childhood and over time we find ourselves with children of our own, coping with the relentless responsibilities that accompany raising a family. We yearn for the time when the daily grind eases and then are disappointed to find the empty nest is surprisingly empty.

Don't just get through the current season of your life, embrace and fully live it. The Little League season you thought would never end came to a sudden death finish and you find yourself missing it. You didn't realize how much you enjoyed cheering from the stands until it was over. Don't let this be a metaphor for your life.

Life emulates earth's natural climate cycle. Spring brings hope, growth, and opportunity. Your spring season ushers in the fresh and new allowing you to blossom and thrive. Summer represents contentment and possibly a little laziness or complacency. Autumn might find you feeling wistful for seasons past. Babies grow up too fast, you age and slow, life happens. And then the cycle of life comes full circle and winter swoops in to test your strength and you lose your job, a loved one, or your way in the world.

If you're having a 'winter moment' reach out to friends and family. Surround yourself with people and things that shore you up and offer hope and reassurance spring is just around the corner. Find the lesson and the purpose in your current season and celebrate the cycles of change. Recognize the value in the present and step up to claim your share of happiness right this very moment.

EXERCISE A LITTLE PATIENCE

"Have patience with all things, but, first of all with yourself."
– Saint Francis de Sales

If good things come to those who wait, why do we all seem to be in a race against time? We demand instant gratification and will settle for nothing less than what we want, when we want it. Usually, right now. Thanks to generous credit card limits, and even more generous criteria for raising the bar when that limit is exceeded, we have become a nation of debtors with a lot of stuff we no longer need or want. And storage units to hold it all.

The next shiny object doesn't need to end up in your closet or garage. If you curb your enthusiasm and wait twenty-four hours the urge may pass, and your wallet will be spared. If you decide this is something you really want, you should buy it…when you have the money. Exercise patience and save for future purchases. When you have the funds, if it's still important to you, buy it.

Life is a process. Sometimes things take a little longer than you would like. Recovering from an illness or injury can be frustrating. It's good to test your boundaries, but trying to do too much, too soon, may trigger a set-back. Relationships take time to develop. Be patient and let them blossom and bloom, or if need be, wither and die.

The best things in life are worth waiting for. It might be necessary, and prudent, to prod them along from time to time, but honor the process and put one foot in front of the other. If you miss an all-important step the foundation might be compromised, and everything important in life requires a solid foundation.

Walk before you run, think before you speak, and trust the universe to deliver what you really need when you really need it.

MAKE YOUR BED

"I you want to change the world, start by making your bed."
– Navy Seal Admiral William H. McRaven

Making your bed every morning may seem like a trivial task, but it's an important one and will set the tone for the rest of the day. Mornings can be chaotic and more than a little stressful, but just a few minutes spent smoothing and tucking is a calming and powerful act. It brings order to your environment and counts as one task completed first thing in the morning. Check, and next. It might feel so good that you are motivated to straighten up a few more things before leaving the house. Making the bed is a small, manageable undertaking that gets you started and forms a healthy habit. You're motivated to do it again and again until you're addicted to the very act of getting your act together.

Little wins accumulated over the course of the day add up to big wins. You start the day ahead of the curve with a positive attitude and a sense of accomplishment. It's a good feeling you will want to experience again, by checking tasks off one by one all day long.

It feels good to know that even if no one else sees it, your personal space is tidy and civilized. There's a world of difference walking into a room with an unmade bed versus one that's neat, tidy, and inviting. Getting into a well-made bed feels luxurious and organized space offers peace and tranquility, just what you need at the end of a long day. You might enjoy the ritual of turning down the bed before climbing in at night, signaling the end of a productive day. You've made your bed, now you can comfortably lie in it.

IT PAYS TO BE PUNCTUAL

"Better three hours too soon than a minute too late."
– William Shakespeare

You scheduled a meeting across town and have a vague idea of commute time, but double check with Google Maps to be sure to arrive on the dot. When it's go-time you press send on one final email just as another drops in. A response will only take a minute, so you quickly dash one off. Then you grab what you need, make a quick stop at the restroom, and head for the parking lot where you run into an old friend, enjoy a brief exchange of promises to connect, and finally reach your car, which is predictably low on gas.

If this sounds all too familiar you know the rest of the story. You arrive late, panicky and frustrated. Instead of using the drive time to mentally prepare for the meeting, you beat yourself up for being late, again. The stress created in those crucial few minutes takes a toll. Racing in late with flimsy excuses and embarrassed apologies puts you at a distinct disadvantage.

Arriving late to seminars, appointments, and events does not go unnoticed. Serial tardiness sends a clear message that you value your time above others. The truth is you're not trying to be selfish or arrogant. You genuinely want to be punctual, but everything takes longer than you think, and last-minute interruptions foil even best laid plans. Set yourself up for a timely arrival by planning to reach your destination fashionably early rather than 'on-time'. Calculate travel time from the minute you walk out the door until the minute you walk into your appointment. Allow for distractions on the way, parking, elevator delays, and walking in. Pad the estimate with a buffer of at least fifteen minutes as an additional safety net. You will arrive focused and calm with a little time to catch your breath.

FAIL FAST

"I have not failed. I've just found 10,000 ways that won't work."
– Thomas Edison

You won't succeed if you don't try…and try again. This is as true for relationships as it is for business, hobbies, projects, and ideas. You will never make progress if you don't step out of your comfort zone and at least try something new. Here comes the hard part: innovation is key to staying ahead, but it involves risk. We're human and inclined to be risk averse. We allow our innate fear of failure to hold us back.

The more you try, the easier it gets. When you take more chances it's easier to recognize success or failure. You're agile instead of stuck, more experienced and able to take a step back, regroup, and go in another direction, if necessary. No one likes to fail so reframe this thought and approach it from a positive perspective. If at first you don't succeed you're probably farther ahead than you were before you launched and it's easier to adjust once you have momentum.

If you are in a relationship that has stalled, or you keep modifying who you are to fit your partner's idea of a perfect mate, it's time to move on. You can waste a lot of time trying to be someone you aren't, but in the end the square peg/round hole scenario is a recipe for failure and resentment.

When you realize your idea/service/partnership is not as successful as you hoped, make decisive moves quickly. You can choose to give it a little more time, adjust as necessary, or pull the plug and start over. Don't bury your head in the sand and prolong the agony. Take what you learned, refine the process, and give it another shot. Fail fast and you will succeed even faster.

HEART CENTERED LEADERSHIP

"To handle yourself, use your head; to handle others, use your heart."
– Eleanor Roosevelt

We are all leaders in some capacity, even if our employment responsibilities fall at the bottom of the workplace ladder. Our families look to us for direction and friends seek and value our opinion. Step up and be the positive, influential leader they are looking for.

Your mind reconciles in a linear fashion, reaching clear cut, black/white/ or yes/no conclusions. Your heart recognizes there is always more to the story. Heart centered leaders put the needs of others first. They have the power to make a difference in many lives and draw people to them like magnets.

When you lead with your heart, people feel it. They are comfortable opening up to you and sharing their hopes and dreams. Listen to extenuating circumstances that may complicate decisions and help individuals determine a clear path to their goals. They believe in you and look to you for guidance and support. Be truthful, authentic, and relatable. Make it easy for them to see themselves emulating your actions and walking in your shoes. Be human and not only admit to mistakes and failures but accept full responsibility for them. Don't let those failures stop you. Lead by example and try, try again. Ask questions to fully understand their problems, find answers and offer viable solutions. Encourage people to focus on their own strengths by inspiring robust two-way communication.

Don't leave your heart at home when you head out for the day. Continue to build trust as you use your leadership power to connect to others and strengthen relationships with compassion and understanding. Foster an inclusive environment. What's good for one is good for all. Believe that one person really can make a difference and that person is you.

TO ERR IS HUMAN

"A mistake should be your teacher, not your attacker. A mistake is a lesson, not a loss. It is a temporary, necessary detour, not a dead end."
– Anonymous

Sometimes we speak before we think or leap before we look and by the time we realize it the damage is done. Mistakes are a part of life and no matter how hard we try occasionally we suffer a misstep. Don't despair, but don't delay the healing process by letting hurt feelings fester. A sincere apology will show them you are truly sorry for what happened and begin to establish trust again.

An apology should be more than a restatement or defense of the damaging words or actions. Open the lines of communication with two words: 'I'm sorry'. Those two words can be followed by 'and' if you feel further explanation will help smooth the situation. This would be a good time to disclose extenuating circumstances they may not be aware of or to describe changes you will make to ensure it doesn't happen again. The magic words, 'I'm sorry' can never be followed by 'but' or it will appear you are making excuses or placing blame elsewhere and your remorse will not sound genuine.

It's not easy but owning up to mistakes earns respect. Take responsibility, admit you were wrong, and seek to make amends. Ask if there's anything you can do to make this right. You may agree to take appropriate action to appease the injured party or it may require a little time to soften the edges before the healing can begin. When the table is turned, and you have been wronged put yourself in the offender's shoes. If they apologize for their thoughtless remark or oversight accept it with grace and understanding. Let them know you appreciate the gesture. Apology accepted, we're all human.

THE THOUGHTS THAT COUNT

"Try to make at least one person happy every day. If you cannot do a kind deed, speak a kind word. If you cannot speak a kind word, think a kind thought. Count up, if you can, the treasure of happiness that you would dispense in a week, in a year, in a lifetime!"
– Lawrence G. Lovasik

Thoughtful people make a difference in countless small ways. It's possible to make someone's day simply by greeting them by name. If you are hesitant to say it because you're not sure how to pronounce it, ask them for help. Instead of the usual greeting, 'how are you?' which prompts the reflex response, 'fine', ask a more personal and pertinent question. If you sense an individual is facing something emotional ask why they seem so happy/worried/stressed/quiet. They will appreciate your caring interest.

Make it a point to remember milestone events in the lives of those around you. People are quick to dismiss the importance of their birthday, but don't let them. Birthdays are special and should be recognized. Acknowledge times deserving celebration as well as times of difficulty. Anniversaries of birth, death, marriage, and years on the job are noteworthy occasions deserving a few thoughtful words of sympathy or congratulations.

Make someone's day in the simplest way. Hold the door or the elevator if you see someone sprinting for it. Pay attention to and anticipate the needs of people you care about. It's not unusual for new mothers to become exhausted and overwhelmed. Step in and lend a hand. Offer to pick up groceries or give her a few hours to herself while you walk her colicky baby.

They say it's the thought that counts, but that's just the first step. Action creates priceless gifts. Make today and every day special by thoughtfully making others feel valued and happy in some small way.

BE A LINCHPIN

"The linchpins among us are not the ones born with a magical talent. No, they are people who have decided that a new kind of work is important, and trained themselves to do it." – Seth Godin

A linchpin is a small device that fastens the wheel to the end of the axle to pin the wheel in place. It literally is the critical component that holds the moving parts together. In much the same way the linchpin of an organization holds things together, and metaphorically, 'keeps the wheels from falling off'. An individual who brings that much value is indispensable to the team, an enviable position in today's fluid environment.

There are ways to position yourself to become an essential, we-can't-make-it-without-you individual in business, as a part of a team, or on the home front with family and friends. Start by being a generous contributor, willing to give more than you get. Don't do it for the accolades and attention. Do it to help, encourage, and inspire others.

Stay ahead of the learning curve and people will come to you for information, direction, and solutions. Become known as the go-to person and be available to lend a hand even though your plate is already full. Offer to contribute at any time, on any level, when support is needed. Your vocabulary does not include the phrase, "It's not my job".

To become indispensable, you must be the first name that comes to mind when collaboration is needed. Step up, share willingly, and contribute with an open heart and an open mind. Commit to be a positive influence in all walks of life and go out of your way to find opportunities to be indispensable, where you're the one who will make a difference.

MILESTONES

"Without continual growth and progress, such words as improvement, achievement, and success have no meaning." – Benjamin Franklin

No matter how small the achievement, reaching a goal you set is a notable success. When our children are growing we ceremoniously mark the progress on a door jamb memorializing each change and when it 'happened'. Each increment of growth designates an exciting milestone in their young life. And so, it begins. We celebrate every graduation starting in kindergarten. Why waste any opportunity to roll out a little pomp and circumstance?

Never underestimate the importance of a milestone birthday. Who can forget hitting double digits, teens, sweet sixteen, legal drinking age, and every tenth year thereafter? Birthdays in between are certainly worth celebrating but be sure to go big when a milestone comes around. The same goes for wedding anniversaries. Every year brings back loving memories of a special moment in time and the rare twenty-fifth and fiftieth milestone years deserve epic galas.

Milestones are signposts that mark the significant events in our lives. The day you celebrate your final graduation is a turning point indicating the beginning of the next chapter of life. You've grown up, landed a job, fallen in love several times, married, bought your first home, and maybe even started a family. Each new beginning brings a milestone of 'firsts'. Your first holidays as a married couple followed a year or two later by baby's first Christmas.

Meaningful milestones can be found all along life's path. Maybe the dream job was the first of several careers or you found your passion and blissfully followed it. Enjoy the cycles and celebrate each generation of firsts.

SYNERGY

"No one can whistle a symphony. It takes a whole orchestra to play it"
– H.E. Luccock, Professor Yale Divinity School

T.E.A.M. Together Everyone Achieves More. We all enjoy strengths and talents that define us as unique individuals. Combine those gifts with the abilities of others and the power of synergy produces results far greater than any of us can produce on our own. Combined efforts produce a greater outcome than the sum of the parts. Synergy demonstrates one plus one equals much more than two.

Synergy happens when a group of people put their heads together and brainstorm better ways to get things done. Food banks connect with businesses to effectively meet their food collection goals. Corporate sponsors partner to share responsibility, PR opportunities, and marketing campaigns in a joint effort to reach more people. Corporate employees hold food drives to fill collection barrels and the food bank sends trucks to pick up and deliver the food where it's needed. The employees could easily have collected the canned goods, but without the food bank systems in place it wouldn't be easy to deliver the food where it would do the most good.

Two heads are better than one. Put a few people together in a round table discussion or think tank and the ideas submitted will be polished and refined by the concerted effort of the team. Read a book, form conclusions based on your own perception, and discuss the book with friends. You will gain new insight and understanding by processing the information through their lens. Cooperative teamwork makes a huge difference. When everyone participates, knowledge is shared, generating synergy far beyond the potential outcome of one person. We are not only stronger together, we are smarter, too.

THINK YOU CAN

"If you think you can, you can. If you think you can't, you're right."
– Mary Kay Ash

Do you remember the story of *The Little Engine that Could*? It's an excellent example of mind over matter. The little blue engine wasn't built for anything more than work around the station yard. It clearly wasn't big enough or strong enough to pull a train over a mountain. But one day the bigger steam engines didn't feel up to the job and *The Little Engine that Could* jumped at the opportunity. It shut out all negative thoughts, repeated the mantra, "I think I can, I think I can" and against all odds, pulled the train successfully to the top of the grade.

If you think you can, you can. You know that's true, but your inner voice still successfully talks you out of new ideas before you even begin. The next time you're tempted to put off trying something because you're not good enough, haven't practiced enough, or you might fail, replace those negative thoughts with positive affirmations. Follow the lead of that determined little engine and talk yourself to success.

It's all about maintaining a positive mindset. If you let your guard down just a little, self-doubt will step in and do its best to derail your hopes and dreams. Stop self-sabotaging and pay attention to the chatter in your head. Don't allow negative thoughts to erode your confidence and self-esteem. When you hear discouraging self-talk, stop and intentionally replace those harmful beliefs with empowering ones. Take a chance, focus on your next move, and know you can reach your personal peak. As you champion your own cause you earn the right to taunt that relentless inner voice with a new, improved mantra, "I knew I could, I knew I could".

LIFE'S NOT FAIR

"Expecting a trouble-free life because you're a good person is like expecting the bull not to charge you because you are a vegetarian."
– Jeffrey R. Holland

As my children were growing up they sometimes became exasperated by a teacher who assigned too much homework or a coach they felt played favorites. They would present a compelling case about how unfair they were being treated and why it was important to transfer to a fair and unbiased environment. My response was, "life's not fair". Learning to deal with injustice is valuable preparation for real life.

I wasn't trying to discourage or dampen my children's optimistic spirit. I wanted them to understand we don't succeed by blaming and complaining when things don't turn out the way we think they should. Success is achieved by overcoming obstacles and moving forward with the best available option. Some people get more than their share of misfortune and sometimes the bad guys win. None of that is fair, but much of life is out of our control and we're not always able to make it fair or right.

Some days it feels as if the scales are tipped against you but keep an eye on the big picture. An excellent employee, in line for the next promotion, is passed over in favor of an outside hire. Within weeks an announcement is made the company will be under new management. The position is cut in the transition, leaving the new guy unemployed. You can choose to protest or choose to make the best of every 'unfair' situation.

Accept challenges as a part of life, choose a positive mindset, and make the most of the hand you're dealt. Fix what you can and put the rest into perspective by counting the things that have gone right recently. Chances are luck is on your side. Don't take it for granted.

BORING IS AS BORING DOES

"It's better to be absolutely ridiculous than absolutely boring."
– Marilyn Monroe

You take a seat in the meeting and cringe inwardly when Debbie Dull sits next to you and launches, unsolicited, into her 'same story, different day' rant. You've heard it all before, so you nod, smile, and tune her out. Boring is boring, and with no expectation of the slightest interesting bit of information you're stuck until you can tactfully slip away.

An engaging conversation requires the speaker to spark some interest in their audience. Even topics the listener knows little about can be interesting if imparted with a little passion. It's dreadful to be bored, but boring others is even worse. Boring people drone on, oblivious to their audience's discomfort, taking no notice of the patronizing nods and vacant smiles. Turn what could be a dull one-sided conversation into a valuable exchange by including the listener in the discussion. Ask questions that require details rather than one-word answers. Watch for signs they may be losing interest and draw them in with a new idea or perspective.

Once you have successfully generated mutual interest take it to the next level by introducing fresh ideas to sustain the energy. Be inclusive and find a balance between listening and speaking. The interaction will fizzle if the listener doesn't join in. Timid people, too shy to speak up or express an opinion, can be equally boring as conversationalists.

Experience life to the fullest so you're never boring and always have new stories to share. Travel adventures, or misadventures, will liven any conversation. Both sides will jump in with a favorite I-can-top-that exploit. Keep it light but keep it real. Don't be afraid to disagree or voice a differing opinion. Sparks might fly, but your comments are guaranteed to lead to sparkling conversation.

WYSIWYG

"I looked around and acknowledged that what you see around you is proof of what exists within you." – Adam Braun, The Promise of a Pencil: How an Ordinary Person Can Create Extraordinary Change

'What You See Is What You Get' has become a common phrase. You hear people say it when they're referring to something that is 'as advertised', no strings attached. Flip Wilson popularized this catchphrase on his 70's variety show, dressed as sassy Geraldine Jones. The words made it clear that 'she' was authentic and real, with no intention of changing for anyone.

It's so refreshing to speak with people who are transparent and genuine. There's no need to read between the lines searching for a hidden agenda or ulterior motive. They allow us to let our guard down and enjoy an honest, uncensored conversation. A genuine person is comfortable in their own skin and clear about their opinions and beliefs. They don't feel the need to expound on their views at every opportunity but given the chance will decisively and confidently share where they stand on an issue. They can participate in discussions without the need to be right or voice judgment.

What they say is what they mean. A WYSIWYG can laugh at their mistakes and accept the flaws in themselves and others. They won't give insincere compliments only to make a sarcastic remark to the contrary once your back is turned. If you ask them for their opinion, they give it in a kind, straightforward manner. If you don't ask for advice they keep their thoughts to themselves. If you're not quite sure about your new short hairdo, ask a WYSIWYG friend. You will either continue to sport it proudly or hope it grows out quickly. Asked and answered. Authenticity is an admirable trait that requires nothing more than being your true WYSIWYG self.

DON'T WEIGH IN

"I've been on a constant diet for the last two decades. I've lost a total of 789 pounds. By all accounts, I should be hanging from a charm bracelet."
– Erma Bombeck

Decide today to stop being a slave to the weight loss scales. The first thing you do in the morning is step on the scale to check your weight and what it reports will determine the mood for the whole day. Weigh in higher than the perfect number and your appetite kicks in as your confidence slumps. Perhaps the scales tipped a little higher due to extra hydration the night before. Add in a salty meal and you move the needle even further. That's not a bad thing but allowing an imprecise number to set a negative body image 'mood' wreaks unnecessary havoc on self-esteem. There are many variables that affect weight and scales aren't always accurate. It's time to stop gauging happiness and self-confidence on a number that may not tell the whole story.

Fit is the new thin. There are ways to mark progress and assess your weight without being locked into a number. How you feel is more important than digits on a scale. Do you enjoy a sense of general well-being with enough energy to exercise and do all the things you love? If so, you're in a good place. Are you comfortable in your clothes? Zipping up those favorite jeans without a fight is a true test of fitness, but more importantly, are you comfortable in your own skin? Our bodies are as varied and individual as we are, and no good comes from holding them to idealistic or unrealistic standards. Do your best to look your best without obsessing and set your sights on a life of acceptance and contentment.

CHILLS AND THRILLS

"Double, double toil and trouble; Fire burn and caldron bubble.
Fillet of a fenny snake, In the caldron boil and bake;
Eye of newt and toe of frog, Wool of bat and tongue of dog,
Adder's fork and blind-worm's sting, Lizard's leg and owlet's wing,
For a charm of powerful trouble, Like a hell-broth boil and bubble."
– William Shakespeare, Macbeth

Halloween is an eagerly anticipated annual holiday where alter-egos and evil twins can be found lurking around every corner. It began as All Hallows Eve, a Celtic festival where people gathered together and paid homage to the ghosts of loved one's past. It sounds harmless enough, but there was always the fear that they weren't all friendly ghosts. To avoid coming face to face with unpleasant ghoulish apparitions, people wore masks when they went out, left treats on their doorstep to discourage tricks, and lit candles to help wayward spirits find the path back to the other side.

Halloween today is steeped in those early traditions with a few updated twists. It's a day of community where treats are plentiful, tricks have waned, and kids of all ages indulge in festive fun and games. Trick-or-treaters consume twenty-five percent of U.S. annual candy sales, and candle-light flickers ominously in spooky jack-o-lanterns. Hours are spent creating elaborate costumes that magically transform regular folks into other worldly creatures, princesses, and daring super-heroes.

Our scariest holiday reminds us winter is coming, bringing with it shorter days and dark, chilly nights. Halloween sets the stage for the onset of howling winds and things that go bump in the night. Goosebumps required.

C'mon, get into the 'spirit' of things. Lose your inhibitions, hide behind a mask, and let your inner child run wild. The holiday season has officially begun.

PREPARE FOR THE WORST

"After all, to the well-organized mind, death is but the next great adventure." – J.K. Rowling

It's said that humans share two common threads: death and taxes. Many of us put off preparing our taxes until the last minute, but that procrastination pales in comparison to preparing our estate for the inevitable. This is not something we want to face, and preparation requires uncomfortable introspection and conversations. Do it anyway. Your heirs deserve to grieve your loss instead of managing what you leave behind.

Start with the easy stuff. Pass down mementos that might be meaningful to someone else, shred outdated financial information, and toss potentially awkward cards and letters from past relationships. You will be beyond caring, but it might be TMI for others. It's prudent to take some secrets to the grave.

Write your last will and testament and select someone you trust to act as your estate administrator. There are templates available online if you don't want, or need, to go to the expense of hiring an attorney. Add details to take the guesswork out of the decisions. Include your wishes regarding burial/cremation, religious preferences, or special passages or music you would like at your final service. Your family will be grateful you have made it easy to honor your final wishes.

Create a list of your physical assets (real estate, jewelry, furnishings, art) and a list of accounts (bank accounts, life insurance, mortgages). Remember to update your lists as values fluctuate. Keep one copy for yourself and provide one to your executor along with information about where your passwords will be located. Now you can stop thinking about death and go about the business of living.

DIA DE LOS MUERTOS

"Memory is a way of holding onto the things you love, the things you are, the things you never want to lose." – Anonymous

The Day of The Dead is celebrated in many countries to honor those who have come, and gone, before us. The celebrants clean graves, adorn them with flowers, and gather together to reminisce. The day is steeped in tradition as death is acknowledged as the final step on life's journey. Spend some time today paying tribute to, and sharing memories of, loved ones who have passed.

This holiday also provides the perfect opportunity for reflection and introspection about your own mortality. Days are numbered. It's possible that every heart has a finite number of beats before it stops. What would you do if you knew you had only six months or a year to live? Would you set out to right some wrongs, make amends, offer apologies? Would it be important to visit and re-connect with people you care deeply for, but have become distanced from? Fostering relationships and getting them in order should be at the top of the list. Make the phone call(s) today that you have been putting off for far too long. You may not get another chance.

What have you set out to do in your lifetime that remains un-done? If you've always wanted to travel but have never had the time, make time now. Sign up for your pilot's license or schedule a flight with another pilot and parachute down. Today may be the perfect day to start writing that Great American Novel. Do whatever you can to live a richer life and create amazing memories for others to share when you are gone. Make today and every day count by living it as fully and abundantly as possible.

LIGHT BULB MOMENTS

"I read for the 'ah-has', the information that makes a light bulb go off in my mind. I want to put information in my mind that is going to be the most beneficial to me, my family and my fellow man, financially, morally, spiritually, and emotionally." – Zig Ziglar

You know when a moment of inspiration hits you out of the blue? Those life altering ideas featured in cartoon mode would show a light bulb hovering over your head. We all have those sudden flashes where lightning strikes with an inspired idea, or a solution we've been seeking suddenly becomes crystal clear. The problem with these 'ah-ha' moments is they hit at the most inopportune times, like the middle of the night. You're sure you will remember them because they are game changers, but morning finds you wracking your brain to recover the thread leading to the two-a.m. revelation.

Write it down. It doesn't matter if it's trivial or tremendous, if it's not written down chances are good it will be forgotten. Jot random notes on a list in your phone or keep a journal to record 'brainstorms and lightning strikes'. You might list, in no order of importance, a new recipe waiting to be tried, a perfect gift idea, books to read, vacations plans, new business campaigns and marketing ideas. The list can go on and on. Don't waste time alphabetizing or categorizing. The purpose is to isolate the thought and memorialize it until you can act on it. Once items make the list your mind is freed up, so you can get back to sleep or continue undistracted on the job at hand.

Take note. Start today and capture your light bulb moments and let them spark brilliant, unexpected ideas and solutions and truly light up your life.

HIT PAUSE

"Between stimulus and response there is a space. In that space is our power to choose our response. In our response lies our growth and our freedom." – Viktor E. Frankl

When someone makes us angry our initial reaction is to let them know immediately how we feel. Unfortunately, when we lash out without taking the time to think it through, we can come on too strong and say too much. It might feel good to vent, but eventually it results in thoughtless words being said that can't be unsaid, and hurt feelings that could have been avoided. The next time you find yourself in this situation, step away without reacting. Take a breath, hit pause, and put some time in before you respond.

Many times, a short cooling off period will give the perspective you need to realize you don't really care enough or it's simply not worth the energy to fight. If you wait a day and you are still upset, it will be much easier to compose a thoughtful response without inflicting new wounds by saying more than is needed or opening old wounds.

The pause button also works wonders when you're tempted to make an impulse purchase. You know the danger of grocery shopping without a list or, even worse, when you're hungry. Stick to the list and steer clear of the aisles featuring conveniently prepared and pre-packaged foods. If you find yourself drawn to clothing or big-ticket items you don't necessarily need, impose a mandatory twenty-four-hour timeout. Most likely, you won't get around to it the next day and if you do, it won't look as 'have to have it' as the day before.

Patience is a virtue. Exhibiting self-control is admirable. Take a step back, hit pause, and make thoughtful, clear-headed decisions.

WELCOME CHANGE

Change is your friend not your foe; change is a brilliant opportunity to grow." – Simon T. Bailey

Things change in spite of our best efforts to stop them. Inevitably, summer comes to an end and chilly winds replace balmy breezes. We can't make choices that are out of our control, but we do have many areas where we can effect change, such as style, tastes, and our mind.

We often resist new and innovative opportunities, let inertia set in, and miss a chance to grow. We remind ourselves that we have been reasonably happy for many years with our current hairstyle. We hesitate to test the status quo because there's no guarantee it will look the way it did in our mind's eye. The real reason is we fear the unknown and really do not like surprises. Why not try? Even if it's not exactly what you expected it might be exactly what you need. Part of us is up for a leap of faith, but our insistent inner voice wins with, "don't risk it".

We convince ourselves that the pain of staying at a job or in a stifling relationship is not as bad as the unknowns around the bend. We are creatures of habit and doing something 'the way it's always been done' is comforting. We hold on to traditions even when they have outgrown their charm because repeating familiar rituals soothes our soul. Stability is our rock and change rocks our world.

Take the plunge and apply for a new job if your gut tells you it's time. And sad, but true, all relationships aren't meant to last forever. If it's not working, move on and take the best memories with you. Change doesn't have to be the final chapter. Spring will follow winter, hair grows back, and if things don't work out, make another change.

DO THE RIGHT THINGS

"Do the hard jobs first. The easy jobs will take care of themselves."
– Dale Carnegie

The 80/20 Rule states that in any given set of circumstances twenty percent of activities account for eighty percent of the outcome. Take a look at your current task list. For every ten items you have listed, two will be game changers and eight will consume time and resources and produce very little in the way of results. I'm guilty of making long lists just for the pleasure of crossing things off. On the days I curb my enthusiasm and make a short list of what's really important, I generate more rewarding results and real progress. Prioritizing and focusing on twenty percent of potential actions, allows us to be eighty percent more efficient and effective.

Whether you work independently or as a part of a larger team it's critical that you evaluate your objectives to make sure you are putting your time and energy into high value activities and not just busy work. Identify areas of opportunity for growth and focus on only the most important ones. Recognize there's a good chance that twenty percent of your clients produce eighty percent of your revenue. It might be helpful to know what qualities and features they share and concentrate on attracting new customers with similar characteristics.

Take time on both a personal and business level to consider tasks that could contribute the most to your success and quality of life. Weigh and measure the benefits they offer vs. resources required and rank them accordingly. Most of your time and energy should be spent on the activities at the very top of the list. Do the things that get the job done, by doing the right things.

SOUND OF MUSIC

"Music, at its essence, is what gives us memories. And the longer a song has existed in our lives, the more memories we have of it."
– Stevie Wonder

Music plays a significant role in our lives and has been a common source of joy in every culture for centuries. It is considered the universal language evoking strong emotions and opening up channels of communication worldwide. Some birds and animals are known for their communicative songs. The humpback whales haunting pattern of sounds fascinates humans and brings a strong response from the rest of the pod.

Music fuels the mind which in turn fuels creativity. Much of our music comes from within, soothing and centering us. We sing in the shower, absentmindedly hum while we go about our day, and talk in a sing-song voice in the presence of a baby. It breathes life into our memories. Three bars of a familiar song will take us right back to our glory days or a milestone event in our past.

The term "Mozart Effect" refers to a study that established classical music stimulates our brain and, in some way, makes us smarter and more focused. The study was conducted on young adult students and verified that the students who listened to music prior to testing generally fared better. They confirmed it's easier to concentrate without disruptive background noise and music has proven to be an effective noise reducer. Mozart isn't the only musical genius who can stimulate our brain and help us focus. Listening to your favorite music while you work will help, no matter how diverse your taste might be.

What's your favorite genre? Pop, rock, classical, hip hop, techno, country? It's personal. Pick your favorite musical style and allow the sound of music to enhance your life.

CREATE WHITE SPACE

"When you let go, you make space for something better to enter your life."
– Unknown

When you simplify life you feel balanced, contented, and in control. In page layout white space refers to the unmarked area of the page; margins, spacing, graphics, and columns. It is essential to the printed piece and crucial in your home, office, calendar, and mind.

It's not easy, but it is necessary to eliminate the clutter in your life, both physical and mental, to find balance. Clutter smothers, less is more. Creating white space requires the reduction of clutter by getting rid of things that needlessly take up space or time, require maintenance, or in some way complicate your life. Let go of possessions that do not enhance your life. Try re-gifting, re-cycling, or simply tossing out one item for every new item you purchase. It can be that easy. Start with one small area and make quick decisions. Assess each item - toss, donate, or keep. Don't over-think the verdict. Just do it.

Create white space by eliminating individual relationships or groups that don't enrich your life. Some people waste time or drain energy without giving anything in return. They may be wonderful people or organizations, but if you have outgrown them, move on. Gracefully distance yourself when you responsibly can or relegate them to a reduced capacity in your life where they use up less space.

Create white space in your calendar. Leave room for unanticipated events that pop up in the course of a day. Cancel commitments that have lost their luster or are no longer aligned with your goals. Fill the time doing things that are meaningful to you, move you closer to your goals, or simply allow an opportunity to relax. De-clutter and run your life before it runs you ragged.

MAKE YOUR OWN WEATHER

"Wherever you go, no matter what the weather, always bring your own sunshine." – Anthony J. D'Angelo

It's easy to perform at the top of your game when the world is sunny and bright. Positive, focused energy is sustainable when the people around you reflect your optimistic outlook and strong commitment. Teamwork and productivity feed off one another in a spirit of cooperation. It's more difficult to maintain focus and motivation in a stormy or overcast environment.

The world is filled with over-competitive co-workers, jealous or insecure people, and supervisors who micro-manage and are reluctant to acknowledge your contribution. A negative environment forms a little black cloud that follows you around and dampens your spirit. When it happens take responsibility and make your own weather.

Is there anyone's opinion you value more than your own? It's generally advisable to seek the advice of people you respect when faced with a big or difficult decision. But once you gather opinions, the final choice is yours. Have the confidence to weigh the beliefs of others against your own and make the decision that is in your best interest. Once a clear choice is made the fog will clear and the sun will shine bright once again.

Maintaining balance in an emotional climate requires a little forward planning. You encounter negative people and situations every day and can minimize the effect they have by checking your own emotional temperature before engaging with them. A positive mindset provides clear, focused intentions which will keep you on track. Become a skilled and valuable rainmaker and make your own weather.

THE POWER OF PRAYER

"Never underestimate the power of prayer! Constant prayer, with full conviction, without loss of hope, really does create miracles."
– Ritu Ghatourey

The power of prayer is shrouded in mystery. It sounds good in theory, but with no concrete proof it's tempting to downplay the significance. It's important to make time in your busy life to pray, even if you don't understand how and when it works.

Prayer is a powerful thing that should never be underestimated. I truly believe God listens carefully to every prayer sent into the universe. Sometimes it doesn't feel that way, especially if we don't feel our prayers were answered. Actually, they were answered. Maybe it just wasn't the answer we wanted. It helps to remember He has responsibilities bigger than us and your request may not fit into His master plan at this time.

There are no rules that govern prayer. It doesn't require your presence in church, on your knees, or with your eyes reverently closed. They don't need to be wordy, memorized, or formal. A simple wish or request from the heart, said with faith and love, is a perfect prayer.

God offered us the vehicle of prayer to communicate directly with Him. The pathway is always open, and God is listening day and night. Feel free to share your joys, sorrows, uncertainties, and worries with Him. Ask questions and then listen for His response. Your prayers may be answered immediately, and you will have clear direction or support for a decision. If the answer is 'not now' the light bulb of understanding might suddenly flash months down the road. Whenever it does, recognize the importance of it, and send up a few sincere words of gratitude.

HONOR OUR VETERANS

"This nation will remain the land of the free only so long as it is the home of the brave." – Elmer Davis, American Journalist (1890-1958)

The national holiday we observe today was originally known as Armistice Day in celebration of the end of World War I. The war was officially in the history books at the 11th hour on the 11th day of the 11th month, 1918. It was known as the 'war to end all wars' and the day was dedicated to world peace. Sadly, the hard-won peace didn't last long.

November 11th is dedicated to honoring those who have served in our armed forces. Parades and ceremonies are held across the country to thank those men and women who selflessly left their homes and their families to fight for our freedom. Enjoy your day off but take time to acknowledge the reason for the day and make a difference in some small way. Reach out and thank every veteran you know with a phone call or handshake. Write a note to someone in a veteran's home or hospital or to an active service member and express your gratitude. Send up a silent prayer of thanks. Donate money or give the gift of time to the National Veterans Foundation or similar organizations. Take the kids and join the flag waving fun at a Veterans Day parade or hang the stars and stripes from your porch to demonstrate your love of country and gratitude to those who gave so much to keep it free.

Veterans Day is a day to recognize individuals who devoted years of service to our country and to thank those who currently serve. Send heartfelt thanks to the brave Americans who fulfilled this patriotic duty to ensure and protect our continued freedom.

THE LAW OF DIMINISHING RETURNS

"Knowledge is the only instrument of production that is not subject to diminishing returns." – John Maurice Clark

Remember the last time you indulged a craving for an excessively rich dish or sweet dessert? You can't wait to take the first bite and it doesn't disappoint. You savor every bit until it becomes a bit too much and you slow down until you can't consume one more morsel. Once your hunger or sweet tooth is satisfied the return is gradually less rewarding and the experience can eventually turn from a positive to a negative. The 'point' you reached indicated subsequent bites would not transport you like the first few, and they might even make you feel a little queasy.

If you plant tomatoes in the same soil year after year they will be more susceptible to disease and less robust. Rotating crops will shore up your returns. Work on the same project all day, every day and your creative spark will dim and eventually go out. Read until your eyes cross and your retention will be greatly reduced. Do anything for too long and your results will be limited.

While this term is usually related to accounting it certainly applies to everyday life. When you feel your energy flagging stop what you're doing and work on something else. Focus on a different project until you recognize the signs and then shift back. Keep it fresh by capitalizing on more of the beneficial first steps. Schedule a break when you realize the returns are diminishing. Optimize your time and energy by starting something that interests and inspires you. Until it doesn't.

In other words, stop eating when you're full, give yourself options when your attention wanes, and make necessary changes to rev up your returns.

INSPIRE KINDNESS

"No one can help everyone, but everyone can help someone."
– Ronald Reagan

If we want to see more kindness in the world let it begin with us. I suggest we start a movement right here, right now, to make the world a better, more compassionate place. One small act of kindness at a time. We can change the world by doing little things that make us and others feel good. Give back, spread joy, and send positivity into what can sometimes be a pretty negative world.

I love the idea of random acts of kindness, but that's not what I'm suggesting. Let's extend kindness to others every day in every way, on purpose. The kinder you are, the kinder others around you will be. Change the approach by going out of your way to do things that make you, and others, feel good. Now sit back and wait for the ripple effect as one good deed inspires another.

A little effort and simple changes will make a big difference. If you pass a homeless person on the street say hello and look them in the eye when you do so. They are human and deserve respect. On the home front, instead of claiming the television remote for yourself, relinquish control to someone else. Give a sincere compliment or write an overdue thank you note. It's never too late to do the right thing.

There's no need to overthink this idea. Practice spontaneous generosity and selfless cooperation – just for the sheer joy of it. Be a contributor but give the credit to others. Build them up and they will be inspired to do the same.

I see a flood of purposeful acts of kindness coming together in a tsunami of understanding and compassion. Inspire kindness. Join the movement today.

BE CRE8TIVE

"Once we believe in ourselves, we can risk curiosity, wonder, spontaneous delight or any experience that reveals the human spirit.'
– E. E. Cummings

Your days can become pretty routine and predictable if you don't inject a little creative energy into them. Do you enjoy music, but are tone deaf with two left feet? There are classes for every level of competence, or incompetence, to strengthen your skills and heighten your musical experience. Too much, too soon? Simply playing background music while you work will inspire creativity in other areas. If you take great pleasure in a good book pick a different genre and make yourself look at life differently. Take the leap from reading to writing and pen your own whodunit.

It's fun to shake things up and throw caution to the wind on occasion. If you get tired of preparing the same meals day in and day spice things up with new exotic spices. Add them to the humdrum, tried-and-true recipes and surprise and delight your family with out of character spontaneity. Challenge yourself to create with new menus and broaden your culinary horizons.

Put a little spark into your life by trying something fresh and innovative. If you've always been a conservative dresser, adopt a bold, more colorful style. Mismatch instead of coordinating your outfit just once. Learn to knit a cap or make a simple dress. Get crafty and make gift-giving extra special with handmade and meaningful gifts. The only thing better than saying, "I made this" is saying "I made this for you!"

Get on the path to creativity by testing yourself as a novice. Take a beginner's class on any subject at the ripe old age of whatever you are. You won't need to become an expert to become more interesting, motivating, and attractive. Find ways to add more fun to what could have been another routine and predictable day.

CREATURES OF HABIT

"I always wonder why birds choose to stay in the same place when they can fly anywhere on the earth, then I ask myself the same question."
– Harun Yahya

Humans are creatures of habit and take comfort in familiar routines. You find yourself ordering the same lunch, at the same place, with the same people every day. There are no questions asked when you take your customary place in the boardroom, at the dinner table, or your favorite recliner at the end of the day. Where you park and where you sit for Sunday services are foregone conclusions. You are habitually drawn to the pew where you quietly belong.

Good habits and comfortable routines make our lives easier. We can allow ourselves a little downtime when small decisions have already been made. Habits improve our well-being by lowering stress levels and adding structure, but too much of a good thing can sometimes be too much. Life on autopilot can lead to complacency and limit the brains need to stretch and grow.

Try breaking the mold. Dine somewhere new, peruse the menu, and make a thoughtful, bold selection instead of rattling off your customary, uninspired order. Think outside the metaphorical box and revitalize your day. Shake loose the constraints of mindless living and tackle something innovative and different. Just once take the longer, scenic route to work and soak in the view. Create a simpler morning routine or upgrade your predictable workout to a cardio dance class to kick start your metabolism.

You might find repetition isn't always fulfilling and can easily become mundane, same old same old, day in and day out. Hit pause and try something new. Offer someone else your seat at the table today. Step out of your comfort zone, spread your wings, and fly.

WHAT WOULD YOU DO IF YOU WON THE LOTTERY?

"Forget the lottery. Bet on yourself instead." – Brian Koslow

It may sound glamorous and exciting but hitting the jackpot doesn't guarantee a life on easy street. Statistics indicate lottery winners are more likely to declare bankruptcy within three to five years of their windfall than the average person. Friends, relatives, gold diggers, and scam artists come out of the woodwork to stake a claim, creating tremendous stress and pressure on the winners. People who mismanage money and are constantly trying to make ends meet exhibit those same bad habits when balancing more zeros. Given the one in umpteen million odds of winning and the inherent problems linked to the payouts it's better to see how your lottery winning fantasies will improve your current life.

Would you keep working if you won? If you answered a resounding 'no' rethink your career. Winners who enjoy their current occupation continue showing up for work. If your job is unfulfilling or no longer challenging look at other opportunities to test your skills and bring value.

Would you share the winnings? If you imagine supporting a cause or lending a financial hand to family and friends in a mega-lotto-winning way resolve to make a difference with what you have. Begin by dedicating the funds you're tempted to spend on lotto tickets to the cause. You have the power to find and spread happiness wherever you are, whatever your means. If you would fund scholarships, champion the underdog, or feed the hungry on a huge scale, start now by collaborating with other like-minded, generous souls. You've always wanted to travel the world, own a better car, or bigger house. Don't hold out for all or nothing. Change your world one small gesture at a time. Set your sights, create an actionable plan, and make your lottery winning dreams come true.

1000 FT VIEW

"When you are a giraffe and you receive criticism from turtles, they are reporting the view from the level they are on." – Bishop TD Jakes

It's easy to focus on the minutiae of life and lose sight of the big picture. If you're overwhelmed by constant distractions and day to day details, stop what you're doing and take a step back. Zoom out and widen your perspective. A broad view approach clarifies priorities and sheds light on areas of wasted energy which lead to frustration. Take a good look, zoom back in, and compare your actions with your values and goals. What else should you be doing and what activities can you let go? Armed with clear vision, the next most important steps are clearly revealed.

A narrow perspective will limit your growth so use your wide-angle lens. Expand your information base by seeking the opinions of others. Widen your focus, broaden your mind, and enjoy the 1000 ft. view of life. Go beyond your normal sources, area of expertise, and comfort zone. Explore new possibilities by asking questions of people who are knowledgeable in that arena. Just be sure to direct those questions to lofty thinking 'giraffes' who share your vision and not glass half full 'turtles' who, by their very nature, keep the bar low.

Broadening your perspective is a work in progress. Once your mind is open, it's possible to improve and advance incrementally. Small victories fuel momentum uncovering more and better solutions along the way. Confidence builds as you break through to higher limits and enjoy a sense of accomplishment. Start today. Reconfirm your direction and re-dedicate yourself to the big picture. Take in the 1000 ft. view from where you are today, determine where you want to be, and determine what must be done to get there.

GIVE PEACE A CHANCE

"The life of inner peace, being harmonious and without stress, is the easiest type of existence." – Norman Vincent Peale

Some people seem to go through life with a black cloud hanging over their head. At least that's their story. According to them everything that can go wrong, does. They participate in every cold and flu season, toxic relationships come and go, nothing happens until the final deadline looms, and chaos reigns supreme.

Does your story consistently begin with 'woe is me' and star you as the victim? If so, it might be time to write a new chapter. Slow down, lower the volume, and make room for a little peace and quiet. You can't do it all, and if you insist on trying, you won't do anything well. Take a breath, think about what lies ahead, and don't lock the car until you're sure you're holding the keys. The next time something goes wrong, take the time to quietly and privately fix it. Resist the urge to share your sad story with BFF's or 'friends' on social media.

We are responsible for the chaos or calm in our lives. We don't consciously create bad luck but if we're not paying attention we allow it in. You're late for work so you grab your morning coffee on the run. In your rush you fail to secure the lid and now you're wearing the contents. Upsetting? Yes. Surprising? No. Set yourself up for success instead of failure. It's not as exciting and doesn't make a very interesting tale, but a little proactive, forward thinking will save you from of mishaps and misfortune.

If you're the calm one, don't get pulled into other people's chaotic existence. Choose friends and activities mindfully. Distance yourself from drama addicts and crisis situations whenever possible. Make the conscious choice today to live a life of peace and harmony.

BE THE SOLUTION

"You're either part of the solution or you're part of the problem."
– Eldridge Cleaver

Not often, but every now and then, it's okay to indulge in a good old-fashioned tantrum. Blowing off steam reduces stress and leaves you better equipped to solve the problem that caused your meltdown in the first place. A healthy vent session is a satisfying way to clear the air, but if your outburst devolves into chronic whining and complaining it is time to re-direct your time and energy to more productive things.

Think about what is behind the need to grumble and gripe. Are you unhappy, in need of attention, or so insecure that you shine a light on outside difficulties in hopes your own shortcomings will go unnoticed? No matter the reason, complaining is not going to solve your problems, so change your focus from problems to solutions. You don't have the power to control every area of your life so don't try to resolve issues that are impossible to overcome. Embrace the undeniable truth, change what you can, and let the rest go.

Life is fraught with unpleasant and disappointing experiences. You can choose to be a victim, or you can choose to accept responsibility, take positive action, and be a problem solver. If you feel you can't do it alone enlist a friend or two. Brainstorm, share ideas, puzzle it out, and find the positive in each situation. Stop zeroing in on what's wrong and start noticing all that is right. Become a problem solver and channel the time and energy wasted complaining to more constructive purposes. The next time something irritates or upsets you ask yourself this one life-changing question, "What am I going to do about it?" You will no longer be part of the problem. You will be the solution.

NURTURE LOVERS

"We've got this gift of love, but love is like a precious plant.... You've got to keep watering it. You've got to really look after it and nurture it."
– John Lennon

Relationships, both business and personal, will wither and die if not properly nurtured. Nurturing is not something you do for a while and then let nature take its course. Solid, long-term relationships are built on trust, mutual respect, and making sure each person feels heard. It's a fine balance. The goal is not to gain control, but to make sure the needs of both sides are fulfilled.

It starts with open and honest communication. When one side speaks the other really listens. Relationships maintain a healthy balance when expectations are reciprocal and collaborative. A 'we're-all-in-this-together' philosophy honors the feelings of all parties. Life requires compromise. It doesn't guarantee one will get their way, just that they were heard.

There will always be differences. Acknowledge them and work through the rough spots without giving up. Your preconceived expectations of a much sought-after perfect relationship might need a reality check to help you work through and resolve problems. There's usually more than one right way to do something. Productive negotiations sometimes call for holding tight and sometimes for giving in, but the wishes of both sides should be taken into consideration in the search for middle ground.

Pay attention as your nurtured relationships evolve to ensure you're on the same page, working toward a common goal. It becomes less about being right and more about being happy. Maintaining balance and joy requires cooperation and acceptance of the priorities of everyone involved. Established, long-term relationships are to be treasured and never taken for granted. Eventually, less work is required to maintain stability, making the effort worth it and the results invaluable.

COUNT YOUR BLESSINGS

"When I started counting my blessings, my whole life turned around."
– Willie Nelson

Thanksgiving is more than a feast day. It's a day for families to come together and express thanks for the bounty and the beauty in their lives as they usher in the holiday season. Count your blessings and the spirit of Thanksgiving will live in your heart every day, not just on one day at one dinner.

Consider keeping a gratitude journal where you document everything good that you are grateful for every day. You can set aside a few minutes in the morning to declare your intentions for the positive things the day will bring by journaling a list of people and things you are grateful for. This sets an optimistic tone for the entire day. You might choose to make it an evening ritual to help you relax at the end the day by listing the positive events that transpired and what they meant to you. Either way it's a powerful tool that offers fresh perspective and keeps you focused on the good that is happening right here, right now. You will be happier and more motivated by day and stress free at night allowing for sound, peaceful sleep…followed by another day of gratitude.

Starting now journal five or more things you are grateful for every day during the holidays. It doesn't matter if you're thankful for small favors, life-changing developments, or the same things every day. Celebrate and honor all that is good in your life. By the time the official season comes to an end you will have created a beautiful life habit that will stay with you all year.

Start here. I am grateful to you and count you as one of my many blessings.

LIFE'S TOO SHORT

"Life is too short to wake up with regrets. So love the people who treat you right. Forget about those who don't. Believe everything happens for a reason. If you get a chance, take it. If it changes your life, let it. Nobody said life would be easy, they just promised it would most likely be worth it."
– Harvey MacKay

You hesitate to invite friends over because you feel your house isn't clean enough or you don't have enough time or talent to prepare a Pinterest worthy meal. Your bar is set so high that you give up without even trying to reach it. The truth is your friends just want to spend time with you. They would be perfectly happy clearing the coffee table to make room for a takeout pizza.

Life is too short to major in the minors. Perfection is overrated, unachievable, and completely unnecessary. It's a beautiful afternoon on your much-anticipated day off. You have a long list of errands and tasks that will take the better part of the day to complete. Weigh your options and decide to do what must be done and let the rest slide. This does not mean opt out of responsibilities, just prioritize them. Load the washer and take a walk while it does the work. Buy groceries for the week ahead and add a few items for a spur-of-the-moment picnic. Check a few more must-do's off your list and then meet with friends for a fun, easy alfresco dinner.

Lighten up, stop talking yourself out of opportunities, and be grateful for who you are and what you have. You will attract the people who deserve you and appreciate what you bring to the party. Recognize and lay claim to the bright spots in every day, let go of the past, and start living your best life right now, in the present.

GET A LIFE

"You only live once, but if you do it right, once is enough."
– Mae West

Do you remember Ferris Bueller's infamous day off? He justified his truancy with these thoughtful and oh-so-true words: "Life moves pretty fast. If you don't stop and look around once in a while, you could miss it."

You want to live a full life, but responsibilities and commitments compete for every waking moment and leave you completely spent at the end of the day. It's unrealistic to attempt sweeping change in light of so many existing obligations, but a few small adjustments will enrich your quality of life.

Do what must be done, but don't fall prey to regularly cleaning up other people's problems. As a good friend you are always willing to lend a hand, but catering to chronic neediness makes you an enabler and doesn't help anyone in the long run. Your co-worker didn't complete her part of the project in time to present at the sales meeting, so you have no choice but to meet early to get it done. The extra time would have been better spent on an activity that brings personal satisfaction or joy. You might need to consider delegating some of your tasks to capable individuals to add valuable time to your day and, as a bonus, make them feel more valuable. Carve out an extra thirty minutes to practice piano, enjoy a walk, journal, or read, and don't allow distractions to encroach on your special time.

Doing a little less to please others frees you up to do the things that matter to you. Make nonnegotiable appointments with yourself and honor them. Time spent on things important to you will increase the significance of daily activities. Spending even a little time every day doing what you love will enhance and improve the magnitude and quality of your life.

TAKE A STAND

"Get up stand up, stand up for your right. Get up stand up, don't give up the fight." – Bob Marley and the Wailers

There are numerous examples of famous whistleblowers who courageously exposed unethical or unscrupulous behavior in the business world and political arena. The lights they've shined in dark corners have caused government and corporate powerhouses at all levels to fall from grace. Some of the good guys never recovered from the backlash they faced for pointing out illegal business practices or dangerous working conditions, but they did what they believed was right and risked personal consequences for the good of the whole.

If you see something, say something. Be prepared and willing to defend others when needed. Speak up or report unacceptable behavior to someone in a position to help. Be a friend and have their back. If someone shares an offensive or mocking view, not joining in the laughter will communicate your feelings loud and clear. Standing up for what you believe in doesn't mean you have to call someone out, start a confrontation, or draw a line in the sand. It means you are your own person, exercising your right to decide what you feel is right and what is wrong. Take a stand and apply your own free will to respectfully disagree with what has been said or done.

Many people are easily intimidated and back down when someone offers an opposing view. They go along, don't ruffle feathers, wanting and needing to be liked. There's no need to fight every battle, but by not making your beliefs clear you send the message that you agree with the opposition. Take a stand and bravely, but calmly, voice your opinion. You may not change anyone's mind but sticking to your convictions and upholding your values will earn respect and build self-confidence.

LIFE IS NOT A DRESS REHEARSAL

"Your time is limited, so don't waste it living someone else's life."
– Steve Jobs

In his play, As You Like It, Shakespeare declared, "All the world's a stage, and all the men and women merely players". Practice makes perfect in the world of theater, but the world stage offers little in the way of do-overs. Real life doesn't offer edits and re-takes until we get it right. Mistakes follow us and the decisions we make shape our lives, for better or worse.

You gave up chasing your dream and settled for a job that would pay the bills. Now you're frustrated, stuck doing work that isn't meaningful or fulfilling. You can choose to play it safe, become complacent, and waste your talent, or you can take a leap of faith and choose to live life, your way. What will it take to set the right scene? The clock's ticking.

Are you content to merely pass time and tread water or do you want to live a satisfying and purpose filled life? You've always known what you want but have lulled yourself into believing there will always be time to correct your course at some point down the road. Life doesn't come with guarantees for tomorrow, so today is the day to cue the spotlight and raise the curtain on the act that will manifest your best life.

Don't waste another minute. It's time to shake things up and live YOUR life. What were your wildest hopes and boldest dreams before everyday living got in the way? What changes will you put in place to bring those dreams to life starting today? This is the story of your life and you are cast in the starring role. You were born for this moment. Break a leg!

GIVE THANKS

"Cultivate the habit of being grateful for every good thing that comes to you, and to give thanks continuously. And because all things have contributed to your advancement, you should include all things in your gratitude."
– Ralph Waldo Emerson

Giving thanks and appreciating what you have fosters joy and hope. Living in gratitude keeps your mind/body/spirit healthy, happy, and gratified. The mind can only focus on one emotion at a time. When you think happy thoughts it's virtually impossible to entertain negative ones simultaneously. Focus your mind on what you are thankful for and your spirit will soar. Brains are powerful tools and given the chance will turn your day or your life around.

This is the time of the year when we are encouraged to be thankful for the many blessings we enjoy. Somedays that's easier said, than done. It's human nature to dwell on what we don't have instead of celebrating what we do have, including life's many simple pleasures. We get so distracted by demands on our time and energy that we forget to reflect on what's good in every day. We live in reactive mode instead of proactively recognizing positives. When we aren't mindful it's easy to sit back and expect, or in some cases feel entitled to, all the good we enjoy in our lives. We are truly blessed to live in peace and comfort in this land of endless opportunity. It should never be taken for granted, but it happens. And when it does wake up, take a little time to reflect, and give thanks.

Make the commitment to dedicate a few minutes every day to giving thanks. In this way expressing your gratitude won't be just a seasonal holiday tradition. It will become a wonderful, healthy life habit.

DO OR DARE

"Go confidently in the direction of your dreams! Live the life you have imagined. As you simplify your life, the laws of the universe will be simpler." – Henry David Thoreau

Do you dare to dream big about an adventure or achievement that will eventually define your life, but keep putting it off until you retire or have more time? Sharing the same endless loop of your vision is not enough to fuel your journey. Talk without action won't get you very far. Someday will never come until you make the decision, commit, and take action.

Before you buy a plane ticket or book a safari verify that this is really your life's quest. Sometimes we focus on a future event and never make it happen because our heart's not truly in it. What appealed twenty years ago may not be as exciting today, but that is not an excuse to give up or give in. Do some soul searching and find or refine your calling.

Once you have identified your purpose you must let go of the fear that prevents you from achieving it. You believe it will absolutely happen, but sometimes life gets in the way of your best intentions. Set visual reminders to keep your dream in the forefront of your mind. Use a tantalizing photo as a screensaver, tape it on your mirror, and post it above your computer. Name your dream and use it as your password. The act of logging into your personal accounts will provide frequent reminders to keep you on track.

Now take action. What must be done, what is the timing, and what actually must happen to realize your dream? Once that plan is in place take the first step, then the second. DO it every day until it becomes a reality. What you DO determines your future. Take a chance. I dare you.

COOKING WITH LOVE

"One of the very nicest things about life is the way we must regularly stop whatever it is we are doing and devote our attention to eating."
– Luciano Pavarotti

Serving others is an honor and serving food made with love, for people you love, is both an honor and a blessing. It doesn't need to be complicated. The point is to bring people together. Think back to mealtimes when you were young. Some of our fondest memories involve Jell-O molds with marshmallows or morsels of fruits or vegetables suspended in it, tuna casserole, and sloppy Joes. Comfort foods - the ties that bind, and keep, people together.

Today's families find it difficult to sit together for regular meals. After school sports and various extracurricular activities combined with dual career parents makes shopping, planning and meal prep a challenge. Food is often consumed on the fly, between commitments, but don't accept that as the new normal. It's worth the effort to get loved ones to sit down, 'break bread', and connect.

It doesn't require a complicated event. Making and serving food with love can be less about the food and more about the love. Keep it simple and serve breakfast for dinner. Whip up a tall stack, brown up some sausage, relax and share the events of the day. Another sure hit involves personal-sized pizza, with a variety of savory toppings.

Take the time to plan ahead and organize a get together with friends where everyone contributes. It's easy and delicious when others showcase their favorite dish. If it's adults only, nothing says love like crackers, cheese and your favorite wine at the end of a hectic day. The simplest meal becomes memorable when it's topped off with a make-your-own sundae fest. Sharing food is sharing joy so cook up a little love today.

NICE GUYS FINISH BEST

"Be honest, be nice, be a flower not a weed." – Aaron Neville, American R & B Singer and Musician

Why do people find it so hard to be nice? You wake up in the morning to breaking overnight news and then take your chances on the highway vying for position with less than courteous drivers. Once you're in the real world you interact with disagreeable, self-absorbed individuals and are expected to be nice in return. In a world that can be not-so-nice, nice people make a huge, much needed difference.

Be nice just because you can, with no strings attached and no expectation of favors due. There's no shortage of 'nice' people who will readily help you out and then come back asking for something in return, usually bigger. Be nice for 'nice' sake, with no hidden agenda. Nice does not mean weak. Pleasant people have the confidence to call out mean spirited individuals or the self-control to ignore them. They demonstrate strength by standing up for themselves and the underdog. There's nothing submissive or weak about doing the right thing.

Genuinely nice individuals attract people to them as they spread positivity. It feels good just to be around them. Look for opportunities to lend a hand, smile, or offer a few kind words. Something that simple can turn a day or a life around. You won't feel the power of nice at first but bless one person at a time with compassion and multiply the goodness over time. In small ways you can and will change the world.

You've heard girls are made of "sugar and spice and everything nice" and you've witnessed nice guys finishing first, not last, many times. So be a nice human. It really isn't that hard.

WHEN LIFE HANDS YOU LEMONS

"Failure is simply the opportunity to begin again, this time more intelligently." – Henry Ford

You have a zest for life second to none and a goal to squeeze every last drop out of every day. You refuse to admit failure and in your quest for success zest a little too deep and end up with the bitter tasting pith. Now what? Regroup and start again.

When faced with a problem out of your control, think about the things you can control and work from there. You don't dictate the weather so what can you do when rain threatens the backyard barbecue you've been planning for weeks? Ranting and complaining won't make it go away, so take a productive approach and make a list of possible solutions. Offer the guests a raincheck, put up a tarp, or bring the party inside. Proactively solving the problem puts you in control again.

Count your blessings. When you stop to think about everything that is right it's difficult to dwell on what went wrong. You consider quality time with friends a blessing and make a practical decision to move the party indoors for pizza. Instead of spending the day manning the grill you are able to relax and really connect with your guests, proving once again that something good comes from everything.

Look for the lesson in every failure. Sometimes you try too hard, zest too deep, and overcomplicate your life. Keep it simple and keep it real. Refocus on a new, positive goal. The pizza party was such a success the group decided to get together monthly and take turns hosting the no muss, no fuss event. When you count your blessings put the rain at the top of the list. It was the catalyst for a fresh start and new perspective. Be the sugar and turn bitter lemons into sweet situations.

YOUR REASON FOR THE SEASON

"My idea of Christmas, whether old-fashioned or modern, is very simple: loving others. Come to think of it why do we have to wait for Christmas to do that?" – Bob Hope

For many people the holiday season is primarily a time for religious celebration. Christians rejoice in the birth of Jesus, the Jewish religion observes Hanukkah, and various other faiths honor important days and spiritual ceremonies during this time. Individuals with diverse beliefs and cultures may celebrate in different ways or for different reasons, but regardless of one's faith the holiday season signifies a time of joy for all.

This month is the perfect time to reach out to loved ones and share traditions and good cheer. It's a time for families and friends to spend time together, grateful and appreciative of loving connections. People tend to show more compassion and care during the holidays. We become a kinder, gentler society where courtesy prevails, and smiles come easily.

The plight of the homeless and less fortunate is stark in contrast to the festivities enjoyed by so many during the time between Thanksgiving and the New Year. People are moved to open their wallets and give generously. Food banks overflow with donations, favorite causes and charities flourish, and many contribute time and energy to their local soup kitchens.

A highlight of the season involves the exchange of thoughtful gifts. Shopping can be hectic and draining, but moods are lifted by the classic holiday carols and cheerful buzz in the air. The spirit of giving makes hitting the malls a much-anticipated holiday experience.

The reasons for the season are as many and varied as there are individual cultures, traditions, and religious beliefs. Whatever your reason, celebrate the holidays in your own personal way, and spread love and joy at this most wonderful time of the year.

ROUTINES AND RITUALS

"The quality of your life is in direct relationship to the quality of your habits and rituals." – Stan Jacobs, The Dusk And Dawn Master: A Practical Guide to Transforming Evening and Morning Habits, Achieving Better Sleep, and Mastering Your Life

A good morning ritual will set the stage for a successful day and save you from flying by the seat of your pants and playing catch-up all day. Wake up at the same time, do the same things, in the same order, day in and day out. Being fully aware of what must be done saves valuable time and energy and eliminates the need for repeat decision making. Stressing about loose ends and details is draining and unnecessary. Daily rituals empower you by putting your best foot forward before you step out the door.

The tea ceremony is very important in the Japanese culture. The ceremonial preparation and serving of tea are step by step rituals that are not focused on drinking tea but on preparing and serving guests 'from the heart'. Europeans routinely enjoy cappuccino at breakfast with quick espressos grabbed on the run in one of many available cafes. Americans sip Venti lattes while meeting friends or taking advantage of alone time and free wi-fi. Sweden's coffee/tea ritual known as "fika" defines time set aside solely to slow down, take a much-deserved break, and connect and communicate with others.

Develop wind-down rituals at the end of the day to gradually slow your spinning mind before your head hits the pillow. Turn off blue screens, brush/floss, and read to unwind at the end of a hectic day. Calming activities practiced regularly before you turn out the lights will help you disengage from the day's events and enjoy a good night's sleep.

HONOR TRADITION

"Ritual is important to us as human beings. It ties us to our traditions and our histories." – Miller Williams

Rituals become time honored traditions that take some of the guesswork and decision making out of holidays and celebrations. The Christmas tree is always placed in the same corner and is decorated with beloved ornaments, collected over the years as joyful reminders of special times the family has shared. Each household has a routine for opening gifts; one at a time in an orderly fashion or all at once in a frenzied free-for-all. One or all gifts can be opened on the eve of the holiday, or the day of. It never changes, it's tradition.

Holidays wouldn't be the same without relatives and food. Traditional activities and recipes are associated with many holidays, often in celebration of a family's heritage or religion. Tamales are served in traditional Hispanic households, and Jewish families enjoy potato latkes, sufganiyot (jelly doughnuts) and other rich symbolic foods to celebrate the miracle of the Festival of Lights. It's possible your holidays would not be complete without a classic green bean casserole with French fried onions on top.

Family style cooking is an integral part of seasonal celebrations. It's not unusual to see three generations, both male and female, donning aprons to construct a graham cracker 'gingerbread' house or to bake cookies to decorate, exchange, or give as gifts to neighbors and friends. It's more about the time spent together than the success of the undertaking. It really doesn't matter if the house collapses or the cookies crumble.

These are the ties that bind. Take pride and comfort in familiar routines and add new twists as needed. Rituals and traditions form lasting bonds and create meaningful memories to be fostered for the enjoyment of generations to come.

HAKUNA MATATA

"Nothing can bring you peace but yourself." – Dale Carnegie, How to Stop Worrying and Start Living

'Hakuna matata' is a Swahili phrase meaning "here there are no concerns" or as popularized by the Lion King, "no worries for the rest of your days". It's a problem-free philosophy that encourages us to stop worrying about anything and everything, especially things we cannot control.

Our lives are filled with circumstances and outcomes we can't change or control. So rather than fight them, learn to handle your response to them. You are understandably furious your car was towed from the fire zone. After all, it was only there for a few minutes while you ran a quick errand. Ranting and raving won't help. It will only aggravate and create a spectacle. Put that energy and effort into solving the problem of retrieving your car. We all make mistakes and things often go wrong. Learn from those mistakes and move on.

We attribute the most common forms of worry to outside stressors. Worries about work, relationship issues, financial problems, and health concerns play on a continuous loop in the back of our minds. We blame outside stress, but it begins internally. The good news is we started it, therefore we have the power to put it to rest.

If only your self-talk would foster patience and understanding instead of one-sided debates. Do you spend your nights writing indignant letters in your head to everyone you feel has wronged you? You're not alone, but since absolutely nothing positive will ever come of it wouldn't it be better to give in and enjoy a good night's rest? Let the catchy little tune, "Don't worry, be happy", smooth the way. Say it often and empower yourself to be patient, positive, and peaceful. Make the right choice.

THE ART OF GIVING

"May no gift be too small to give, nor too simple to receive, which is wrapped in thoughtfulness and tied with love." – L. O. Baird

December plays host to the biggest gift giving events of the year. It's a time to demonstrate love and friendship for those we are close to, as well as appreciation for those we have worked with throughout the year.

It really is better to give than to receive. Making someone happy when they receive something unexpected from you is very gratifying, inspiring you to do even more. If someone surprises you don't feel the need to rush out and buy something of equal value for them. Graciously accept it and express your gratitude. Gifts are meant to be given from the heart, with no expectation of reciprocity.

Gifts are not one size fits all. Thoughtful, personal gifts mean so much more than cash or a check. Consider gifting an experience. Tickets for a favorite event or venue that you will attend together, or a promise of a day hike followed by a lovely picnic create lasting memories that strengthen the bond between you.

Give a memorable gift of yourself by contributing your time or expertise. It may not take much sacrifice on your part, but to the receiver it is very valuable. Look over your list and find opportunities to surprise and delight your recipients in ways that won't cost a dime but are truly valuable. An evening of baby-sitting that allows a young couple peace of mind and alone time is priceless.

Gifts made with love are the best. The neighbors will welcome a plate of home baked goodies and crafty handmade items will serve as a reminder you care. With a little forward thinking this year's gifts will be cherished for years to come.

THE TRUTH OF THE MATTER

"Oh, what a tangled web we weave when first we practice to deceive."
– Sir Walter Scot

Honest people are respected and trusted, which is a good thing since trust is the cornerstone of solid relationships. The truth is known to set you free and allow you to sleep well knowing you did the right thing, but sometimes that same truth exacts quite a price by ruining relationships with people who don't want to face it. Honesty, as the best policy, sometimes comes at great expense.

Have you ever kept your thoughts to yourself or dodged the right answer in an effort to avoid hurt feelings or confrontation? We all do, but it just never seems to work out. Lies by omission become the elephant in the room and eventually must be faced. We hesitate to tell people close to us we are unhappy, hoping the situation will blow over, or we recognize someone is making a bad decision and elect to remain quiet for fear we're overstepping our bounds. Our best intentions come back to haunt us and no matter how bad the truth is, the lie will be viewed as worse.

Pesky little white lies create a web that complicates and obscures the truth. Whatever caused you to resort to lying in the first place will surface again. When it does you will need to recall what really happened, which is easy, and the spin you felt it needed, which gets thorny and ultimately tangles you in the web of deception.

The fact is, being less than honest comes with a price and being truthful is priceless. Relationships survive with open, honest communication. It's not necessary to be brutally honest, but a frank, straightforward opinion, when asked, will earn respect and build trust in the long run.

TIS THE SEASON

"Nobody's walking out on this fun, old-fashioned family Christmas. No, no. We're all in this together." – Clark Griswold

The holiday season is approaching, and the masses are hastily falling into two opposing camps. There are the over the top Christmas lovers who think Halloween is the perfect time to deck the halls and start the fa-la-la. And then there are the 'humbugs' who dread the stress and pressure and would be grateful to skip Christmas, given the chance.

It's important to be empathetic to one and all in the coming weeks. We were pushed to our limits time-wise and energy-wise before we faced additional seasonal expectations. Feelings of loss are magnified during this time and spending demands aggravate money worries. Not everyone has a family and if they do they may not fit into the 'fun, old-fashioned' category. We're expected to be jolly, participate in obligatory gifting, hosting, celebrating, and endless traditions. We are tempted to over-commit, always seem to under-deliver, and end up spent and exhausted. If you are of the pro-Christmas mindset, it's all part of the process. If not, it can be a very tough time.

Let's agree to approach the weeks ahead with an attitude of peace and goodwill – toward ourselves, as well as, others. Ease financial pressure by limiting your gift giving and stay within your budget. Be selective about the luncheons/cookie exchanges/cocktail parties you attend and try to fit in a little stress reducing exercise and much needed sleep.

Christmas doesn't heal the sick or comfort the lonely and it might create rather than resolve conflict. It can be the most wonderful time of the year in many ways and a most trying time in others. Reach out to someone who may be struggling, share a little holiday spirit, and help make it a peaceful, happy season.

CALLING ALL ANGELS

"Make yourself familiar with the angels and behold them frequently in spirit; for without being seen, they are present with you."
– St. Francis De Sales

Angels are God's messengers and their mission is to protect and to serve the living. We are familiar with, and accept the existence of guardian angels, our assigned protectors who guide us through life's ups and downs. Consider for a moment the possibility that we might be blessed with an army of angels, some very familiar to us and some unknown. There's something comforting about believing departed loved ones are still here with us. We trust they are in a better place and possibly that place extends beyond Heaven.

Who else leaves those inexplicable stray pennies that keep showing up and turns lights on you know you turned off. We can't explain it, but we accept that angels enhance our lives and give us hope. Angels are free to watch over us, keep us safe, and come to our rescue when asked or needed. They remain invisible, but we are very aware and blessed when we feel their presence.

It's okay to call on your angels for assistance in reaching an impossibly high shelf, locating a rare parking space in a crowded lot, or finding the perfect words of comfort for someone in need. Be sure to send them a prayer of thanks when, for no apparent reason, you wait a beat when the light turns green giving the car going the opposite direction a chance to run the red light thus avoiding an accident.

Your angels are watching over you right this minute. Feel free to ask for help in any area of your life. They have infinite resources and the luxury of time. Be grateful and smile, knowing you're always in good hands.

HEAVENLY PEACE

"The life of inner peace, being harmonious and without stress, is the easiest type of existence." – Norman Vincent Peale

The holiday season is a magical time to connect with people you love but creating holiday joy is fraught with stress-inducing activities like shopping, wrapping, baking, decorating, and endless social events. Canapes and cocktails take the place of balanced meals, we're up way past our bedtime, and our exercise program is on hold until New Year's resolutions shame us back to it. How can we possibly maintain a calm spirit and inner peace while still exhibiting holiday spirit?

It's important to find positive outlets to let off steam, de-stress, and regain some measure of peace for your mind and body. Start by going for a spirit lifting walk. It will clear your head, calm nerves, and improve your mood. If you're feeling completely spent a few minutes on the move will rejuvenate and energize you for the next round of festivities.

When your tilt-a-world is spinning out of control take three minutes to breathe and find your center gain. Whether you call it meditation or simply a quiet interval to gather your thoughts, the time spent will increase your overall sense of health and well-being. Treat yourself to a professional spa treatment or a leisurely bath in the comfort of your own home, complete with scented oil, candles, and soothing music. It will replenish your sense of self – Happy Holidays to you!

Be selective when accepting party invitations. A request for your presence is not a call to action. Admit you can't show up everywhere with the perfect hostess gift. Bow out when demands threaten to stretch you too thin. Stay home, enjoy a healthy bowl of soup, and turn in early with a good book. Once all is calm, all is bright, sleep in heavenly peace, sleep in heavenly peace.

SHORT CUT OR SHARP ANGLE

"There are no shortcuts to any place worth going." – Beverly Sills

Looking for the shortest distance between two points isn't a bad thing unless it defines you as a minimal standard person. Taking a calculated short cut very often eliminates unnecessary steps which is valuable when streamlining an operation or trying to navigate red tape. However, habitually taking short cuts is a lazy approach and risks creating an existence of cut corners and settling for the quickest, cheapest solution. Sharp angle mentalities use their time and energy looking for ways to jump the line by inappropriately cutting corners, rather than seeking ways to succeed.

A short cut through the neighbor's back yard or the grocery store's parking lot will usually shorten the distance between you and your destination, but constantly searching for the easiest route might leave you shy of the goal. Get rich quick schemes rarely work because a solid foundation must be firmly in place to provide sustainable support. Some individuals get lucky and skyrocket to stardom, but success usually requires putting one's head down and working for it.

Before you submit an incomplete or hastily thrown together report, stop and consider what it says about you. Take pride in building a reputation as a person who excels, not someone who simply gets by. It might take a little more time, focus, and energy, but the resulting feelings of satisfaction and self-respect will be worth it.

If something is worth doing, it's worth doing right. When you do choose short cuts be sure they are time saving measures that get the job done well. Cut the fat, simplify wherever possible, but leave the corners intact. Always looking for the sharp angle will short cut your life. Take the long way and enjoy the ride.

FAD VS FASHION

"Good style - regardless of fads - means the thing that suits your body."
– Natalie Dormer

Take a wistful look through the pages of family photo albums and you might discover a time release capsule of fashion forward outfits that, in retrospect, were often unfortunate choices. The 80's made quite a statement with shoulder pads, power suits, disco colors, and big hair. You weathered the inexplicably expensive grunge look, low-rise jeans that caused 'muffin top', and decades of denim in every shape, size, and color. You've followed the trends and worn your jeans torn, skinny, bleached, embroidered, and possibly way too short.

Every year fashionistas plot and present styles and designs that will be 'in', relegating everything else to so-last-year. One season they tout black eyeliner and layers of black lashes and the next they caution us to avoid an overdone, 'spikey' look. They select color trends to define a look that may or may not work for you. If orange doesn't brighten your complexion, don't embrace a trend featuring orange-by-another-name. Tangerine, peach, and coral may sound enticing, but will leave you looking equally washed out.

Choose styles that make you feel comfortable and confident regardless of the latest fads. Try different looks and colors until you find the ones that suit you best. Design your wardrobe around well-fitting, age appropriate clothing, with or without a fancy label. Squeezing into too tight pants or shirts that hug every curve won't help your self-esteem. Dressing for success means putting your personal best foot forward every day, which in our diverse culture could mean anything from a step above yoga pants to buttoned down business attire. People do judge books by their cover. Cover yourself in clothing that makes you feel good and face the world relaxed and confident.

BLESSINGS IN DISGUISE

"What seems to us as bitter trials are often blessings in disguise for which we are later, in the fullness of time and understanding, very grateful for!"
– Oscar Wilde

A family of ten planning to celebrate the New Year with extended family in Singapore missed their flight because they didn't check phone messages informing them of a schedule change. They arrived at the airport minutes before the AirAsia plane departed, two hours ahead of the original departure time. The family was angry and disappointed until tragedy struck and they grasped how narrowly they escaped death. The plane encountered bad weather and went down in the Java Sea taking all 162 souls on board with it. The shocked family believed it was God's plan and described it as "a blessing in disguise".

Not all setbacks are life or death events, but many are life-changing. You have just been told the company is moving in another direction and your department is being phased out. The news throws you into a tailspin of self-pity. When the party's over you get busy networking, fluffing your resume, and filling out job applications. By the time you've boxed up your cubicle a very promising job interview is scheduled for a position perfectly aligned with your talents and interests.

If you never experience obstacles you can't appreciate the wins. Doors close, relationships end, and roadblocks divert your best laid plans. Look for the opportunity behind every door. There's a reason relationships crumble and viewed through the lens of hindsight's perfect vision the reasons are usually obvious. Of course, you were devastated when you lost your job, but your new role is much more rewarding, challenge-wise and money-wise. How often have you been faced with unwelcome change only to look back and realize you should have made a move sooner?

WORK BACKWARDS FROM THE GOAL

"Instead of looking at the past, I put myself ahead twenty years and try to look at what I need to do now in order to get there then."
– Diana Ross

When we set long-term goals we usually start from Point A and list the steps that will get us to the finish line at some point in the future. Stephen Covey encouraged us to 'begin with the end in mind' in his best-selling book, The Seven Habits of Highly Effective People. Set a target and create a schedule by working backwards from the desired outcome to develop a comprehensive plan of action. The traditional 'start to finish' practice can be greatly improved with a fresh perspective based on time sensitive benchmarks and deadlines. Implementing a backwards approach sets the stage for a smooth, sequential rollout with fewer opportunities for details to slip through the cracks.

Your daughter and her fiancé have happily announced their engagement. You immediately launch into wedding planner mode. They have a date in mind and clever 'Save the Date' announcements are in the works. But not so fast. The first step in event planning requires establishing a budget, securing a suitable venue, and determining the number of guests the site and price will comfortably accommodate.

Once you have locked down the time and place make a detailed plan of action. Work backwards from the big day and set milestones, such as finalizing the guest list and ordering/mailing invitations. Once the framework takes shape fill in the blanks with a chronological list of what actions are needed, when, to guarantee a memorable event. Select a theme and color palette, contract with vendors, put a weather contingency plan in place, to name a few. Implementing a 'backward plan' will call attention to potential errors, omissions, or overlooked details to be avoided on the path to your goal.

A NEED FOR CIVILITY

"Don't ever forget that you're a citizen of this world, and there are things you can do to lift the human spirit, things that are easy, things that are free, things that you can do every day: civility, respect, kindness, character."
– Aaron Sorkin

Turn on the news, any network, at any time, and be prepared for confrontational and contentious chaos with newscasters, politicians, and policy makers trying to out-shout one another. The failure is top down and crosses the full political spectrum. It's almost impossible to determine a political candidate's campaign platform in this hostile climate. Instead of advocating for their personal beliefs, values, and goals, they hurl insults and relentlessly attack the competition.

Where are our manners? The First Amendment guarantees Americans freedom of speech, but please air your views when appropriate and in a civilized manner. Questioning is healthy, but to be effective it requires listening to the answers and no one seems to be listening. Robust discussion fosters understanding and perspective if it isn't taken too far. If opposing viewpoints fail to find some acceptable middle ground, respectfully agree to disagree.

Showing courtesy and understanding strengthens relationships. Give peace a chance by leaving your strong, but possibly divisive, opinions at the door. Exercise diplomacy and good manners by steering clear of prickly subjects. Don't poke the bear at the dinner table or family gatherings. Life would be pretty boring if we all thought alike, so respect the conflicting opinions of others the same way you want them to respect yours.

When it becomes clear the sides are polarized, let go and find some higher, neutral ground. Nothing clears the air like a good laugh so change the subject and lighten the mood with a bit of humor. Let go of angst, be nice, and mind your manners.

SILENT AND LISTEN HAVE THE SAME LETTERS

"Never miss a good chance to shut up." – Will Rogers

Offering your full attention to the words of another is a skill that, properly honed, can become a powerful communication tool. Listen carefully to what is being said and thoughtfully craft a reply based on what you heard rather than what you expected to hear. The better you listen, the better, more effective, and succinct you will be as a communicator. Paying attention to the spoken word minimizes the risk of creating confusion or misunderstandings with a thoughtless or ambiguous reply.

The Bible tells us "there is a time for everything… a time to be silent and a time to speak". Silence sometimes feels awkward and we are tempted to talk our way through it. Your good friend is ill, and you visit regularly to bring a few magazines or a frozen yogurt and brighten her day. There's no need to keep up a one-sided conversation if she's not up to talking. If she does feel like sharing be an attentive listener and give her the floor. Sometimes just being together in companionable silence will say it all without the need for words.

From now on make it a point to let others have the last word. You confidently stated your opinion and listened respectfully to theirs. You are not looking for validation from them and words alone won't change your mind, so there's nothing left to do but bow out gracefully.

Listen without judgment and speak only when you have something to say. A wise individual doesn't feel the need to weigh in on every conversation. People who value their time want to listen to people who add value when they speak. Use Gandhi's question as a guide and before you begin, ask yourself, "Does it improve upon the silence?"

DRIVEN TO DISTRACTION

"By prevailing over all obstacles and distractions, one may unfailingly arrive at his chosen goal or destination." – Christopher Columbus

From the minute we wake up until we call it a day we are bombarded with non-stop interruptions and distractions. Some are necessary and should be dealt with as quickly and efficiently as possible and others are trivial and can be handled at a more opportune time. The problem is less about how we avoid distractions and more about how we prevail over them to allow us to focus on the priorities needed to meet our goals.

Every individual is blessed with the same amount of time in the day. What you do with it is the key factor between success and another day of explanations and justifications for putting off important things because you allowed yourself to be distracted by unimportant things. Disruptions, interruptions, and distractions accumulate like grains of sand until you're buried up to your neck with no way to dig yourself out.

Determine what must be accomplished and estimate how much focused time is needed to complete the task or tasks. Now find a distraction free environment and turn off the alerts and pings on your computer and smartphone. Let your family or coworkers know you will be unavailable for a certain amount of time. Next comes the part where you struggle and fall short. Get started and stay disciplined and focused until the job is complete. No excuses.

Design an hourly/daily/weekly plan and create a strategy around it. Prioritize, time block, tune out the diversions of social media, and feel free to say 'no' as needed. Once you lay down rules, follow them relentlessly. At the end of each day celebrate your accomplishments and generously reward yourself for good behavior.

TO DO OR NOT TO DO

"Rename your "To-Do" list to your "Opportunities" list. Each day is a treasure chest filled with limitless opportunities; take joy in checking many off your list." – Steve Maraboli, Unapologetically You: Reflections on Life and the Human Experience

Year after year he makes a list and checks it twice. Maintaining an organized list is the only way Santa is able to keep his commitment to the many children who rely on him at Christmastime. There are far too many details/choices/sizes/names/addresses to commit to memory and his mission is far too important to miss even one.

Lists keep the loose ends battened down and allow room for new, possibly loftier thoughts by clearing our conscience minds. They are powerful tools that clarify and create order out of chaos and help us organize what could otherwise be an overwhelming life.

If you dare to grocery shop unprepared you are more apt to impulsively buy snacks or ready to eat foods. A well thought out shopping list contains the items needed to prepare healthier, more creative meals. Ongoing honey-do and to-do lists can be journaled along with your wish or bucket list which hopefully is growing longer by the day. Keep your gift list handy all year. When you find the perfect something for a special someone, buy it on the spot. Make a note of it or you run the risk of forgetting and settling for something less perfect when the time comes.

Chipping down a list one item at a time is exceptionally satisfying. Checklists spur you into action and provide a positive way to help you be more productive and to measure forward progress. Sit down and gather your thoughts, notes, and haphazard scribbles into one organized laundry list of tasks and responsibilities. Now one at a time check, check, check.

JUST RIGHT

The best and safest thing is to keep a balance in your life, acknowledge the great powers around us and in us. If you can do that, and live that way, you are really a wise man." – Euripides

We're all familiar with the classic children's story of *Goldilocks and The Three Bears* where young Goldilocks discovers the bear's lair while walking through the woods. The bear family is out for a walk as their porridge cools. Goldilocks tastes each bowl of porridge and decides she prefers the one that is just right, not too hot or too cold. She prefers the just right chair, and so on. The tale conceptualizes what has become known as the Goldilocks Principle, a study of 'just the right amount'.

The Swedish subscribe to a similar concept, known as 'lagom', which translated means 'not too much, not too little'. It's about finding happiness by balancing all areas of your life and learning to enjoy everything in moderation.

Today's environment applauds individuals who consistently maintain a healthy work/life balance over the chest-thumping of self-proclaimed workaholics. Homes are lighter, both literally and figuratively. The heavy drapes have been replaced with simple blinds that let in 'just enough' natural light. Less clutter, fewer trinkets, and simple furnishings soothe and center the occupants.

Apply logam to your life by culling through and paring down your wardrobe and belongings. Once you experience the joy in 'just the right amount' of material possessions consider the value of balancing commitments vs. over-commitments and adjust as necessary. Not too much or too little. Just enough to fill your life with happiness and serenity.

ASSESS THE YEAR

"There will come a time when you believe everything is finished. That will be the beginning." – Louis L'Amour

It's mid-December and you're tingling with excitement in anticipation of putting the year behind you and starting fresh. But not so fast. The best way to set goals and expectations for the coming year is to assess the triumphs and failures of the past twelve months.

Before you spend time committing to big sexy goals, sit down and review last year's wins and losses. Consider your ROI (return on investment) in all areas. We understand ROI in business but think about the service club you joined because you set a goal to give back to the community. Were you able to make a difference or would your time and expertise be more valuable elsewhere?

Weigh and measure. What worked and what didn't? Don't just add numbers, raise the bar. You fulfilled your reading resolution last year, but beach reads didn't expand your mind or improve your life. Tighten the criteria to books of substance this year and count frivolous reads as extra credit. You may be content with last year's income goal, but if you paid off your car re-direct the amount of the payment to your savings or a grander than usual vacation.

Check your calendar and journals to identify projects and accomplishments that were not included in the annual goals. The blog you started just for fun has attracted a following and it might be time to monetize it. Take note of all the little wins and where you found the most joy. Recognize the disappointments and honestly assess why you failed. Possibly your fitness/weight loss/debt reduction goals were unrealistic, and a little adjustment will motivate and inspire success. Taking the time to set current goals based on past performance will lead to future success.

ZEAM

"A mistake is to commit a misunderstanding." – Bob Dylan

Zero Errors and Misunderstandings. The acronym represented a campaign by an influential ad agency whose focus was publishing an annual directory. One small mistake followed them for the whole year. Is ZEAM a lofty, stretch goal or an impossibility? "To err is human", but how often are mistakes and misunderstandings avoidable?

Sometimes we're just moving too fast. We hastily compose a text or email and press send without taking the time to review the message. Between our own typing errors, imprecise phrasing, and autocorrect much of what we send is flawed. One way to eliminate mistakes is to slow down and make corrections before we share them. Spell check, fact check, and then post.

In a world where information travels at lightning speed, 24/7, it's hard to believe there continues to be so much communication breakdown. We rely heavily on the written word, even though it can come across as terse or abrupt at times. Texts and emails are intended to be succinct with no warm greetings or pleasantries leading into the message. An old-fashioned telephone conversation would provide a better platform to work out prickly details to ensure both parties have a mutual understanding before the results are memorialized in an email that might be misinterpreted.

Expect errors and misunderstandings to occur when you assume the solution will be either black or white. Most situations resolve in a shade of gray. Make concessions, give, take, and then settle on a happy medium. If you want to decrease needless mistakes and misunderstandings think before you speak, look at the situation from other perspectives, and consider other options before you leap.

YULETIDE

"Winter is the time for comfort, for good food and warmth, for the touch of a friendly hand and for a talk beside the fire: it is the time for a home."
– Edith Sitwell

Today is the Winter Solstice, the shortest day of the year. It has been celebrated worldwide for centuries as a landmark day that signifies hope and optimism as the sun now begins its ascent in the sky, gifting us with more and more sunlight every day. It's a perfect time for families and friends to come together to celebrate and create a new version of an old-world tradition.

The Scandinavians called the Winter Solstice "Yule" and their customary festivities included the burning of the Yule Log. Early ceremonies included many rigid customs that were believed to protect the household from misfortune in the coming year. A kinder, gentler version of the ritual might be a better fit for today's lifestyle. Invite family and friends to join you in their comfy clothes for a casual evening of fun and comfort food. Gather around a cozy fire, dim the lights, and ignite your own festive Yule log. Take time to sit quietly together as it burns and bid farewell to the past year. Now contemplate the coming year, visualize your hopes and dreams, and share with those around you. You may want to include a bit of the old tradition by saving some charred remains of your Yule log and place them under your bed to keep your home safe throughout the year. Use it to ignite next year's fire and continue the tradition.

The holidays can be hectic and exhausting. Think of this as a timeout from the hustle and bustle of the season. Use the longest night of the year as an opportunity to slow down and savor what is truly important. Eat, laugh, reminisce, and simply enjoy each other's company.

YOU BETTER BELIEVE IT

"The future belongs to those who believe in the beauty of their dreams."
– Eleanor Roosevelt

There's a lot of talk about hope, as in hoping something will work out or come together successfully, but commitment and belief don't come as easily or as often. Consider these two thoughts: "I hope I will be promoted to the new position at work" vs. "I believe I will be promoted to the new position at work". There is a definite difference. Hope expresses an element of uncertainty or doubt. Belief demonstrates determination. Don't stop believing.

Believers are not victims, they are doers. They don't look for easy outs or reasons why a situation won't work for them. As long as you trust your judgement and are willing to try new approaches until one works, you will succeed. Believe that you can reach your goals and you're halfway there.

Being hopeful is optimistic, upbeat, and positive, but it is an emotion and not something that proactively drives you toward your goals. You cross your fingers and hope for the best, even when you aren't in a position of strength or in control of the outcome. Only when you are 'all in' and 100% committed to making something happen will you be able to reach the desired outcome and manifest your dreams. By taking ownership, maintaining faith in the outcome, and striking out confidently in search of your dreams, you are controlling your destiny.

The major difference between successful people and unsuccessful people has little to do with opportunity, means, or intellect. It's directly related to their belief in themselves. They believe they alone are responsible for bringing their dreams to life. The combination of unwavering confidence and resolute belief will make all the difference in your life.

PAUSE TO REFLECT

"Follow effective action with quiet reflection. From the quiet reflection will come even more effective action." – Peter Drucker

As the year draws to a close it's important to take time for serious thought about what you achieved, what you learned, how you grew, and how you served during the past year. Did you lose your way or set yourself up for failure by setting unrealistic goals? Take time to step back and reflect.

It's tempting to skip this step in the hustle and bustle of the holidays, but it's critical to identify guidelines and review benchmarks to keep you on your best path. Just a few quiet moments of introspection will clarify your objectives and get you going in the right direction.

Revisit your core values and personal mission statement. Ask yourself a few questions that focus on essential areas of your life before you set new goals: Did I honor my relationships by spending time with the right people? It's important that the people most important to you get the best of you. Did I strengthen my body and mind by eating healthy, staying fit, remaining positive, and getting enough sleep? Did I meet my financial goals by retiring debt and saving for the future? Did I live within my means? What are my career goals? Am I operating at my productive best? Did I fuel my soul spiritually? Have I lived up to my full potential? Did my actions make a difference?

By taking this important step you are living your life by design, not default. Set aside just a few minutes to control your destiny and manifest your best life.

SET PERSONAL GOALS

"By recording your dreams and goals on paper, you set in motion the process of becoming the person you most want to be. Put your future in good hands – your own" – Mark Victor Hansen

This year is ending and a new year is looming. It's time to set goals that will challenge you to live your best life. Next week you will thoughtfully evaluate where you are now compared to where you want to be next year. Setting goals helps clarify your objectives and channel your random hopes and dreams into an actionable plan. A plan that, when followed, will create many wonderful memories.

This is the perfect day to think about your personal relationship goals. Reach out to the important people in your life with holiday greetings. Find ways to strengthen relationships by purposely and deliberately staying in touch. Identify positive influencers and set goals to interact with them in a bigger way. Who makes you feel good when you're around them? Make a list of those people and commit to seeing them regularly. Identify people at the other end of the spectrum who tap your resources, mentally or physically. Make a determined effort to move closer to the 'fountains' and farther from the 'drains'.

If you have outgrown your friends, nurture new ones. Choose carefully. The individuals closest to you greatly affect your attitude, motivation, and decisions. Make a goal to surround yourself with positive people who are dedicated to your success, and you to theirs.

What professional relationships can you strengthen? Find and invest in networking opportunities to cast a wider net. All relationships grow and strengthen when you show a sincere interest. Reach out and make a difference.

LOVE, HOPE, AND JOY AT CHRISTMAS

"Christmas isn't a season. It's a feeling." – Edna Ferber

It doesn't matter where you live or what you believe, Christmas Day could very well be the most wonderful day of the year. It's about the love of family and friends and being happy just being together, making new memories. The sparkling lights and seasonal scents entice and excite us. It's a day where everyone gathers round the table to eat, drink, and be merry and the house is filled with infectious laughter and holiday cheer.

The month of December is a time when many religions celebrate their faith, reinforce their beliefs, and express hope by paying tribute to a higher power. Christians around the world celebrate the birth of Jesus, our Savior, on this auspicious day. Buddhists acknowledge the date when Buddha gained enlightenment, the Jews celebrate eight days of Hanukkah, the Festival of Lights, and Kwanzaa is a week-long festival that honors classical African cultures. Interfaith families set aside their set-in-stone beliefs and honor the best of both worlds. They strengthen family bonds and respect their differences as they create new family traditions. The lines have blurred a bit and the religious celebrations blend with the secular side of the season and Menorahs, nativity scenes, Christmas trees, and Santa with his helpers all peacefully share center stage.

The spirit of Christmas is real. It brings a special joy which can be felt and seen. Share your joy with others as a treasured gift. Open your home to someone in need of a friend today. Find the real joy of Christmas by offering love, hope, and peace to everyone you see. The more you give, the more you have, so give generously. Wishing one and all a holiday filled with joy. God bless us, everyone.

SET PROFESSIONAL GOALS

"All successful people have a goal. No one can get anywhere unless he knows where he wants to go and what he wants to be or do. "
– Norman Vincent Peale

The holiday season has past, leaving a trail of wrapping paper, leftovers, and lasting memories. It's time to pack up, store the decorations, and prepare for the new year. This week spend time looking forward to the future.

Now is the time to dream big! Be bold and don't let any self-talk or preconceived ideas hold you back. Does your career energize and fulfill you or have you settled and let fear of change or fear of failure hold you back? If you're not feeling passionate about your current vocation it might be time to change direction or find a new path to follow.

If you feel your situation could be improved, go deeper. Ask yourself some soul-searching questions and listen carefully for the answers. What satisfies and fulfills you? Is it necessary to head in a different direction? If so, what steps will get you there? You might realize you are essentially in the right place, but there's room for improvement. If that's the case, think about changes to make things better. Raise the bar and enhance your personal fulfillment, salary, or position.

Regardless of where you are professionally, it is always advisable to step up your skills and expand your résumé. Sign up for a class, obtain a designation, or let it be known you are ready and willing to assume more responsibility. Determine what it will take to get to the next level, make a plan, and enlist support. Ask for guidance. Make sure the people who can help you reach your professional goals are fully aware of your intentions.

SET CLEAR FINANCIAL GOALS

"You've got to tell your money what to do or it will leave."
– Dave Ramsey

Setting well thought out financial goals is essential to successful money management. Those goals must be in place before you can create a financial plan or budget. Are you looking forward to retirement? Depending on how much time you have and where you stand currently this could be a major priority. What costly expenditures are you facing this year? It might be time to replace your car, air conditioner, or roof, but you may not be able to replace big ticket items, pay off debt, and save for retirement at the same time. You need a plan.

Start by listing all your assets and debits. Now set your priorities. If you have children approaching college age you will need to plan for that expense, but if you are carrying high interest credit card debt the interest you accrue will cut severely into your ability to save. Hence, priorities.

List your credit card debt starting with the highest interest rate. Pay that card off first. Begin a rainy-day savings account because you can count on unplanned expenses to crop up, and without emergency funds you will be forced to borrow on the credit cards you just paid down. Now that you have identified the expensive necessities start shopping before you absolutely need to invest in them. A replacement roof might be less daunting if you contract for it in the summer when roofers with free time are more competitive. The same for air conditioners in the winter or this year's autos right after the new models are released.

Determine where you want to be financially this year, next year, and in five years. Create a realistic budget, commit to living within your means, and set yourself up to enjoy financial peace.

HEALTH AND WELLNESS GOALS

"Every day is another chance to get stronger, to eat better, to live healthier, and to be the best version of you." – Unknown

Give serious thought to how you want to look and feel. Do you want to lose weight, gain strength or just feel fit, less stressed, and more energized?

If you are setting goals around weight control, frame them as positives. Instead of deprivation think portion control and fresh, healthy choices which might be more manageable if you commit to eating at home more often. Every body has individual needs so don't try to transform your body into a size that doesn't work or an inappropriate diet program that sets you up for failure. Be true to your body and to yourself.

Daily exercise keeps you fit and is excellent for peace of mind. It reduces stress and anxiety and is generally good for the soul. There's no need to break records or set the world on fire. Exercise in small, but consistent, doses is sustainable and will probably serve you better in the long run. Say 'yes' to gain without pain and improve, one day at a time.

Keep your commitment by counting every step/calorie/sit up/hour of sleep but keep it real. If your goal involves giving up something that has been a big part of your life, start by cutting down. Enjoy one cup of coffee or soda per day instead of the amount you usually consume. If your goal involves adding something in, ramp up slowly. Start with one lap, one salad, one no-thank-you to dessert and build momentum from there.

Who doesn't want to live a long, healthy life? Make it happen by setting realistic goals, making good decisions, and sharing a cheerful, hopeful outlook. Laugh, be happy, and add joy to your life as you become a shining example of healthy living to others you connect with daily.

GIVING BACK GOALS

"Life's most persistent and urgent question is, 'What are you doing for others?'" – Martin Luther King, Jr.

There are many ways to do the right thing. Each opportunity won't be life-changing, but in small, seemingly insignificant ways, what we decide to do, can and will, impact the world.

We all want to matter, so set some goals and embrace that need and do your part to make a difference. What acts of kindness will you be known for? Do you want to help individuals or work at the community level? Look for opportunities to offer support. Find one area that calls your name and it might lead you to another, possibly greater, cause.

My niece is known for her generous contribution to the American Red Cross Blood Bank. One pint can save up to three lives and as of this writing she has donated almost fifty pints and she's not planning to stop any time soon. She didn't wake up one day and decide this was her calling, but at least one hundred and fifty people are grateful she did.

Find a charity or a cause that reflects your values. Resolve to support them monetarily or with the gift of time. It's impossible for you to help everyone, but never forget your commitment to the community has real impact, even if you help just one. Be a good neighbor, set a goal for giving, and lead by example. There are hundreds of worthy charitable causes to support. Commit to a goal of dollars raised or donated, or time spent on behalf of the cause. Make a bigger difference by inviting family and friends to join you. Combined efforts make it more fun and competition boosts morale and raises the bar on good deed productivity.

SCHEDULE GOALS FOR FUN

"You can't stop the waves, but you can learn to surf." – Jon Kabat-Zinn

All work and no play is simply no fun at all. Recreation and hobbies round us out and center us, but unless we intentionally schedule rest and relaxation our days turn into months and opportunities for fun pass us by.

It's time to set goals just for the fun of it. How you do it is up to you as long as you follow your own personal passion. Playtime makes you more interesting and much happier. Some people enjoy sports and interacting with friends in their spare time. Others like to curl up quietly with a good book. If you are involved in an activity that is legal, ethical, relatively safe, and gives you pleasure, go for it!

There are an endless number of choices, so don't just stop at one. If you select an activity that involves other participants, you will be supporting your goal to network and build relationships. If going out to play sounds unproductive and doesn't inspire you, find something creative that motivates you. Hobbies might add purpose to your downtime as you pause to refresh. Sign up for painting lessons, become a master gardener, join a book club, or gather friends and form a gourmet cooking group. Still stumped? Think back to your childhood for inspiration. Did you enjoy crafting or did your creative juices flow through song, dance, or drama?

Explore new avenues for growth and learning and build measurable goals around them. What time/days will you set aside to indulge in your new or reincarnated passion? Will you need to invest in supplies or lessons? And finally, how will your life be enriched and improved as a result? It's time to go out and play.

ALL'S WELL THAT ENDS WELL

"Although no one can go back and make a brand new start, anyone can start now and make a brand new ending." – Carl Bard

Another year has come and gone, faster than ever before. Some years are better than others, but they all consist of a combination of joy/pain/success/disappointment. If this was a particularly challenging year, put it behind you and start fresh. If it was largely a good year take full credit for what you did right. It's too late to worry about what could have or should have been, but it's the perfect time to identify areas in your control that you will handle differently going forward.

You've devoted time to an honest and open annual review. Use those past defining moments as opportunities to learn and acknowledge the value in that thoughtful look back on your life. It helped you redefine what success and happiness mean to you. Maybe you decided this is the year to stop settling, set your sights higher, and become an even better you. You understand the need for health, meaningful work, and consistent attention to important relationships. You know how you want to give back and make a difference. When you are clear about what is truly important you can commit to realistic, reachable, and authentic personal goals and resolutions.

No matter how you rate the past twelve months, learn from the life experiences you encountered, and move on. Be grateful for what worked and put practical strategies in place to change what didn't. Focus your hopes and dreams on the future and create a plan of action to bring them to life. Move forward resolutely with optimism and decide now to make next year your best year ever.

ACKNOWLEDGEMENTS

I'd like to thank my wonderful husband, John Karelius, for his constant encouragement and honest feedback and for everything he does to make "Me, Improved" every day.

Many thanks to my sons Cole Archuleta and John Archuleta for their ideas and insight that inspired many a daily dose.

I'm very grateful to my daughter, Lauren Purdy, my sister, Evelyn Brady, and my friends, Nancy McCracken, Heather Jones, and Susan Papageorge's for proofing excerpts and offering suggestions, edits, and support throughout the process.

Sincere thanks to everyone who aided, abetted, inspired, and cheered me on believing I could create a manuscript that would become this beautiful book.

Made in the USA
San Bernardino, CA
15 August 2020

77075100R00211